Dear Target Friends,

Thank you for picking up this book and deciding to join me on this wellness journey!

Eating right, exercising, and nourishing my body are my essentials—these are the things that keep me going day to day, whether I'm on the road, in the recording studio, or enjoying some downtime at home. I didn't always know all that I know now about health and fitness. I have been through some trial and error, and now that I have found my path, I want to share what works for me with you. The tips, strategies, and recipes in this book are part of my every day, and I hope that is how you will use them—7 days a week, 52 weeks a year.

This special edition of *Find Your Path* includes a bonus chapter at the end, just for you. If you don't know this about me already, you will discover in these pages that I love veggies! I'm going to show you how to get fresh garden veggies at home like I do. It's easier than you think. In this exclusive chapter, I will also share a few of my favorite go-to plant-based recipes. I absolutely love these and make them all the time. I hope that you will too!

Are you ready? Let's go! It's time to *Find Your Path*.

xoxo,

Carrie

find your
PATH

HONOR YOUR BODY, FUEL YOUR SOUL, AND GET STRONG WITH THE **FIT52 LIFE**

CARRIE UNDERWOOD

with EVE ADAMSON

PHOTOGRAPHY BY CAMERON PREMO

DEY ST.
An Imprint of WILLIAM MORROW

THIS BOOK IS DEDICATED TO ALL OF YOU OUT THERE WHO WANT TO MAKE POSITIVE CHANGES IN YOUR LIVES AND WHO WANT TO PROMOTE POSITIVITY IN THE WORLD AROUND YOU.

I WOULD ALSO LIKE TO DEDICATE THIS BOOK TO MY FAMILY, WHO ARE MY MAIN REASON FOR PURSUING A HEALTHY LIFESTYLE. I LOOK FORWARD TO SO MANY MORE FIT-FILLED YEARS TOGETHER!

contents

introduction
FITNESS SHOULD BE SIMPLE

Sometimes I go a whole day without sitting down once. When my work is done, my babies are in bed, and it's just my husband and me on the sofa drinking a little red wine and watching a little TV to unwind, I'm probably already planning for the next busy day. I'm usually ordering up groceries, household supplies, clothes for the kids, diapers, or Lord knows whatever else through one of the apps on my phone. Or I might be writing in my journal, answering emails, and figuring out what I've got to get done tomorrow, when I probably won't be able to sit down again until after the sun sets.

One of the most common questions people ask me is, "How do you do it all?" How do I live this crazy life as a country singer, on the road half the time, while also being a good mama to my kids, a good wife to my husband, a good daughter, and a good friend? How do I still find a way to eat what my body needs and get in a workout so I can be strong enough to put on a show in high heels (no easy feat, I'll tell you that) or carry a toddler up the stairs or a basket of laundry down? And somewhere in all that rushing and doing and fixing and loving and living, how do I find a little time for myself?

My answer isn't all that surprising: I had to find my path. I'm just a mom. All moms have to do it all. We all have work to do, children to tend, relationships with husbands or partners or friends to maintain. We all need to be strong, not just for carrying toddlers on our hips but for doing our jobs and all the other things we have to do every day. I call it "mommy multitasking." And it's not just moms. Dads have to do it all, too.

Or maybe you don't have kids, but you're still trying to do it all—working, playing, cleaning, cooking, running around all day, helping your family, and spending time with your loved ones, while also trying to eat right, find time to work out, and stay healthy. That was me for a long time, so I know what that world is like, too. We are all incredibly busy, and I know how hard it is to juggle eating well and staying active with everything else you have to do. Every single one of us has to find the path to taking care of ourselves, a path that works for us. We all have a path to better health, fitness, and energy, and while yours may turn out to be different than mine, in this book, I want to help you find it.

My life is no crazier or more stressed out than the life of any other working mom with a demanding job and a husband and a house and laundry and meals to cook (I still do most of that stuff myself, to be honest—that's how my mom did it, and that's how I'm doing it, too). I love my work, but I also love my family, and I've got to make time for both. I spend a lot of time on the road performing shows, which is probably different from your situation, but you likely have other challenges and things to get done that are just as important and just as difficult to balance, in different ways. We're all trying to figure it out as we go along. We're all trying to do the best we can.

That's why my approach to health can be summarized in one word: simple. I'm not about fancy cooking or complicated workout routines. Heck, I can't even figure out yoga. I'm a vegetarian, but I'm not soaking dried beans and making hummus from scratch. I've seen a lot of books out there about fitness and diet and health, and I swear, some of the things they recommend sound a little crazy or just plain confusing to me. Not to judge what anyone else wants to do—everyone has to find what works for them, but I sure don't have the time for all that. I don't know about you, but it's rare that I get a proper vacation, and it'll probably be a while before I have the time to squeeze one in. Every minute of my day is precious, and I'm not going to waste any of them rehydrating seaweed or chopping up ten different vegetables when I can get a bag of mixed stir-fry veggies for a couple of dollars at the grocery store.

I know you all have similar issues. I know because you tell me. You tell me before my shows, when you come by to meet me. You send me messages or write me letters. One of the main ways I get to interact with people is when they tell me their stories. Sometimes these stories are about how a certain song helped them get through something, and sometimes they're about how something I said on TV or in an interview made an impact on their lives.

I'm always surprised that people listen to what I say, but I guess they do! I've had people tell me they finally got in shape, they lost fifty pounds, they changed how they ate, because of something they heard me say about the easy ways I swap out healthier ingredients in my favorite comfort foods, or how I do pull-ups at the playground while my son is running around, or my philosophy about working out on the days I can, even when I don't feel like it, because I know there will be days when I can't.

I want to be healthy and fit fifty-two weeks of the year, but that doesn't mean I have to be perfect every day. That would be impossible. I have to make sure I have time with my kids, with my husband, and for my faith, because those are the things that make the rest of it worthwhile. I want to be a good example for my kids. I want to live as long as I possibly can. I want to cherish every day of this life, and when I don't feel good, when I don't have energy, when I'm not nourished, I can't make the most of the minutes God's given me to be here on this earth.

That's why I developed the Fit52 lifestyle, inspired by my own experiences and by some of my friends who are fitness and nutrition professionals and who have guided me and taught me much of what I know today (you'll meet them later). This philosophy is a year-round common-sense approach to health and fitness that involves doing your best *most of the time*—and by that I don't mean being naughty for three days and good for four. I mean doing your absolute best in most instances, every

Meet
Penny Jean Fisher!

week, fifty-two weeks of the year. Be good on all the days you can, so that on the days when you slip up or want to indulge, you don't sabotage your whole plan. Your goal isn't to be perfect every second of every day. It's to be mostly in line with what you want for your life over the course of each week. You messed up today? That's okay. Your week is what matters. What you do on the other six days matters. One bad food choice or one lazy day on the couch isn't going to wreck everything, because when you look at a healthy *week* as your goal instead of a single healthy day, you always have a reason to get back on the horse. Fit52 is all about balance. And let's be honest—who couldn't use a little more balance in their lives?

To do good, you have to feel good, and to feel good, you have to do good. You have to be strong and steadfast and remember what's important to you. In this book, you'll find out that I am disciplined. I enjoy having a game plan and adjusting my plan to meet my goals. It's not about doing what's easy. It's about doing what's simple. It's easier not to work out. It's easier to go through the drive-thru than to cook something at home. But it's simple to walk more and it's simple to make meals and snacks that don't take too much prep time. I'm not willing to pay the price for those so-called easy shortcuts (at least, not most of the time), but I'll take the simple swap of a decadent food for a healthier food any day of the week.

But sure, I'm human. I have days when I indulge, or don't have time to exercise. There are always birthday parties and girls' nights out (okay, they're rare, but they do happen) and holiday time with family that I want to make sure I get to enjoy and not feel like I'm depriving myself. I have days when I don't make the best choices for my body. But they are not *most days*. They are my exceptions, not my rules. The trick is to make the things you want to do for yourself as effortless as the things you are tempted to do but know you shouldn't.

There are ways to make working out simpler. There are ways to make healthy eating and cooking simpler—and sometimes even faster than ordering a pizza. It shouldn't be a hassle to be healthy, but sometimes, it seems like it is. I wrote this book to show you that it doesn't have to be that way. You can be fit and healthy and gain strength and confidence every week, all year long, year after year. You can be Fit52.

About This Book

Most of the time, I feel like I'm just Carrie, living in my bubble of family and work. I make music and I want people to like it, but I don't really think about people caring about what I do in my personal life every day. I'm a pretty private person, and I don't usually talk a lot about personal things in public. The little bit I do say, I guess people hear, and I hope

that means I can be a positive influence in someone's life. Maybe I can help some of the people who might feel they need some direction or inspiration to get healthy and take a little bit better care of their bodies and souls. Maybe I can help you. That's my purpose in writing this book.

I didn't always know what I know now. Over the years, I've tried a lot and been through a lot on my own fitness and health journey, not to mention my journey from Oklahoma farm girl to Nashville country music singer. I had a pretty normal childhood. My adult life has been anything but. I'm not gonna lie—I've done some dumb things. I've made some big mistakes. When I started on this journey, I didn't know much, but at a certain point I got a handle on what I needed to do to achieve my goals. And I'm still learning, of course. But if I can save you some time, help you avoid some of my mistakes, and show you how to get right down to the business of feeling better about yourself, well, that's all I'm going for. I'm just me and you're just you, but being who we are in the best possible way every week of the year is what we're meant to do in this life. I believe that.

To me, "Carrie" is someone very different from "Carrie Underwood." "Carrie Underwood" is the public me—the person you see on the stage or on TV. That's me, living out my dream. "Carrie" is just me, without all the bells and whistles. My friends aren't celebrities or, for the most part, even music business people. They are moms and wives and people who started their own businesses. "Carrie Underwood" might write a different book than this book (although I did name each chapter in this book after one of my songs—maybe that was a "Carrie Underwood" move, but I hope you'll enjoy recognizing some of those titles). The real everyday me—the mom, the wife, the friend—is probably a lot like you, and this is the book "Carrie" has always wanted to write.

So here I am, sharing my life with you a little, and telling you how I found my path and what I've learned along the way about how to be healthy. If you want some of my drive, some of my discipline, or some of my resolve, or even if you're just trying to get your legs to look a little more like mine (for some reason, I get a lot of questions about how I got

my legs, so I'm going to do my best to tell you), then this is the place to find it. But I promise not to tell you to eat weird foods or try fad workout routines or do crazy cleanses or anything like that. I'm just going to tell you what I do, and as you'll see, it's a pretty commonsense approach: a basic (but fun) workout I love to do and ideas for getting moving in all the other parts and times of your life, along with some easy advice on how to eat for health at home or wherever you are (and what to do when you're tempted to go off track). And hey, a little storytelling thrown in for good measure.

You and I both know how much energy and strength, physical and emotional, it takes to get through a busy day when everybody depends on us. That's why it's so important to get strong and fit and healthy—to eat and move to fuel your life, so that you can experience joy and connection and a bigger capacity for love in all that you do.

I've always believed that to get where you want to go, you need to push yourself just a little outside your comfort zone, and you've got to keep forging ahead, even when it's hard. This book is about making those hard times easier. What it all comes down to is how each one of us learns to walk that path between pleasure and health, staying busy and wheel-spinning, stress and ease, disconnection and love. On most days of the week, I find my path. Let's find yours.

PART ONE

the girl you think i am

HEALTHY LESSONS FROM THE SOFTBALL FIELD TO THE STADIUM STAGE

Meet my firstborn, Ace Underwood!

THANK GOD FOR HOMETOWNS

Growing Up and Growing Roots

There are a lot of books I *could* have written. I could have written a book about the story of my life so far, or about the music business, or about faith or family or even career success. But at this point in my life, I really want to write about health and fitness, two subjects that I am truly, deeply passionate about.

I wasn't always into fitness. As a kid, I didn't really know what "being fit" meant. Today, exercise is one of the most important parts of my life. It's my "prescription" for feeling good, strong, and capable. It is the best mood-booster I know, and I love the way it helps me cope with the stresses of both parenting and performing. I don't know how I would survive without it.

I'm also devoted to healthy eating and to living a lifestyle that makes me feel energized and strong, that keeps me lean, and that has me

looking on the outside the way I feel on the inside. But again, it wasn't always this way. When I think back to how I ate as a kid, it's hard to believe I'm the same person. I've come a long way, and I've learned a lot about health and fitness, and my hope is that I can help you along your way, too.

To me, fitness and health should be simple, sensible, and a fully integrated part of life. These aspects of life should feel natural, like the way you felt as a kid, playing on the playground or eating an apple straight off the

tree or just relishing that feeling of being alive in a beautiful world. My goal is to help you figure out how to make health a priority in your life— not by adding one more thing to your endless to-do list, but by turning the quest for health into part of who you are.

So who are you? Where did you come from? What has your path been up to this point? How were you raised, and how did that shape you? How have you changed over the years, in terms of your awareness about what you need to feel good about yourself, to be strong, and to live your truth? What you learned as a kid tends to stick with you. Maybe you are still living with many of the health habits that you picked up when you were young or that you learned from your family—and maybe not all of these habits are good for you. Or maybe your childhood has influenced you by teaching you what *not* to do in your current life. Either way, who you were influences who you are.

In that spirit, I'll begin this book by telling you some stories about where I came from, where I've been along the way, and what I've learned over the years about how to live healthier. Slowly but surely, I've figured out how to calibrate my life to be in tune with who I am and who I want to be for my family, for my fans, and for myself. But it wasn't always this way. It took a while for me to figure out the kind of life that was right for me, especially when things happened in my life that I could never have predicted. I certainly didn't always know what I know today. In the beginning, I was just an active kid in a small town, with good-hearted, well-meaning parents and a lot to learn.

Growing Up, Oklahoma-Style

I grew up in Checotah, Oklahoma, population 3,500. Checotah is a small country town full of wide-open spaces, pastures and woods here and there, family farms, and, best of all, decent people who look out for each other. We're about sixty-five miles southwest of Tulsa, we've got a Civil War battle site, and we're the self-proclaimed "Steer-Wrestling Capital of the World." Once you get outside of downtown, about all you'll see are farms and ranches, Interstate 40 running just south of town, and Lake Eufaula, where people like to go on the weekends. Checotah is pretty flat, not overly wooded or green, and sometimes we get tornadoes outside of town, rumbling over the plains. My husband, Mike, likes to say, "It's

so flat, you can watch your dog run away for two days straight around here!" But what I love about Checotah, other than the people, is the quiet. Step outside, and all you'll hear are birds singing, cicadas buzzing, the wind. It's peaceful. It's simple. It's home.

My mom was an elementary school teacher for twenty-five years, mostly teaching fifth grade. My dad worked in a paper mill, but we also lived on a small cattle farm of about 160 acres. My parents bred the cattle to sell for extra income. We raised up those baby calves and my dad baled hay and fed them in the winter. I helped out, bottle-feeding the ones that needed some extra attention and naming them—they were like pets to me. Sometimes I had to help move the cows in and out of different pastures and pens. The more bodies you've got for a job like that, the better. We'd shut down different parts of the pasture at different times of the year. When a fence went down because a cow trampled through it (this always seemed to happen when my dad was out of town), Mom and I would have to go down there and get all the cows back in, then rig the fence so it was strong enough to hold until my dad got home to repair it.

I have two older sisters, but they were out of the house by the time I was in grade school, so I grew up like an only child in a lot of ways. That was okay with me. I had a nephew about my age, and there was another girl in my class who lived nearby in my spread-out neighborhood. I had friends from Girl Scouts and school, and we would have sleepovers and roam the countryside around whatever house we were playing at together that day. Most everyone lived outside of town.

I think I was lucky to grow up in a place and at a time where kids didn't need to be overly supervised, although the older neighbors who were home most days usually kept one eye on us kids to be sure we were okay. In a place like Checotah, everybody knows who's coming and going. You'd see this person's car or know when that person had a visitor. My friend's grandpa lived across the street from us and he always knew when we were climbing his trees. He'd come out and sit in a lawn chair in the grass. We'd throw apples down to him, and he'd peel them. It was a win-win. We had fun, and he had his apples for the week.

My friends and I spent a lot of time outside, hunting for snakes, scooping tadpoles and turtles out of the pond to look at them, catching frogs in the ditch or fireflies in the fields at dusk (and letting them go again), chasing each other through the pastures and backyards and little stands of trees here and there. My family didn't have cable, so we had maybe five TV channels. What else was I gonna do but go play outside? When we weren't in school or sleeping or called in for family dinner, we were usually out there running wild.

To be honest, I was always filthy with pond muck or dust or dirt from the cow pasture. I remember going to a friend's house when I was seven or eight. I caught a frog outside and brought it into their kitchen and put it in the sink. At my house, that was a completely acceptable thing to do, but my friend's mom flipped out. "Take that thing outside! It's filthy and disgusting!" I wasn't sure if she meant the frog or me. Another time, my father brought me a wild rabbit he found, and I accidentally let it loose in our house. It took us days to find that little guy.

I'm grateful for my free-range childhood. It was fun and interesting, and I had the freedom to explore and learn about what I loved—animals, sports, and singing. And I was always active. My friends and I were always running around. It wasn't something we even had to think about. It was just the way we all were—and if you ask me, that's the way life is meant to be.

The Beginning of My Fitness and Health Evolution

When I was a kid, I was into sports . . . sort of. I loved basketball, but I'm not very tall, so I wasn't great at it. I preferred T-ball when I was really young, then I moved on to softball and also cheerleading. But we weren't a "sporty" family, necessarily, and by the time I was fifteen, I was out there singing in talent shows around Oklahoma and Arkansas and didn't have time for sports anymore. When I was in high school, I joined a country music band and we played in bars on the weekends. (It's not as shady as it sounds—my mom always came along as a chaperone.) You can only miss so many practices before you get benched, so I moved on from sports. I knew I wasn't going to be a professional athlete, but sometimes I imagined becoming a country singer. I thought that would be a fun career. A dream? A little unrealistic? Sure, but I didn't care. I was an ambitious kid and I wanted to make it happen, so other than studying to get good grades, singing is where I put most of my efforts.

My parents weren't exactly exercise fanatics, either. They liked to go to my games, but they were just as happy going to see me sing. Every once in a while, they would get on "health kicks." For a couple of weeks, my mom would do Jane Fonda workout tapes in our little living room. I remember watching her doing these leg lifts on the floor with ankle weights and thinking, *What does that even do? I could do, like, a thousand of those and not feel a thing.* It seemed silly to me, and annoying that she would take over the TV and our entire small living room just to lift her legs up and down like that. As for my dad,

whenever he decided he needed to drop a few pounds, he'd skip breakfast for a couple of days, do some curls with a dumbbell or a few chest presses on the floor, and that was that. It was so *Dad.* He's still like that. What I didn't realize at the time was how hard it can be to stay fit when your life is busy. With their jobs and three daughter to raise, my parents didn't exactly have a lot of leisure hours for exercising.

As for how we ate, well . . . I'm going to throw my mom under the bus a little bit by saying this, but I don't think she'll mind. She'll be the first one to tell you she's not a cook. We'd have fried Spam and shells-and-cheese from a box and call it dinner. We never had fresh vegetables—only canned or frozen—and not a lot of fruit. We had a lot of potatoes, but no fresh broccoli, no fresh corn on the cob. Recently, my mom came to visit us. We had corn for dinner and she kept commenting on how delicious it was. "It's because I shucked it myself, Mom,"

I said. "You know, under those husks, there's something called a fresh vegetable!" I think that's why I grew up not liking vegetables. They were always so . . . mushy?

Sometimes my mom made taco salad, but it was fatty ground beef and iceberg lettuce and a ton of cheddar cheese, topped in Fritos and Thousand Island dressing. It was a salad . . . I guess . . . but there wasn't much nutritional value in what we were eating. We fried everything—even hot dogs—and I remember eating big brownies or chocolate chip cookies before school. Literally three brownies, or five Chips Ahoy! super-chunky chocolate chip cookies, and that was breakfast. Who lets their kid eat like that for breakfast? I was the last of three kids, so by that point, I think my mom was just like, "Eat whatever." I guess that was one fight that wasn't really worth it for her.

Many Sundays after church, we went to my Grandma Nell's house. We always sat in her little eat-in kitchen with the avocado-green appliances and she always made pot roast with small potatoes and carrots, with cobbler for dessert. It was our fanciest meal of the week. And of course, since it was Oklahoma, beef was pretty much a dietary staple.

In our small town, there weren't many restaurants or any health food stores. Most folks had to work and didn't have a lot of time to spend in the kitchen, but I was always curious about eating better. When I first saw a TV commercial for Silk soy milk, I wanted to try it. I wasn't much of a milk drinker, but I thought, *This looks interesting. I might be willing to drink this.* Sometimes I would beg my mom to let me try other "health foods" I would see in the store, like almond milk or tofu. My experiments weren't usually very successful. If you don't know what to do with tofu, it's pretty gross. I remember being excited to get Lean Cuisine meals, so I could make some chicken and rice for myself because I felt like that had to be healthier than fried hot dogs. Somewhere deep inside my teenage self, there was a healthy eater trying to get out, but inevitably, like my mom shelving her exercise videos and my dad putting away his weights and eating breakfast again, I would go back to eating whatever I was eating before. It was easier.

Then something happened that changed the whole course of how I would choose to eat for the rest of my life. It began with something that had been right in front of me the whole time, and I never saw it: our cows.

An Awakening

One afternoon when I was about thirteen years old and my parents were out in the pasture taking care of the calves (or so I thought), I decided it would be a nice daughterly thing to do to bring them some iced tea. I filled up two glasses and carried them outside. Instead of taking my usual shortcut by climbing over the corner of the fence and then going through the blackberry briars, I walked down the road and up the worn path to the gate. I walked directly into the pasture and down the hill to where we had a kind of setup with chutes, where they would bring the calves in to do the banding (basically, this is how they neutered the male calves).

Our calves were always adorable. They would jump around and play, and they were so sweet. Think of the most adorable baby cows you've ever seen at a petting zoo. In my memory, that's what they looked like. And for some reason, I had never seen my parents do the banding before. Or I just hadn't paid attention. This time, I noticed the contraption that would stretch out a teeny tiny rubber band and put it around each calf's "male parts." I looked, and then I looked again. And for the first time, I saw and actually realized what was happening. I was horrified . . . and confused.

"Mom . . . why are you doing that?" I asked.

"It makes the calves grow bigger," she said.

I let that sink in, and then it hit me. "Whoa, wait, you mean . . . you mean so people can *eat them*? You mean, so they can end up on somebody's *plate*?"

Now, my mom probably knows me better than anybody else on this planet, and I'll never forget the look on her face when I asked her that question. She knew exactly what this knowledge would do to me, but she also knew she had to tell me the truth. She looked at me and just nodded. She wasn't going to sugarcoat it, and in retrospect, I appreciate her honesty.

But I was utterly shocked. I was the kid who would pick up worms off the road and put them in the dirt so they wouldn't get fried in the sun or run over by a car (I still do this when I'm out for a run—old habits die hard, I guess). I was the kid who snuck out of the house at night with a package of hot dogs to feed the stray dogs. I have this deep and unshakable love for all life. It sounds weird, but somehow, at thirteen years old, I had never really thought about the purpose of our farm. There were always cows. I always helped with them. They were a part of our lives, but I had never considered where they went when they left us. And like most kids, I had never considered where the meat on my plate came from, either.

At the same time, I realized, in a flash, that I had been a participant in this process my whole life. A huge wave of guilt washed over me, and I wanted to burst into tears. I had eaten the hamburgers and the pot roasts and never once connected those with the baby calves I loved so much. I had a lot of friends in various farming organizations and after-school programs who would raise cows and show them and spend all this time with them, and then . . . send them off to be butchered when they were done? How had I not seen it before? How could I have been so blind?

This was a transformational moment for me, and in a matter of seconds, my course was set and my resolve was firm: I would never eat beef again. I announced it to my parents. And that was that. This was probably the response my mom expected when she realized the jig was up, but I bet she was wondering what the heck she was going to feed me now. She soon realized she didn't have to worry. I was self-sufficient by thirteen, and when she served beef, I always made something else for myself, like chicken and rice or Boca burgers. (At the time, I still ate

chicken—in the context of my family, it was hard to imagine another alternative.) I've never gone back to eating beef, and I never will. Instead, I've progressed in the opposite direction, eventually dropping all animal meat out of my diet as I felt ready to. I don't feel that my body needs it.

I do want to say that this is just my decision, and that brings me to an important side note, and the last point I want to make on this subject: I respect what my parents did to keep food on the table for our family. I also respect farmers. I know that dietary choice can be a controversial subject. Not eating meat is a personal decision of mine, and I would never expect anyone else to do it if it wasn't the right decision for them. I don't expect you to avoid meat just because I do. You can eat whatever you want—it's not my business to judge. We all have to live according to our own beliefs, and this is one of mine, but to each his own. I hope you won't judge me, either, or think that I'm trying to tell anyone else what is right and what is wrong. My husband eats meat, and that's his choice. In this book, the recipes are vegetarian, but you could add some animal protein to some of these meals like my husband does, if you want to make that choice—the recipes my husband adapts will include those suggestions, for those of you who prefer to eat that way (look for the "What Mike Likes" notes throughout the recipe chapter).

Bottom line: We're all born with a sense of right and wrong, and each of us chooses what is most important to us. I believe that life feels better when you have convictions and you live by them, no matter what they are. If something doesn't feel right to you, and you don't follow your heart, you are the one who has to live with it. With that said, the choices that are right for me are not necessarily the ones that are right for you. And that's all I'm going to say on the subject.

How I Left Checotah

Before I knew it, I was graduating from high school and going off to Northeastern State University in Tahlequah, Oklahoma, to major in mass communications with an emphasis on broadcast journalism. My dreams of being a country singer were fading as I got older and more practical and realistic. I imagined I would become a journalist, or maybe a reporter or even a news anchor. I still participated in a summer performance program, dancing and singing for college credit, but it was just something fun to do so that I could keep music in my life a little longer. I knew that it was time to get serious about a career. I'd always had good grades, and I wasn't going to blow it now for some silly dream of stardom. Sometimes, when I missed performing, I would tell myself, *Everybody wants to be famous. What makes you think you're so special?* And I'd go back to studying.

But then, the summer before my senior year in college, I was at home, watching TV in the living room, and I saw a news program talking about people auditioning for *American Idol.* I got online and saw that the auditions closest to me were in St. Louis. *That might be fun,* I thought. *Just to see.* I called out to my mom, "How far is St. Louis?"

She said it was six or seven hours away and I thought, *That's too far. Out of the question.* She asked me why I wanted to know. "Oh, nothing," I said. "I just saw they're having *American Idol* auditions."

She came into the living room and looked at me with her arms crossed. Then she said, "If you want to try out, I'll take you."

"No, it's dumb," I said. "What are the chances?"

"Oh, I don't know. Just think about it," she said. "I'll drive you if you want me to."

We went, I auditioned, and the next couple of days were a blur, but eventually I got my "golden ticket" that meant I had made it through to the next level and I was going to Hollywood! That ticket is every auditioning contestant's dream, and it had

happened to me. I couldn't believe it! Then the reality hit me: I was going to have to go to California . . . alone . . . on an airplane . . . for the first time in my life. I was twenty-one years old, and I'd thought I had an idea of where my life was going. Turned out, I didn't have a clue.

The day I was scheduled to get on that plane, I was terrified—to go to Hollywood, to sing with all those other people who were so talented, and especially to leave home and go that far away all by myself. On the way out of town, we stopped at a grocery store so my mom could run in and grab me some lip liner. I sat in the front seat with my dad, just the two of us, and suddenly I thought, *What am I doing? This is scary! Am I really doing this?* And I started to cry. My dad turned to me and said, "Carrie, we can go home right now, and we don't ever have to talk about this again."

I took a deep breath. I didn't want to be afraid. "No," I said. "I'll do it. I'll go." And so I did.

Looking back, I see how everything that happened to me happened for a reason. There was a reason I grew up on a cattle farm. It was God's way of helping me define my values. There was a reason I didn't get famous until I was an adult. I wasn't ready before then. I had to grow up a little first. There was a reason I went to college, even though I didn't go into broadcast journalism. It got me out into the world a little and taught me how to manage my own life and balance my responsibilities. And there was a reason I was born in that small town, and lived there for eighteen years, and in Oklahoma until I was twenty-one. It gave me roots, and the chance to grow them deep and strong, to figure out what I believed, what mattered to me, and who I wanted to be—even if the life in store for me would turn out to be full of surprises.

Those roots have served me well over the course of my life so far. Whenever life throws me a curveball, they help me to remember what is truly important: family, faith, friendship, following my dreams, doing the right thing even when it's hard, and honoring the body, the mind, and the life God gave me. Those roots also helped keep me grounded once I got to California and my whole world changed.

Go Outside to Get Healthier

Remember when you were a kid, how you used to play outside, running around, rolling in the grass, climbing trees? There's no reason you can't do some of that now, as an adult. These days, many of us don't get outside much, but it's healthy to be out in the sunshine and the fresh air. You could start by taking a walk or a hike in a local park or wilderness area, or even just around your own neighborhood. Take your kids to the playground and don't just sit on the bench—play with them! (See page 174 for some exercises you can do on the playground.) Run around, walk barefoot in the grass, take deep breaths of the fresh air. If you're up for it, you could even see if you remember how to do a cartwheel, or climb a tree, or just run for no reason.

Spending too much time inside, especially staring at a television or a computer screen, can make people feel disconnected from themselves. Going outside and looking around at the real world can feel like waking up again. Get out there and reconnect with your physical body. Start by trying to be outside for just a few minutes every day and work up from there. You don't have to do anything fancy. Even if you just step outside and breathe the fresh air and feel the sun and the wind and listen to the birds, it can totally change your mood.

Meet Zero Fisher!

My Secret for Comfort Food Indulgences: Healthy Swaps

MOM'S BISCUITS WITH CHOCOLATE GRAVY
Active time: 10 minutes
Total time: 10 minutes

Serves 2

MOM'S VERSION
¼ cup unsweetened cocoa
   powder
½ cup sugar
¼ cup flour
2 cups milk
½ teaspoon vanilla extract
6 Pillsbury biscuits, baked
   and torn into small pieces

CARRIE'S VERSION
¼ cup unsweetened cocoa
   powder
¼ cup real maple syrup
¼ cup flour
2 cups unsweetened vanilla
   almond milk
½ teaspoon vanilla extract
1 (whole) Thomas' Light
   Multi-Grain English
   Muffin, split

One of my favorite things my mom used to make when I was a kid was this amazing breakfast of biscuits with chocolate "gravy" on them. (I know it sounds more like dessert, but occasionally this would kick off my Saturday morning.) So good! Today, I still make this dish every once in a while, but my recipe is a little bit different. I'm going to share it with you here because this is an example of one of the most important things I do to keep my diet on track: healthy (or rather, healthier) swaps.

I still make food I love, but whenever I do, I swap out some of the ingredients that are the least nutritious or the highest in fat or sugar. With a few healthy adjustments, an indulgent recipe can taste almost exactly the same, but it will be a lot less of a nutritional disaster. This recipe always reminds me of home, and it's a way for me to have a piece of my childhood in my life . . . once in a while. Know that chocolate gravy, even with swaps, is still a treat. It's certainly not health food, and I don't eat chocolate gravy every day. It's something for special occasions only—but this version is still better for me than the one I ate back in Oklahoma.

Here's the recipe, with my mom's ingredient list and then mine—I put my healthy swaps in bold. Notice that I only swapped three things (simple!), but that alone saves 160 calories, 1 gram of fat, 20 grams of carbs, and over 35 grams of sugar in the gravy alone. Add the difference between the biscuits and the English

390 calories, 6.5 grams fat, 65.5 grams carbs, 11.5 grams protein, 59.9 grams sugar, 3.5 grams fiber, 122 grams sodium (doesn't include the biscuit)

CARRIE'S VERSION:

230 calories, 5.5 grams fat, 45.5 grams carbs, 4.5 grams protein, 5 grams fiber, 24 grams sugar, 163.5 mg sodium (doesn't include the English muffin)

muffin and the total savings is **360 calories, 2 grams of fat, 40 grams of carbs, and 36 grams of sugar.** *See what simple swaps can do? (On the left side of this page, you can check out the more specific nutrition information for the chocolate gravy only.)*

Note: If you use a high-quality cocoa powder, it really improves the taste.

In a small saucepan, whisk the dry ingredients together. Whisk in the milk. Heat over medium heat, stirring continuously, until the mixture simmers and gets thick like gravy. Remove from the heat and add the vanilla. Serve the chocolate gravy over biscuits pieces or (in my version) an English muffin.

all you have to do is start writing

I keep a journal, and it means a lot to me. It keeps me honest and accountable. I don't tell very many people about every detail of my life, but I tell my journal. I record what I did that day, anything unusual that happened, what I ate and how many calories and macronutrients (protein, carbs, fat) I had that day, how much I exercised, and other things that are important to me. If you would like to do this, too, then look for these journal boxes throughout the book, where I'll give you suggestions for what you might want to write about. Use this space to reflect on the way your life is now, and the kind of life you may ideally want to have. You can write these thoughts by hand in a real journal with actual pages like I do, or you could keep your journal on the computer. Whatever method you are most likely to stick with is the best way.

In this chapter, I've reflected on my childhood. This can be a valuable way to look back and discover why you feel the way you do about who you are, how you live, or how you got to be where you are today. In your journal, you might want to answer one or more of these questions:

1. What are your earliest memories of physical activity? Were you into sports? Did you like to play outside?
2. What was the most fun active thing you did as a kid? See if you can remember how it felt to move when you were young.
3. Do you still feel that way about exercise, or has your attitude or practice of it changed since childhood?
4. What are your earliest food memories? What did you love to eat? What did you dislike?
5. What kind of attitudes did your family have about food? Was health a priority in your family, or not so much? Do you remember things your parents or friends said about food that stuck with you?
6. Do you still feel the way you felt then, or have your ideas about food and health changed?
7. What is important to you? What are your beliefs? Think about what matters to you and whether you live by those beliefs. If you don't, what's stopping you?

I AIN'T IN CHECOTAH ANYMORE

How American Idol (and a Few Extra Pounds) Happened

Somehow, without knowing how airports worked and missing one of my flights, I made it to Los Angeles on my own. When I got there, I was in a different world. There were so many people! I'd never been in a taxi before. I left Oklahoma in February and arrived in Los Angeles to weather like summertime. My head was spinning.

I was a fish out of water, and it was exciting but also intimidating. Everything was new, and I wasn't sure how I was supposed to act. It seemed like every chance they gave me to say something awkward, I managed to do it. I swear I said intelligent things, but they never had the camera on when I did. Shortly after we all arrived in Hollywood, Ryan Seacrest was taking us around the city, and he did an interview with me. I guess he'd heard that the little country girl was taking pictures of palm

trees, so he asked me if I'd ever seen one before. Nope. Then he asked me if I had seen any stars yet. I said, "No, it's been pretty cloudy."

He said, "No, I mean celebrities."

In our interview, we had been talking about outside things like the trees and buildings, so that's where my mind was. It was so embarrassing. I felt like people were thinking, *Aww, isn't that cute, she's never been on a plane before, she's never seen a palm tree before, she's never been to Hollywood before, she thinks stars are in the sky—how quaint.*

But there were some great parts of the California experience. For one, I was singing every day. I felt like part of my life that had long been buried had reemerged, like a surprise visit from an old friend. For another, being a vegetarian was actually pretty common in

California—I couldn't believe they had whole restaurants just for vegans! (Even though I was not vegan at the time, the idea thrilled me.) They had whole stores with nothing but health food! They knew how to cook tofu so it actually tasted awesome! I obviously wasn't in Checotah anymore.

Everybody in California seemed to be into exercising and being healthy, and that was all new and interesting to me, too, but I could only admire it from afar, because for the contestants on *American Idol*, there was hardly any time for things like going on hikes or going out to eat, and I didn't have any money for that anyway. They kept us busy constantly, and they fed us, but those craft service tables they had for us in the rehearsal spaces were piled with junk food all day—bear claws and doughnuts in the morning, big vats of pasta or fried rice for lunch, stacks of pizzas or tacos and platters of cookies for dinner, and big trays of food they brought around to everyone to keep us going on the late

My fellow Idol alum Bo Bice!

nights. Chips and cups of ramen noodles and mini tacos or quesadillas— there were probably some carrots and hummus, too, but I didn't bother with those. I grabbed what was easy and what I knew I liked. All I had to do was tell them I didn't eat beef and they catered to that, like, "Bring Carrie some spaghetti!" I wasn't eating beef, but I certainly wasn't eating healthy.

We started out in a dormitory sort of situation with roommates, but as the rounds progressed and the group got smaller, they moved us into apartments. We each had a small budget, and I should've thought to buy some egg whites and vegetables now that I had a small kitchen to cook in. But since I never had much money to spare, I waited to get to the set

and have one of those bear claws instead. Why pay for food when I could get it for free?

For the first few months, we would film some shows, go home for a while, then come back for more cuts and filming. Before long, as the group dwindled, we stayed in California all the time. I couldn't believe I was living there. I still wasn't used to being in the spotlight, but I knew one thing, and that was how to sing. That carried me through, and I gradually got used to my new environment and my strange new life.

One day—it must have been when I was in the Top 12—I was getting my hair and makeup done and they brought lunch and it was KFC. I was still eating chicken at this point, but it was more a matter of convenience. I didn't particularly enjoy it, and the longer I lived in California, the more I encountered people who didn't seem to think it was necessary to eat animals at all. I couldn't help thinking that maybe I didn't need to, either. But there was that convenient bucket of fried chicken. I remember eating it like I always did, but this time, I questioned it more seriously and consciously. I thought, *Why am I eating this? I don't need this. I'm in California. They have all the vegetarian food I could want. I don't need to eat fried chicken ever again.* The few of us that had advanced this far were getting more special treatment, and we actually had a chef to make us dinner in the apartments where we lived. Why would I eat fried chicken when I had a chef making my dinner? I didn't make a bold declaration about it or anything like that. I don't think I told anyone, but in my heart, I knew that was the end. I never ate any kind of meat again after that day.

But there was another reason, too—a reason why fried chicken suddenly seemed like a bad choice. It was definitely about not wanting to eat animals anymore, but it was also a kickoff to a whole new attitude about my health and my weight. And it all started with internet message boards.

A Rude Awakening

Back in 2005, the internet wasn't anything like it is today. Facebook had just been invented but most people hadn't heard of it, and social media wasn't really a thing yet, but there were message boards. Remember those? It's hard to believe things have changed so much since then, but message boards were the main way people communicated online. These boards were all devoted to different subjects, and were places people could write posts and talk about their common interests.

One evening, I was playing around on the computer with some of the other contestants and we found a message board devoted to *American Idol*. At first we were excited to see what people were saying about us, since we didn't have any kind of feedback from the people out there watching us on television. It was fun reading what the fans had to say. There were a lot of them out there—who knew? (Not us!) But then we saw the negative comments.

These days, everybody knows that online comments sections can be brutal, but back then, this was all new, and we were not prepared for it. Most of the things people wrote were sweet and supportive and encouraging and even flattering to all of us, but then there was that 1 percent that was just awful. And I guess it's human nature to focus on the negative, because we did. We were obsessed with the negative comments. The naysayers picked us apart—our appearances, our performances—with comments like, "He totally blew that song," or "What was she *wearing*?" or "Why does he make that weird face when he sings?" or "Why is she so fat?"

We were all a bit shocked by the mean-spiritedness, and we started to feel like targets. I think this was the first time I really recognized that we were in the public eye. We had been living in a bubble, and the bubble had burst. Every week, the only people we saw were the few hundred people who fit into the studio. We knew there were people out there watching us in their living rooms, but we didn't really know how many, or where they were, or who they were. The only access we really had to our viewers' opinions were those message boards.

Every night after rehearsal, back at the apartment, we would all log in to see what people were saying. We didn't want to read those mean comments, but we couldn't stop ourselves. And some of the negative comments about me really made an impression—in particular "Carrie's getting fat," and "What is up with her fingernails?"

Now that I'm a little older and wiser, I look back and think, *Those are not your average good-hearted, nice people. Don't listen to them, younger Carrie!* If I could go back in time and tell myself that, I would. And of course now I never read the comments section on anything about myself because I know some of it will be mean, and I know how that feels. I take it all very personally, and it hurts my feelings. Hey, I'm human, too! But there was a bright side to all of this. First, I'd been a fingernail biter all my life, and those comments about my nails made me quit biting them, right then and there. And second, I realized my pants *were* a lot tighter than they had been. I *did* have less energy. I *wasn't* feeling that great or weathering the stress of the show all that well. My steady diet of junk food, along with all that time we spent sitting around waiting on set or rehearsing songs in the studio all day and late into the night, was taking its toll. Why hadn't I noticed it before?

I am not excusing those mean commenters, and I am also not trying to be anything other than body-positive. I think that everyone should love the body they are in, no matter what. But the fact of the matter was that I knew I could do better. I knew this wasn't the version of myself that I wanted to be. I wasn't taking care of myself. That was what really struck me. How had I let this happen?

In retrospect, I think seeing those comments was a blessing in disguise. For the first time in my life, I took a good hard look at my lifestyle. It wasn't so much vanity as wanting to feel like myself again. So when I had that last meal of fried chicken, I was already thinking hard about getting back in touch with who I was and who I wanted to be. I wanted to live according to my values and career goals. I wanted to look and be healthy. Part of me recognized that if I really wanted to have a career in the music business, I was going to have to work on my public image. How I looked was a part of that—it's the reality of being a performer. But I also wanted to find what I needed to do to get where I wanted to be. Life on *American Idol*, not to mention in the music business, requires energy, strength, and commitment. Those message boards lit a fire under me, and it was like I unearthed my old forgotten dream, dusted it off, and reinstated it in my head. That gave me a new vision for how I wanted to present myself and take care of myself. It was the best and most effective motivation I had ever experienced.

But it's one thing to want to get yourself into great shape, and it's another thing to know how to do it. I had no knowledge at all about fitness or healthy eating. I set the intention, but I didn't know how to execute it. It would take me a while to figure it all out, because at first, my ideas about how to get from here to there were all wrong.

My Calorie Conundrum

Once the show ended, the Top 10 contestants went out together on the *American Idol* summer tour. We all traveled around together, performing in different cities, and I decided this was the perfect opportunity for me to change my lifestyle and take more conscious control of my health and my body. My first thought about how to do that was pretty simple: *Why do people gain weight? Because they eat too many calories. Okay, cool. So, if I just eat fewer of those, I'll lose weight.*

I started to look into how many calories different foods had, and that was an important step in raising my awareness about how I was eating. For the first time in my life, I started reading labels, and making some changes. I noticed a difference *immediately*, and that was gratifying.

I started dropping some weight and feeling better. A lot of that probably came from cutting out all meat, but being a vegetarian can be tricky if you don't know what you're doing. You can end up eating nothing but a bunch of carbs and sugar all day long. That's where the calorie counting helped. Those were my main goals: Eat no meat and count my calories.

This had a few different results. I started eating better. It wasn't like I was saying, "No more fried foods ever." It was more like, "This doesn't fit into my daily calorie allowance, so I'll pass." I also figured that if I burned more calories by exercising, I would lose even more weight. Another big "first" for me was starting an actual organized exercise

Getting Started with Fitness

If you are new to fitness like I was back in my early twenties, it can be pretty intimidating. Sometimes, people feel like they have to overhaul every little part of their lives to get fit, but that's too daunting. All you have to do to get started is get moving! You know how to walk. You don't need special fitness information to walk. So get out there and walk! Just try to be a little more active in your day, and your body will adjust. When being more active becomes a regular part of your life and isn't as hard as it used to be, that's when you know you're ready to start a more organized fitness plan.

These are my two most important pieces of advice for anyone who is just starting to think about getting healthier: Get moving and make healthy food swaps. Just doing these two things will make a real difference if you are currently not moving much and aren't eating well. Start where you are right now and decide to move forward at your own pace. Even if you only walk for ten minutes, or go back to the gym for the first time in months and get on the elliptical trainer and sweat just a little—it will make a difference. Even if you only make one healthy swap in your favorite meal, like using whole-grain pasta instead of white pasta, or olive oil instead of butter, or a veggie burger instead of a big bacon cheeseburger, it's a step in the right direction. Even if you skip just one can of pop that you would normally drink, or cut your regular portion size down just a little bit, that's progress. Good job! Keep going. Make it a good week.

routine. It wasn't complicated—it was mostly just cardio on the elliptical trainer. But that had an impact, too. I was getting in better shape, feeling less winded, and I experiencing more endurance. All good.

But then I started to experiment, to see how low I could go on calories and still function. If cutting calories is good, isn't cutting more calories even better? If burning calories is good, isn't burning more calories even better? I didn't realize that I was taking it too far. Some days, I went as low as 800 calories! That was a mistake. I didn't know any better at the time, but I was cheating myself out of nutrition, and

I suppressed my metabolism so much that it took me a long time to get it revved back up again. All I knew at the time was that it seemed to be working and that I was continuing to lose weight. However, I was also starting to lose energy again, and strength, too.

At the end of the summer, the tour was over, and before I knew it, I was moving to Nashville. By the time I attended the Country Music As-

Ramen Swap

Back in my *Idol* days, one of the things I ate all the time was ramen noodles. They were always available, they were quick, and they were filling. But those cheap packages of ramen are actually quite unhealthy. One package is two servings, but a lot of people probably eat the whole thing (I always did). Regular ramen noodles have a ton of calories and surprisingly, a whole lotta fat. Not surprisingly, they are also full of sodium, preservatives, additives, and MSG. I had no idea what I was eating at the time. I thought it was "just noodles."

Now I make a different choice that is just as quick and easy: Dr. McDougall's instant soup cups. My swap costs a little more than those 99-cent packages of ramen, but it's still an economical choice at under two dollars for a big two-serving cup. Dr. McDougall's soups have hardly

any fat and about a fourth of the calories of regular ramen noodles, are much lower in sodium, and are just as good and just as filling. My favorite is their vegan pad Thai noodle soup. Just add boiling water, or add room-temperature water and microwave. All the ingredients are real foods that I recognize (like vegetables, bean starch, sea salt, lime, and chiles). When I eat them, I feel like I really am eating "just noodles," without all the junk.

I don't usually make these at home (they are still a little high in sodium and the ingredients aren't fresh), but I consider them great "on the go" food. At home I prefer to make real (not instant) pasta, with fresh vegetables added for an even better swap. But when I need something quick, Dr. McDougall's soups are my current go-to.

your potential

Did you ever surprise yourself by doing something you didn't think you could do? Did you dig deep and make something happen that you didn't think was possible? Did you "get lucky," but recognize that you were in the right place at the right time with the right mind-set to help take advantage of that luck?

Think back to something you did that was a real achievement, large or small. Write about what happened and consider what it took for you to accomplish that. What qualities do you have that allowed that thing to happen? What did you learn? Could you nurture those qualities and bring them out in yourself, to bring even more success or good things into your life? What other things could you do to put your best self forward?

sociation (CMA) Awards in November 2005, anyone who had been paying attention could tell I'd lost weight. Sometimes I thought, *Hey, message board people, what do you think of me* now? I looked thin, but I wasn't feeling great anymore, and I definitely wasn't healthy. Fortunately, I'm a bit obsessive about information, so as I settled into my new life pursuing my new career in the country music capital of the world, I also decided to pursue better health. It was like a challenge: *Can you be better, Carrie? Can you do better than this? Can you feel better than this? Let's see you figure out how!*

3

LOVE WINS

Getting Strong, Finding Balance, and Prioritizing Body Love

nce I was settled in Nashville and busy with my new career, I was in the public eye like never before. There's a lot of pressure to look good, and I felt that pressure—it was partly my competitive nature and partly being the new young upstart in the industry and knowing I'd better make a good impression. Not everyone agreed that you should be able to be famous after a few months on a TV show, so I really felt that I had something to prove. I had to sing great, and I had to look great. That's how I saw it.

My new low-calorie regimen was beginning to wear on me. I was thin, and I knew I should probably be doing something differently, but I was so busy that it was hard to find time to figure it out for myself. I was on the road all the time, or in the studio, and it was all I could do to grab food when I could. When I was onstage, the adrenaline took over, but otherwise, I gotta tell you, I was hungry *all the time*. I was eating barely enough to get by, and my body was finally rebelling because it wasn't getting the nutrition it needed.

Afraid of losing all the progress I'd made on my body, I wasn't letting myself enjoy food. There was no pleasure. When I went out with my friends to eat, I wouldn't let up at all. I would literally ask the servers if they could bring me a big ol' bowl of steamed vegetables. I love pizza, but there was no way I was going to eat even one bite of the stuff, especially if I knew I had an awards show coming up. I'd have a little veggie burger patty with no bun for dinner, and that was it. It was no way to live.

I'm a determined person, and I'm so competitive that I even compete with myself. I have a lot of willpower and I take pride in being able to tell my body what to do and then pushing myself to the limit, but I was using that determination to deprive myself of good nutrition. If I had to make an appearance on the red carpet, I would tell myself, *I have to be perfect!* But of course, there is no such thing as perfect. I was punishing my body and depriving myself. It was completely unsustainable.

I was also trying a lot of things that were just plain dumb to stay thin. I found these diet supplements at the health food store that would give me a buzz of energy and kill my appetite. I had no idea how terrible they were for me (how ironic that these were in a health food store!). I thought that if a health food store sold them over the counter, they must be fine. But they made me sick to my stomach, and I would get all wound up after taking one and then crash.

I finally decided that I was not going to be able to figure all this out on my own. There were so many things out there marked "healthy" that were *not actually healthy*. I thought, *Hey, wait a minute. Maybe there aren't any quick fixes. Maybe there aren't any magic pills to make me perfect. Maybe this is not my area. And maybe there is a better way.* I knew that I wanted to look great, but I also wanted to feel great at the same time—I know, crazy concept, right? I knew I needed a new strategy, a new game plan. I needed a *professional*. For the first time in my life, I decided to consult with an expert who actually knew about fitness and nutrition. It was one of the best decisions I ever made.

Falling in Love with Fitness

I hired a trainer. A trainer was a good solution for me because I find gyms intimidating and uncomfortable. There is so much equipment in a gym that even today I still can't figure out what to do with, and I always feel like I'm getting in the way of the true hard-core fanatics when I'm at the gym (not to mention the fact that I'm sure they're judging me and my lack of gym-spertise!). Working with a trainer in private is more my speed. And it was only once I started working with a trainer that I realized how much I didn't know! Since then, I've worked with multiple trainers, both at home and on the road, and I credit them for teaching me how to be healthy without completely depriving my body.

My first trainer introduced me to fitness basics, but it was my next trainer, Basheerah Ahmad, who went with me on the road, and who really opened a door in my mind. Exercise and nutrition became a fascinating new world that I could step into and learn about. It wasn't just about burning calories anymore. It was about getting stronger, smarter, and healthier. Basheerah dared me to learn more and to do better. When I worked out with her, the stress of living on a bus and out of hotels and doing big shows every night just melted away. Before, when exercise

was just about burning calories, I hadn't seen it as a way to help relieve my stress. But beginning with Basheerah, exercise on the road became a blessing in my life. She took advantage of my competitive nature and gave me goals. Goals! She was speaking my language. I was burnt out on calories in/calories out, but this was a new frontier. I was learning how to make my body and my mind work better for me.

She taught me about lifting weights, which I had never done before. As ladies, we have often been told that lifting weights would make us bulky and man-like. Boy, were we ever lied to! Lifting weights altered my body composition in amazing ways, and it also helped me get out a lot of my excess nervous energy. And it was fun to track my progress as I felt myself getting stronger and stronger. My arms got firm. I got abs (well, as close to abs as I, personally, can get—everyone has that one area of their body that is the hardest to get to do what they want, and mine is my midsection)! People often ask how I got my sculpted legs. Well, before I started a real fitness program, my legs were just kind of skinny. Now they're strong, and they do everything I need them to do. (I'll talk more about my legs and how I've changed them in chapter 6.)

This is Basheerah!

My trainer Basheerah (that's her on the right) also bought me my first heart rate monitor. When I worked out, I could strap this thing on and it would tell me how many calories I had burned during my workout based on my heart rate. I remember being on the treadmill and thinking, *I've got twenty-five more calories to go until I reach five hundred!* I know those things aren't entirely accurate, but it was so helpful for me to have numerical goals to use to my advantage. I've always liked information and numbers, and she turned that quality from a detriment (obsessive calorie counting) into a benefit (using the numbers to get stronger, eat smarter, and feel more balanced).

She also taught me things about nutrition that I'd never known before. Being a vegetarian was great, but I wasn't maximizing my nutrients. She started to help me manage my diet. One important thing she taught me was that eating whatever you can find on a tour bus or in a hotel is not a good strategy for feeling good or looking the way you want to look. On her recommendation, I started bringing my own food around with me everywhere I went, so that I'd never be stuck somewhere without a healthy option—easy things like protein bars or tomato or mushroom soup. She had me eating three meals a day, plus a snack after every workout—I felt like I was eating all the time! She wanted to keep my metabolism up and she had me volume eating to keep me full on healthy plant foods—sometimes I had to tell her I couldn't eat one more bite! But instead of focusing on what I wasn't eating, she taught me to focus on what I *was* eating, and that made a big difference in how I felt. I was learning how to make food work for me.

I'm grateful I had Basheerah with me during those early Nashville years because I was on the road a lot, and the road is a brutal place to try to stay healthy. My very first tour after the *American Idol* tour, I opened for Kenny Chesney. The next tour, I opened for Brad Paisley, and after that I toured with Keith Urban. Then, finally, I was the headliner on my own tour. Sometimes I felt like I was never home—or like the tour bus was my home. It was stressful and intense at times, but two things really helped me get through it. One was my faith. I had to ask God to help me deal with all the stress of my crazy new life. The other was exercise. I think maybe God sent me the gift of exercise, knowing that it was what I needed.

Once I was exercising regularly and getting in ever-better shape, it became a lot easier to keep up with my grueling schedule. Performing, which is physically demanding, also got easier. I had more energy and strength to be up there in those high heels for those long shows. I could move better, and my clothes fit better. I was more comfortable in my own skin. It was awesome. I wasn't just living. I was optimizing myself.

Everything felt different, and one day it occurred to me that exercising, then feeling hungry, then eating good whole food, was *how it should be*. It's not natural to be hungry and to refuse to let yourself eat. It's not natural to exercise so hard that you feel like you're going to faint or throw up. It's not natural to take weird supplements or follow insane schemes to trick your body into getting thinner. It's not natural to starve yourself. That's what puts your body to sleep. I wanted my body to be awake and alive and fully participating in this amazing life! God put us here to love the lives he gave us. It's not natural to deny that gift.

The scary part for me at the time was that at the beginning of this new health makeover, I actually gained some weight. I hadn't been eating enough, and now I was eating a lot of healthy food. I panicked a little when I saw that number on the scale go up, but my trainer told me to give my body some time to figure out what was going on. I had to wake up my metabolism and get it revved up again. I had to get my body back into working order.

I also had to learn that the numbers on the scale don't tell the whole story. I realized that although I'd gained weight, I wasn't any bigger. I was just stronger. There have been times in my life when I weighed what seemed like a lot for my five-foot-three frame, but my clothing size never changed, and I felt a million times better than I had when I was starving myself and was thin, but had no muscle tone. It was a difference in body composition. Don't let the scale play mind games with you! What matters is that you feel good, that you have energy and strength to get through your day, and that you like the way you look. What matters is that you feel like the best version of yourself. When you can look in the mirror with real honesty and self-awareness and say, "Yes, this is me!" then you know you are on the right track.

Settling into Life

As time went on, I got used to my new life. I adapted to the pressure, I got fitter and stronger, and, in 2008, I agreed to meet my bass player's friend's friend Mike Fisher. The idea of a blind date was too weird to me, so Mike came to one of my shows and I met him backstage. He was a hockey player and he lived in Canada and I thought, *Sure, Carrie, get into a relationship with a guy who lives in another country. What a good idea.* But we had chemistry like I'd never had with anybody before, so . . . that was that. We were engaged about a year later and married in July 2010.

Four years later, we had our first child, Isaiah Michael, and as I was working on this book, we welcomed baby number two, Jacob Bryan. I'm so grateful for my beautiful little family (and of course that includes my dogs, Ace, Penny, and Zero).

I am one lucky lady for many reasons in my marriage. But when it comes to health, I feel so blessed that my husband is just as interested in fitness as I am, being a former professional athlete and all. In the mornings, we take turns going to our home gym to work out while the other does kid duty. Exercise will always be one of the most important priorities for us and for our family. For dinner, we usually cook at home—I make my veggie version of dinner, and sometimes he adds meat to his. We don't have time to go on many vacations, but we do prioritize family time, and every night, whenever we can, Mike and I try to spend time alone together after the kids are in bed to unplug, relax, and check in with each other. We are both private people and we like to have a quiet home life to balance out our very public careers. We've created this life for ourselves, and we're happy. It works well for us.

But exercise will always be one of the most important priorities for our family. I've come to rely on it so much that I know my day won't go as well if I skip a workout (which inevitably happens—nobody can fit in a workout every single day). Exercise is my antidepressant, my anti-anxiety "medication," and my stress relief. In fact, exercise has become so important to me that I even started my own fitness lifestyle brand with DICK'S Sporting Goods, called CALIA by Carrie Underwood. I plan to keep exercising until my last day on this earth, or as long as I possibly can. And even if I can't squeeze in a full workout on certain days, there is always a way to do a little something to be more active.

I don't claim to have it all figured out, but through trial and error and plenty of mistakes, I've finally found a delicate balance: a fitness routine I've committed to and that I love, a dietary strategy that energizes me and makes me feel great, a passion for music and a dedication to a career I feel blessed to have, and a devotion to my faith and my family. Whether on the tour bus, in a hotel, or at home, I always try to exercise on the days that I can (even when I've got a show that night). I always try to eat for maximum energy. And I always try to fit in some necessary downtime to recharge.

Stepping back for a moment, here's how I see it: God is the engine that powers our lives. Love is the oil that keeps the engine running smoothly. And healthy living is the fuel that powers the engine and keeps us moving forward. Let's start with the fuel. In the next part of this book, I'm going to tell you more about what I do to stay strong, and how you can do it, too. Because your body is a gift. Let's honor it.

The Family That Exercises Together Stays Together

Exercise is a big priority for both my husband and me, and we try to find physical activities we can do together whenever possible. When the weather is nice, we might take a walk with our sons after dinner instead of defaulting to sitting on the couch to watch TV. You might try an evening walk like we do, or riding bikes to get frozen yogurt after dinner instead of sitting at home eating ice cream from the freezer.

Mike and I also work out together sometimes, especially when we travel together. My current trainer, Eve Overland, sometimes gives us things to do at the same time. Mike might hold plank position while I do 25 push-ups, or I might do wall sits while he runs ¼ mile on the treadmill. This is motivating because when one of us knows that the other is doing something difficult, we work harder and faster. We don't want the other person to be in pain for too long! So I'll do those push-ups as fast as I can. He'll get that ¼ mile behind him as fast as he can. It's a fitness-oriented way to show you care (or to completely torture your spouse—your call, ha!). Here's a more structured way that we do this when Eve is directing the action. You can try it with your partner, with a friend, or even with your kids. In this version, Eve has us doing lunges, but you can do this with any exercise. It's called . . .

I Go, You Go

This is a simple drill that you can do with two people or two teams. There are two exercises: One is to go halfway down into a lunge and hold it—this is called an isometric hold. The other is to go into a static (stationary) lunge and, without moving your feet, lower your knee down and then back up again. While one person holds the isometric lunge, the other does the static lunge, going up and down. Then they switch, like this:

The first person holds an isometric lunge while the second person does 10 static lunges.

Switch: The second person holds an isometric lunge while the first person does 10 static lunges.

Next, the first person holds an isometric lunge (on the same side, using the same leg) while the second person does 9 lunges (on the same side, using the same leg). Then they switch.

This pattern repeats, working down: 8 lunges (while the other holds), then switch. Keep counting down, swapping who holds a lunge and who does moving lunges: 7 reps, 6, 5, etc.

When you get all the way down to one lunge, you both switch to your other side/other leg, and do it all again.

Eve says, "Things start to get real around the eighth set. This is where I see form starting to break down. The isometric holds begin to look more like standing with one foot in front of the other, and the lunges start to look more like quick pulses, probably in hopes of going faster to get this game over with already! For clients that are new to exercise, or in the interest of time, I will often start at eight reps. It is a little less evil."

Yep, she's telling the truth! This exercise is intense, but it's awesome for your leg muscles. I do lunges *a lot*, and this is a way to make them fun. But don't exceed your fitness level. If you get too tired, stop so you don't injure yourself.

Another way to do this is to use different exercises, like alternating push-ups and holding the plank position (like the top of a push-up), or doing squats (or squat jumps for people who want an even greater challenge) and holding a squat position. The possibilities are endless.

Just to recap, here's what we do:

Round 1: Right Foot Forward

- Carrie holds a lunge (or plank or squat) while Mike performs lunges (or push-ups or squat jumps) for 10 reps.
- Mike holds a lunge while Carrie performs lunges for 10 reps.
- Carrie holds a lunge while Mike performs lunges for 9 reps.
- Mike holds a lunge while Carrie performs lunges for 9 reps.
- . . . and so on, down to 1.

Round 2: Left Foot Forward

Same as above, but with the opposite foot forward.

Meet My Current Trainer, Eve Overland

When I was looking for a new road trainer in 2010, we discovered Eve Overland, who was living in Los Angeles at the time, and she's been working with me ever since. Eve has been in the fitness industry as far back as scrunchy socks and leotards and has experience in everything exercise-related that I can think of. She is a former bodybuilder (and figure competitor), has been competitive in powerlifting and CrossFit, participated in obstacle course races, and even works as a stuntwoman! But don't let all this hard-core stuff fool you. She still loves her step aerobics, functional workouts, dance classes, and yoga. All these interests certainly contribute to her ability to keep workouts interesting, creative, progressive, and fun after all this time. She also has an (unnatural) thing for burpees . . . which pretty much means I have a thing for burpees, too.

In addition to being a personal trainer, she is also a certified Krav Maga instructor (Israeli martial arts/self-defense), and has instructor certifications in group fitness, kettlebells, and yoga. Eve currently lives in Atlanta, Georgia. When she and I aren't together, Eve tours with other artists, teaches group fitness classes, works with clients as an online coach, trains via Skype, and trains actors on set to prepare for their roles in films and television shows that shoot in the Atlanta area. She loves to travel and takes as many different fitness classes as she can all over the country. At home, she runs or hikes with her dog, Bo. Like me, she is an animal lover, and one of those people who finds cats (or they find her)—she usually has one (or four). She'll be chiming in throughout this section of the book with fitness advice for you. You can find out more about her at eveoverlandfitness.com.

My On-the-Road Survival Food List

It's hard to eat well on the road. Whether you're on tour like I am or you travel for work or pleasure, junk food always seems like the easiest option. But there are lots of things you can do to make sure you always have healthy options available. One of the best "tricks" I've learned to implement while traveling is to stop by a grocery store on the way to the hotel . . . especially if I'm going to be in the same hotel for a few days. This has saved me on so many levels! Usually, a hotel's idea of food suitable for a vegetarian consists of some type of pizza or flatbread or spaghetti or risotto. Don't get me wrong, all those options are certainly delicious, but eating those foods night after night in a hotel gets boring, and those carbs add up quickly! Plus, hotel restaurant food or room service is so expensive—and so salty! Who wouldn't want to save some money while simultaneously doing their body a favor? Many hotel rooms have some sort of minifridge and some also have microwaves—or you can request one ahead of time for your room (or they may have a microwave in the lobby in the area where they sell snacks).

Some of my favorite things to look for at the store when I'm on the road are:

> **OATMEAL CUPS:** Simply add hot water, or add water and microwave. Just make sure the ones you grab aren't loaded with sugar. I like Bob's Red Mill oatmeal cups. Some have flaxseeds or other healthy additions; some are gluten-free.

> **FRUIT:** Apples or mixed berries are never a bad choice for a breakfast boost or a snack.

> **PREMADE SALADS:** I'm not talking about the ones loaded down with iceberg lettuce, cheese, and ranch dressing like Mom used to make! Instead, pick salads that have leafy greens like romaine, spinach, kale, arugula, or spring greens, and have lots and lots of veggies. I like the ones with dressing on the side so I can decide how much to use (I don't like a lot). If you're a meat eater, you can usually find some with chicken breast or salmon on them. Boiled eggs are a good protein add-on as well, and most stores sell them precooked and peeled.

> **SANDWICHES AND WRAPS:** Most grocery stores have a whole section with premade sandwiches. If you're at a more health-oriented store, you can probably find some good tofu options or things that are organic and healthy. As always, read

the labels, and make sure they're not loaded down with mayo and cheese, and that they're full of lots of veggies!

› **HUMMUS AND VEGGIES:** I may have ignored the hummus and carrots from craft services back in my *Idol* days, but now I depend on hummus as a snack. A lot of grocery stores even sell premade snack-size containers of this veggie goodness. Hummus has a savory flavor that satisfies. I find that hummus and veggies is a super filling combination, and can easily satisfy hunger, especially if you're a late-night snacker.

› **KAREN'S NATURALS JUST VEGGIES:** If you love to snack on chips or popcorn, this might just be the perfect healthy swap for you. These are simply freeze-dried vegetables. They're crunchy and super yummy! This brand also has fruit, which is easy to add to those oatmeal cups in the morning.

› **ENLIGHTENED ROASTED BROAD BEAN CRISPS:** So much better for you than potato chips, but with that same satisfying crunch!

› **RHYTHM SUPERFOODS KALE CHIPS:** I know, I know—there are a few words in the title of this snack that may turn you off, but seriously, these are delicious. Way better than they sound. I like the ranch and nacho flavors. Even Mike loves to eat these.

› **PRIMAL STRIPS:** These are vegan "jerky" strips made of seitan. Surprisingly tasty!

› **RAW ALMONDS:** These are always great to keep in your bag for a quick snack grab. They contain those good-for-you omega fatty acids your body needs, as well as fiber to help sustain you for a while. Just make sure to only grab a handful. Don't eat the whole bag! Even the healthiest of foods can take a turn for the worse if you overindulge.

› **BARS:** These can be a tricky item. Many bars are high in sugar and low in protein (even if they have "protein" in the name). Despite what the package might say, most of them don't do much to keep you going. They'll spike your blood sugar and give you a quick pick-me-up but will likely make you crash soon after you eat them. My husband generally doesn't like bars—he says he'd rather eat real food, and I totally get that. But . . . sometimes convenience is key, and there are a few bars out there that can be beneficial and add to a well-balanced diet. Bars are easy to keep in your purse or briefcase and could potentially save you from derailing your entire day with greasy fast food. They may not be the perfect food, but they can be the perfect swap for a much worse food. Just make sure the bars you're grabbing have a good amount of fat and fiber and don't have a ton of ingredients that you can't pronounce. Here are some of my favorites to have on hand when hunger strikes—try a few, or seek out different ones and see what you like.

› **NO COW BARS:** These are my favorite. I really like these because they have a *ton* of fiber, which fills me up for a long time. They also have around 20 grams of protein and are vegan. My favorite flavors are the peanut butter chocolate chip, mint cacao chip, chocolate fudge brownie, and vanilla caramel. Out of all the bars out there, No Cow is the bar my husband is most likely to eat.

- › **GARDEN OF LIFE PROTEIN BARS:** There are many different types/flavors of these. I like this brand for other foods, too, including protein powder.
- › **RXBARS:** These are simple. They don't have a lot of ingredients, which I appreciate, and they usually include lower-sugar fruits and nuts.
- › **KIND BARS:** These are also made with simple, recognizable ingredients. They contain lots of almonds and they taste really good, too.
- › **QUEST BARS:** If you're okay with whey (a protein from milk), you might like these. They have lots of protein and fiber and many flavors to choose from.
- › **STEVE'S PALEOGOODS PALEOKRUNCH:** This is a grain-free granola bar made up mostly of nuts and seeds. It's super yummy and doesn't have a ton of sugar. If you like granola bars, this could be your new best friend.

- › **MICROWAVE BURRITOS/ BOWLS:** These fall into the same category as bars when it comes to health—they vary widely in terms of how good the ingredients and nutrition are. Some are all right, and some are naughty posing as nice, but again, I like to have a few around for an easy grab—better than going through a drive-thru for junk food. Remember, it's all about convenience and making healthy swaps.

Even if they're a bit processed, microwavable burritos and bowls are probably a lot better for your health than what's on the room service menu. Some of my favorite brands are:

- › **SWEET EARTH BURRITOS:** I love the Big Sur Burrito and the Protein Lover's Burrito, but all the flavors are really good, and they also have lots of protein. I could eat these for any meal of the day.
- › **AMY'S KITCHEN BOWLS:** I especially like the Brown Rice & Vegetables bowl (tofu, brown rice, veggies... what more could a girl want?) and the Brown Rice, Black-Eyed Peas, and Veggies bowl.

These are just a few examples of things I like to look for, but each grocery store is different, and sometimes you just have to do the best with whatever you can find. However, I promise that once you get into this healthy habit and work on your label-reading skills, you'll be able to master any store and any travel situation. You'll learn the things you like and dislike, and you'll be able to stay on track while you're away from home. So worth it!

are you tracking yet?

When I moved to Nashville and started working with trainers and learning more about how to exercise and eat for health instead of just to "be thin," I also started expanding my journal beyond calories to include more comprehensive information about what I was eating and how much nutrition I was getting. I started tracking fat, carbs, and protein. At first, I wasn't sure why I was doing this, other than that I liked information and I wanted to know if my eating was balanced. I wanted to compare my days, and this helped me stay on track.

I began tracking all this information in my journal in 2006 or 2007, and then I discovered that they have actual diet and nutrition tracking apps. Today I use an app called MyFitnessPal to keep track of my calories and nutrients, and it does the math for me. I click on the foods I eat (it has a huge database of foods), and the app adds up the calories and shows me my percentages of protein, fat, and carbs for the day. I can see if my percentages are on target for my goals, and I can look back to see why my percentages are what they are. Maybe my fat percentage is high that day, but then I can see that I had half an avocado, and know that's okay because it was healthy fat. Recording everything in the app helps me keep things balanced, and when I know that I have an occasion coming up where I will probably eat more, I can adjust my other meals accordingly. But you can still call me old school because every morning, I copy the information from the app from the day before into my journal, along with anything else I want to remember.

I think that keeping track of this kind of information is important for accountability as well as health. I write down every single thing I eat, and every bit of exercise I do. Sometimes I might want to eat something "bad," but knowing I have to write it down stops me. I suggest you try this. It might seem annoying at first, but once you make it a daily ritual, it feels more like something you do just for yourself, to stay committed to your health and well-being. To see how I do this, check out the template in Appendix 1.

PART TWO

who are you?

PUSH YOURSELF (A LITTLE)
TO KNOW YOURSELF (A LOT)

4

CHANGE

My Fitness Philosophy

Making exercise a priority changed my life. I don't know how I would have made it this far without working out to keep me going. For me, fitness is my therapy. It's my way to blow off steam. When everything else is nutso in my life, at least I know what I'm doing for the 45 to 90 minutes that I'm working out. That time is just for me. It's critical stress-management time, it's strength-building time, and it's mental decompression time. I'm an exercise junkie. If I accomplish nothing else with this book, I want to convince you that if you're not working out, you should start, and that if you're already exercising, you can make it more of a priority in your life. Because exercise is *just about the most important thing you can do to make your life better.* I truly believe that.

I can't overstate the value and power of physical fitness. To me, one hour of exercise is worth all the massages in the world. I very rarely get massages, and it's even rarer for me to get a facial. That would be nice, but I've got a million other things to do, and I just don't have the time. But if I can go to our home gym and spend one solid hour exercising, or if I can go outside and run a couple of miles, that's what calms me, centers me, clears my head, and makes me feel connected to something bigger than myself. It makes my life easier in countless ways. Exercise actually makes me feel like I have *more* time in my day. Exercise is Carrie maintenance.

But it's more than that. If I had to pick the number one reason I exercise, it's that I want to be around for my children as they grow up. I want to know them as adults. I want to know their children, and their children's children. I want to be that hundred-year-old granny who is out there hustling, who's still bringing it. And I want the same for my husband, and for my children. I don't mean I just want them to live for a long time. I want them to live *well*—healthy, happy, functioning, and mentally sound. That's why exercise isn't just a priority for me. It's a priority for our whole family. That has made all the difference in how we structure our family time together. The family that prays together stays together, but the family that prays *and* exercises together probably lives with a lot less stress and a lot more harmony.

But I'm not gonna lie—my motivation isn't all selfless. It definitely feels good to look good in your clothes. To be comfortable. To be able to move and bend and lift and sit and stand and run if you have to. (You never know when you might need to hightail it out of some bad situation, or just sprint after a wayward and super-fast toddler!) When you are strong and fit, you feel at home in your own skin. You feel more capable and in control of your own life and your place in the world. Who wouldn't trade one hour of their day for all those benefits?

My goal is to convince you that exercise is worth your time and that it can change your life for the better. If you can get that hour in most days, your body will change. Your brain will change. You'll have more minutes in your day (it will feel like you do, at least). You'll be in a better mood. You'll get along with people better. You'll appreciate your life more. You don't have to take my word for it. I encourage you to do your own research. There are countless studies and articles about the proven physical and mental health benefits of exercise. Honestly, there's just no good reason not to do some sort of exercise. We can all make improvements in this area of our lives, no matter our fitness level. So let's see if I can't get you motivated to start exercising today, or to step up your current fitness efforts. Because exercise is not a chore. It's a privilege.

The Fit52 Lifestyle

I am all about living fit, fifty-two weeks of the year. This is the philosophy behind the Fit52 way of life. It's a way to get fit, and it's a way to stay fit. It's also a way to think about health. As I said before, Fit52 means doing what is good for you, *almost* all the time over the course of the week. You don't have to be perfect every day, but if you're staying active and getting some exercise on most days, and you're eating good food in moderation, you are living Fit52. You don't have to do a structured workout every single day. You can still indulge in treats once

ARE YOU LIKE CARRIE?

As with her diet, Carrie likes to record all her workouts in her journal. Some people love to do this. They want to remember how many reps they've done or how much weight they've been lifting so they can keep progressing or keep their workouts organized. Or they may use technology, tracking every exercise minute, step, and calorie burned on their phones or fitness watches. Others aren't so interested in keeping track of every move.

I understand that not everyone is as numbers-oriented as Carrie. However,

I definitely encourage some sort of accountability tracking. Even if the tiny details aren't your style, feel free to just give the overview of your time spent working out or just being active. Record what you need and what will help you, inspire you, and keep you moving forward. Remember, this lifestyle is all about what works for you and what you will realistically implement into your daily schedule.

in a while. You can still celebrate holidays, go out with friends, and live your real life.

The beauty of the Fit52 lifestyle is that it keeps you on track no matter what you're doing. It also means that messing up won't derail you. You won't think, *Darn it, I missed my workout. Oh well, I guess I'm off the wagon. I can lie on the couch and eat cookies all weekend.* Instead, living Fit52 means that when you slip up, you can put it in perspective. The Fit52 way to see that missed workout is, "I missed a workout. It was nice to have a day off, but I'm going to be healthy for the rest of the week. I'll be as active as I can be today, and tomorrow I'll have a great workout and make it count." It's a more logical way to look at health that works in the real world. It's *sustainable*.

For me, sustainability is key. What good is a workout or diet you hate? You and I both know you won't keep it up, and as soon as you stop and go back to what you were doing before, any good work you've done will get undone. Why bother? Instead, Fit52 means integrating healthy behaviors into your life in a way you enjoy so you can keep them up. It's not something you "go on" and then "go off." Fit52 is an attitude about embracing health for your benefit and the benefit of the people you love.

This is a topic that I feel passionate about, and I hope my enthusiasm will be contagious. In the next chapter, I'm going to get you started by introducing you to a great workout. But first, let's talk about fitness in terms of everyday life.

The Exercise of Daily Life

The Fit52 lifestyle is about living fit and healthy for most of the week, every week, all year long. But that doesn't necessarily mean you do 100 sit-ups or 50 push-ups every day without fail. Structured exercise is great and very important, but the truth is that most people can get a lot of exercise just by living their lives in a more active way.

This is important because we all need a way to manage the pressures of our daily lives. We're all under some kind of strain, physically, mentally, or emotionally—or more likely, we're dealing with a combination of these three things every day. Some days are easy, but there are always those hard days. Maybe your work is challenging, or your home life is hectic, or you're just under a ton of stress. I feel you. Trust me—my work falls into that "all those things at some point each day" category for sure!

You need a way to manage that stress and make your busyness more productive. To get through it, we all need endurance. And guess how you get endurance? By moving more and building stronger muscles, a stronger heart, and better lung capacity. Moving more with intention will relieve your stress, not increase it. It will help you think more clearly and breathe easier. You'll feel calmer. Exercise is the trick for making it through the best days as well as the worst ones.

How do you start? The first step is to figure out how to fit more constructive movement into your life. It doesn't have to be formal exercise, especially if you haven't exercised in a while (or ever). Think of all the things you need to do every day. How could you make those things more physical? This is Exercise 101.

I purposefully make my daily life as physical as possible. One easy way to do this is to be more active in my home life. I try to make everything I do around the house an opportunity to get more physical. You might think I have people to do everything for me, but I'm actually really bad at asking for help. Maybe my life would be better if I did ask for help, or let people help me more, but it's important to me that my kids grow up thinking, *Mom is still just Mom.* I do my own laundry. I buy my own groceries. I cook dinner for my family—I don't have a chef. I do have someone in to clean about once a month, but otherwise, I pick up my own house. I don't want somebody doing everything for me and cleaning up after me all the time. That doesn't feel right. I like to be self-sufficient—it's just who I am.

True, my husband helps, but he's also Mr. Social, always off doing charity work or dealing with his various businesses. Even though he's retired from the NHL, he's still just as busy as he ever was. And while I'm really busy, too—I admit to having a pretty cool job and getting to travel a lot and see some amazing places—being home with my kids as much as I can is a priority to me. I'm a mom and a wife, and I consider those job titles to be my most important ones. But that means I take on a lot of the everyday household responsibilities.

One of the ways I get more active at home is by being inefficient. I'll take things up and down the stairs way more often than I have to, just for the exercise. I'm always putting things away, like clothes and toys, and I feel like I'm always running around after my kids. They really keep me moving. Whenever my mom visits and hangs out with them, or other family members spend time with them, they always say something like, "I don't know how those kids don't wipe you out every day. How do you keep up?" I keep up because I have to keep up. Isaiah is an active little

Count Your Steps

Step counters are a great invention. Some are simple pedometers you wear on your belt and some are built into fancy smartwatches, but whatever the mode, I recommend getting one. A step counter has been a great thing for my life. In a way, it makes exercise easier.

Let's say I need to take something upstairs. Maybe I don't feel like it. I might think, *Ugh, I don't want to do that.* But then I'll think, *Wait! I'll get steps!* And then I actually *want* to take the toys or laundry or dirty child who needs a bath upstairs. A step counter makes me go out of my way to do more things around the house, especially if I'm not working out that day. I might think, *Hey, I'm gonna clean the house . . . because I gotta get my steps!*

I'm also grateful for a step counter on my more sedentary days. When I'm in the studio writing all day, I try to be sure I 1) work out in the morning, and 2) get in as many steps as I can before and after the writing session. If you know you have a big day of just sitting, your step counter might motivate you to go on an extra-long walk before or after, or walk around picking things up in the evening instead of watching your favorite show from the couch. Because *you've gotta get your steps!*

By the way, my trainer Eve says that the average American only gets about 4,000 steps a day. That's less than half the recommended daily goal of 10,000 steps and translates to roughly a 30-minute walk with my

boy, and Jacob is well on his way to being the same, and I think that's awesome. I want them to stay that way even when they're grown up, because I know that means they'll be healthier and happier.

My job is also really active some days—although at other times it can be pretty sedentary. When I'm performing, I have to sing a lot of vocally challenging songs. I get a ton of exercise moving across the stage to the music. I need good lung capacity and breath control. And I'm doing it all in high heels. All that makes me more fit, but at the same time, staying fit makes all that possible. I couldn't just get up off the couch with

dogs, Ace and Penny—and they have little legs! (Our dog Zero can go longer.)

You might think this sounds a little crazy, but on days when I don't get to move around very much or I miss my workout—maybe I had something I had to do in the morning and then I had the kids all day—I will just jog everywhere I go in the house. Anybody can do this. You don't even have to put on your shoes. Just jog to put away laundry. Jog around the kitchen while you're making dinner. Jog into the bedroom to grab a sweater. Jog over to your phone when you get a text. Why not? Think of all those extra steps! You might think it's silly or that you'll look strange doing it, but who are you trying to impress in your own home? Trust me, your pets won't judge you. Mine don't judge me (I don't think . . .).

If you sit at a desk all day, maybe you could get one of those adjustable standing desks, or, if you're really motivated and your situation allows for it, one of those treadmill desks. Shift back and forth, take breaks to get up and walk around the office or around the building, or just go up and down the stairs a few times. More steps! Having a step counter helps you think outside the box and be more creative in finding better ways to move more. It helps you roll with whatever is happening in your life while staying as active as you can.

And if you're like me and you love to count things and keep track of things and set goals for yourself, you'll love step counting even more.

no baseline fitness level and do what I do onstage. If I do a sound check in tennis shoes and then I get onstage in high heels, it's a whole different game. I get winded a lot faster, and those gorgeous stilettos force my body to use a different set of muscles.

If you just stand in heels and sing, that's one thing. You're mostly using your lungs. But start walking around, and you're using a bunch of muscles that have nothing to do with singing. I also like to say that I sing with my whole body—and that's strenuous. I can't have my heart rate spiking when I'm onstage. I have to be ready for that level of physical exertion. I once heard that Beyoncé works out in high heels . . . yet another reason to be impressed by Queen Bey. I don't know if it's true, but I can see the benefit. Unfortunately, I am *not* that coordinated! I feel like it might be dangerous—I'd probably (and by "probably," I mean most definitely) break my ankle or hurt myself if I tried it! But I do know that some people really do this. If you work out in high heels, your quads are going to be firing, your booty muscles are going to be firing, and when you do need to bring it in your high heels, you'll be ready. But I *really* don't recommend this, so don't say I told you to do it!

At other times, between tours, I may sit all day long during writing sessions in the studio. I may not get much exercise at all. If I'm not doing something in the morning to stay fit, then my fitness level would decline fast and I could lose all that progress. And when I did have to get onstage, I'd be in trouble.

To sum it all up, life can be strenuous and stressful, and exercise helps. Life can also be sedentary and stressful, and exercise helps. Exercise can also be something you do throughout the day as you go about your life (chapter 7 is all about this), but fitting a more structured exercise session into your day will make all the other parts of your life easier.

About Motivation

You may want to exercise—I mean *really* exercise, like have a whole workout plan you do every day—but how do you make yourself do it when you aren't in the habit yet? How do you get off the couch and tie up your workout shoes and get out that door? How do you get motivated? Here's what motivates me, and what I hope might also motivate you:

> › **JUST START**. It sounds so basic, but sometimes it's just a matter of starting, and then it's all downhill from there. Maybe not

literally . . . you may end up walking or running up an actual hill! But doing that very first thing is sometimes the hardest part—putting on your shoes, packing up your workout gear, or just stepping outside. I do it because I've decided that if I'm not absolutely unable to do it, it's nonnegotiable. When you don't give yourself a choice . . . well, then you don't have a choice. You're going to exercise.

> **BE FLEXIBLE.** Some days, I'm psyched to go hard, but on other days, I just can't. If it's nice outside and I'm not feeling particularly motivated to work out inside, I'll go for a walk. There's nothing intimidating about walking. I live in a hilly area and I can walk for three miles and feel like I did something. Or I might go for a run, if I'm feeling up for it. I always do the loop, rather than go a certain distance and turn back, because once I'm on my way, I have to go all the way around to get home. That means I have to finish—I can't quit early. Plus, think of all that sunshine vitamin D and fresh air I'm getting! My point is that you don't always have to do the same thing, and it's probably better for you if you don't. Change it up. Keep it interesting, think of the positives instead of the negatives of whatever you're doing, and meet yourself where you are. Maybe you're geared up to do a 90-minute workout, or maybe you can only do 30 minutes. Or even 20 minutes. Do what you can do. Anything is better than nothing.

> **LET THE MUSIC PLAY.** Music is a huge motivator for me, as it is for many people. Whether you're a musician or not, I think all people have a connection with music. It taps into something emotional that spurs you on, and when the beat works with what you're doing, it fuels you even more. You have to keep running because the song isn't over yet! Whatever I'm doing, I can do it better to the beat of music.

I once read an article from Psychology Today* that said scientists have actually studied this. They said music is "ergogenic" (meaning it enhances work). Music can keep your energy up longer, increase your physical capacity for exercise, make you process energy more efficiently, and make exercise more enjoyable. They said many studies have proven that during low- to moderate-intensity exercise, music resulted in measurable improvements in endurance. The article said the only reason not to use music while exercising is if you are doing something really difficult and you have to focus for safety reasons. But running, walking, cardio machines, weightlifting? Play on.

Besides all that, I like to put on my headphones so I don't have to hear my footfalls or my breathing. If I'm running and I can hear myself breathing hard, for some reason it makes exercise seem more difficult. I don't know why. There must be a psychological effect of hearing yourself doing something strenuous. It's almost as if listening to music when I run tricks my mind into not noticing how hard I'm working. I know it sounds weird, but try it sometime!

I also like to customize my musical experience, so I make playlists to go with what I'm doing—running, lifting weights, cardio—and something about listening to music that is just the right tempo to match what I'm doing makes it all feel more enjoyable and fun. I also like to match the music to my energy level. Sometimes louder, more intense music or old-school heavy metal helps me channel my energy and keeps me going all the way to the end. Yes, it's true—your little country-lovin' girl likes to get down with some good old-fashioned headbanging music! (You'll find some of my playlists throughout the next few chapters.)

› **SET AN EXAMPLE.** Another huge motivator for me is knowing that my kids are watching what I do. Kids learn who to be by watching

---

* *This article by Jeanette Bicknell, PhD, was posted on the Psychology Today website on January 30, 2013. You can read it here: https://www.psychologytoday.com/us/blog/why -music-moves-us/201301/music-and-exercise-what-current-research-tells-us.*

their parents, and I don't want mine to learn that life happens on a couch. I want them to see that we care about health and being strong and taking care of ourselves and each other. Sometimes, my elder son sees us both working out and says he wants to work out, too, so we'll say, "All right, Isaiah, show us some push-ups." I can't wait to watch him as he grows and see how he makes fitness a priority in his own life. I would have loved for my parents to have taken me to the gym to work out (not that we even had a gym in my hometown when I was growing up, so I guess even if they'd wanted to, it wouldn't have been possible). Sometimes I think about how much further along I could be on my fitness journey if I had started earlier. I want to give my children the gift of growing up seeing how both my husband and I make fitness a priority. We do that for each other, and we do that for our kids. And here's another major perk: I really like watching my husband work out. I think it's hot.

› **CELEBRATE LIFE.** The last big motivator for me is to think about exercise as a celebration of life. God gave us all bodies to live in during our time on this earth, and I believe we have an obligation to take care of those bodies, which are such a gift to us. I would even say exercise is part of my personal value system. Our bodies are sacred and beautiful, no matter who we are, how old we are, or what size we are. Keeping them in the best possible condition is a way to honor the lives we've been given and the creator who made us with love. If God loves you, then who are you to argue that you aren't beautiful and don't deserve the self-care, strength, and peace of mind you can get from exercise? And besides, you have to live in your body for your whole life. It's only logical to take care of it so it lasts as long as possible.

CARRIE'S SQUAT SONG

To describe how music-driven Carrie is, once upon a time, on the Blown Away Tour in 2012, we were in the middle of a workout session when the song "Shots" by LMFAO came on the radio. Carrie immediately started singing "Squats" instead of "Shots." We both stopped what we were doing, and organically started squatting to the rhythm of the music. Slow squats for the verses, fast squats and a jump squat on the chorus, and pulsing squats for the bridge. I have since refined a choreographed routine for this song. I will often add our infamous "Squat Song" to special events for CALIA (Carrie's fitness lifestyle line) or workouts that I lead. It's really fun. To this day, whenever I hear the song (which isn't so often anymore), I stop what I'm doing and get to squatting!

MY WORKOUT PLAYLISTS

As I've mentioned, music fuels my workouts and keeps me energized and inspired. Everyone has their own taste in music. Fortunately, technology is at your service. There are some really great apps out there that actually let you pick the BPM (beats per minute) of the songs you want to hear while you're on the move. As they say, there's an app for that!

When you run to the beat of the music, somehow it takes the pressure off you to set your own pace. It's like the music is driving your body and you just do what it tells you to do. Plus, you can speed up the BPMs as you advance, to improve your time and/or distance. That said, we're all on our own journeys and all run at different paces, so I encourage you to find the tempo you're comfortable with and give it a go!

To get you started, I put together a random list of songs that I feel are good to run to. Most have BPMs somewhere around 170 (I tried to mix in lots of genres).

Note: Some of the songs in some of my playlists have adult or explicit lyrics, so just be aware, in case little ears are listening.

RUNNING PLAYLIST

"The Pretender"—Foo Fighters
"She's Country"—Jason Aldean
"Livin' on the Edge"—Aerosmith
"California Love"—Tupac Shakur (feat. Dr. Dre and Roger Troutman)
"Santeria"—Sublime
"Paper Planes"—M.I.A.
"Take on Me"—a-ha
"All My Life"—Foo Fighters
"Love Is a Battlefield"—Pat Benatar
"Interstate Love Song"—Stone Temple Pilots

"Work It"—Missy Elliott

"Johnny B. Goode"—Chuck Berry

"Danger Zone"—Kenny Loggins

"Loser"—Beck

"Kickstart My Heart"—Mötley Crüe (a personal favorite song that always kicks me into high gear)

"Centuries"—Fall Out Boy

"Part-Time Lover"—Stevie Wonder

"Knee Deep"—Zac Brown Band (feat. Jimmy Buffett)

"Swallowed"—Bush

"Big Poppa"—The Notorious B.I.G.

"Gold Digger"—Kanye West (feat. Jamie Foxx)

"Boys Don't Cry"—The Cure

"Stressed Out"—Twenty One Pilots

"Bang Bang"—Jessie J (feat. Ariana Grande and Nicki Minaj)

"Basket Case"—Green Day

"Karma Chameleon"—Culture Club

"Give It Away"—Red Hot Chili Peppers

"Hey Ya!"—OutKast

"Paint It Black"—The Rolling Stones

"The Middle"—Jimmy Eat World

Should You Hire a Trainer?

I hope I've convinced you that exercise is more than worth the effort. Now let's talk about how to do it. There are a few things to consider, and one of the things people ask me a lot is, "Do I need a trainer?"

A better question might be, "Do I need guidance in creating and sustaining my exercise plan?" I realize that trainers cost money and not everyone can afford extra luxuries like that in their lives. Fortunately, there are a lot of incredible alternatives out there when it comes to finding exercise instruction and creating a game plan. There are free or inexpensive apps and online videos that can up anybody's workout game. But if your question is, "Should I spend my money on a gym membership or hire a personal trainer instead?" well, a lot of that depends on you.

Some people like to go it alone and already know what they want to do. Some people like the camaraderie of a gym, or the privacy of working out with their headphones on and talking to nobody. But if you aren't sure how to start, or you don't know if you're doing the right exercises, or if you aren't making the progress you hoped to make by exercising, a trainer can help a lot. Even one or two sessions can send you in the right direction.

The main reason I hired a trainer is that I'm just not very comfortable going to public gyms. As I said earlier, for me, they're confusing and intimidating, and I never know what to do. Personally, I would hire a certified, experienced trainer instead of paying for a gym membership (for my money, I'd hire a trainer before just about any other personal service). I don't think anybody really *needs* a gym membership if they don't like gyms. Have the trainer come over to your house a couple of times a week or meet you somewhere, like a park. Any place can be a gym. Or, if you don't mind gyms but want more direction, a lot of gyms have personal trainers on staff who can work with you once, or every time you come in. Some are even included in your gym membership.

A trainer can assess your personal needs, condition, and goals, and they can help you design a workout plan that works for what *you* need. That is what they are trained in, so they can give you an appropriate workout, compared to what you might come up with on your own. They can tell you what equipment you need, like bands or dumbbells or a kettlebell or a jump rope. They can show you different exercises and mark your progress. They can say, "You did this last time, so let's go heavier this time" or "You're ready to do more reps." They can make sure your form is correct, so you get the most out of the exercise and don't get injured. It's easy to do some exercises the wrong way, and then they don't do anything for you. For example, I can't tell you how many times I've

More Ways to Score a Trainer

If you don't want to spend money on a gym membership and a weekly trainer doesn't fit into your budget, another option may be to hire a trainer for one session a month. That way, you still have someone to hold you accountable and help you track your progress. The trainer may even be able to write out a monthly workout plan for you to do on your own, then check in with you once a month. Some trainers also take online clients, and that's another option. There are many options for personal training that don't require going to a gym or always having your trainer right next to you. Depending on the trainer, you may have weekly check-ins, Skype sessions, or even the ability to call or text your trainer whenever you need them. There are a lot of ways to get the personalized guidance you want.

Right now, I do a lot on my own, but that's only because I have gained huge amounts of knowledge from my trainers, past and present. I currently train with Eve Overland, but not every time I do a workout. Instead, I meet with her periodically, and sometimes we have Skype workout sessions together. Because she's a professional, I can trust that there's a method to her madness and she has good reasons for every exercise she gives me. And I

like that she can put together different workout programs for me to keep things fresh.

I probably work out with Eve the most when I'm on the road. She makes sure I don't slack off and quit exercising when I really need it. Also, traveling means random gyms and weird hotel workout rooms—some are awesome, but some are just terrible, and a lot of them have equipment that looks good but isn't really useful. With a trainer, I can avoid all that and keep it private. She can find facilities, classes, or great hikes ahead of time, wherever we're traveling, and come up with programs that work for the road. The therapy of exercise gets me through the rigorous schedule of a concert tour, and for that reason, it's my on-the-road splurge.

Yep, I work out on the road, even when I'm doing shows. Is it fun getting up early and working out after I spent the night before doing a show, then dealing with a young child waking up at three a.m.? No. But did it make me feel so much better that the rest of my day was actually productive and energized? Did it make me perform better? Absolutely. On tour, in the studio, or at home, taking the time to exercise makes every day better.

been to a gym and seen people swinging weights around when they're doing something as simple as biceps curls. A trainer would teach you how to do even the "easy" things properly to maximize their effect. Working out with a trainer can also be really useful for motivation. A trainer can encourage you along the way, has a professional perspective on your progress, and can also become like a workout buddy.

Get an Accountability Partner (or Three)

Another thing to think about is accountability. You can tell yourself you're going to do it—get up every morning and work out, rain or shine—but if you have someone else to help keep you accountable, it can make a big difference in how well you actually stick to your resolve. I think everyone should have at least one person who is on the same fitness "wavelength," so you can encourage and motivate each other. This is especially helpful on those mornings when you want to roll over and go back to sleep and skip your workout. If you have something scheduled and somebody else is depending on you, you'll feel like you have to show up. Whether you're meeting a friend, meeting with your trainer, going on a run with your partner, or just sharing your workout on a digital platform like Fitbit, someone else other than you is witness to your workout, and that holds you accountable.

Trainers are good for this, and this is just one more reason to work with one. I'm not going to cancel on my trainer. She has to make a living. This is her job. She doesn't hang out with me for the fun of it (although I do like to think of myself as being a pretty fun gal). If I cancel, then she could have booked another client in my slot, so unless I am legit sick with a stomach virus or the flu, I'm going to get my butt out of bed, even if I don't feel like it.

Welcome to My Mobile Gym

I bought my mobile gym to treat myself. I am fully aware that 99.9 percent of people don't have a mobile gym—most people probably don't need one—but because I'm on the road so much, it has really saved me. Being in hotel gyms is so inconsistent. Sometimes you get nice shiny new equipment, and sometimes you get nothing. I'm okay working with nothing. There is plenty I can do without equipment. But at some point, I really do like being able to do all my regular workouts while I'm on the road. So now I take a gym with me!

My mobile gym is in a big trailer like you would see on the back of a semi. It's got a leg press, dumbbells, an elliptical machine, and a treadmill. It's all spaced out just right. There's not a whole lot of extra room, but I do have the space to do burpees and

floor exercises. I have barbells, and a "captain's chair" (chin dip machine), where I can hold myself up and lift my legs for a great ab workout. I have a cable machine, a bench, and a box. We pull it all with a truck that follows the tour bus.

But you don't need a mobile gym to stay fit on the road. You can pack everything you need in your suitcase. Throw in some workout bands, a jump rope, and an ab wheel that disassembles. You could even get bands with interchangeable handles. None of it is very expensive. Or, if that doesn't seem like your cup of tea, just get out and explore the city you're in. Do it on foot—think of all the steps you'll be getting! Traveling should never be an excuse to be sedentary.

For a complete list of what to bring on the road with you and how to exercise on the road, including in a hotel room, see chapter 7.

Workout buddies are also good for this. If I have a friend who's counting on me because we're meeting in the park to go for a walk, then I'm not going to cancel. Don't be one of those people who flakes. Be one of those people who keeps your word and shows up when you say you will.

My best friend Ivey is that person for me. We've been through the same seasons in our lives, with getting married and having kids and that sort of thing. (Ivey is married to my bass player/musical director.) When we each see the other one making good choices, we're more likely to make good choices, too. Ivey and I keep each other honest and inspire each other. Plus, we have different strong suits that can benefit the other person. She is a cardio queen! She can run for miles and miles and make it look like it's nothing. I love a good running session, but what she can do is definitely inspiring. I'm better with equipment and weights, and that inspires her. We can fill in each other's gaps and push each other to do better in the areas where each of us needs improvement. I'm motivated knowing I motivate her, and we promote positive change in each other. Even when we're not together—and we often aren't—we share our statistics through the Fitbit app, and when her steps for the day are super low, I'll tease her about it. She is more the temptress—as well as being a cardio queen, she is a dessert queen! Try having a best friend who is an incredible baker of cupcakes! But I'll come up with workouts and we both do them and it's long-distance fitness solidarity. It's nice to be on the same page with someone.

My husband, Mike, is my other accountability partner. We both like to eat healthy and stay active together, so that means he's not always trying to get me to do unhealthy things. Thank goodness, since we are together in the same house! It would be really difficult to live with someone who tries to sabotage you all the time, so it's important to get your partner on board with what you're doing. You want to make your partner proud, not feel constantly tempted to skip your workout and order a pizza. I'm lucky that my husband is one million percent supportive, and all partners should be, but obviously that's not reality. If it's not your reality, I advise sitting down with your partner (or all your family members) and explaining how much you need to do this and asking directly for their support. If they know you want to be around for a long time, and you want them to be healthy and happy and long-lived right along with you, that might make all the difference.

Are You a Morning Person or an Evening Person?

The next thing to think about if you really want to be successful at starting a good regular fitness program is *when*. When are you most likely to actually work out? Some people have to do it in the morning or they know it won't happen. Other people are not going to do it in the morning, no way, but have no problem stopping by the gym on the way home from work to decompress and transition back to being home. Think about who you are and how your days go and make a realistic plan.

For instance, I am not a morning person. I wish I were one of those people who can just wake up, throw some clothes on, and go work out. But that doesn't work for me. I have to have some breakfast. I know I can't work out on an empty stomach, or I'll pass out. But everybody is different. I know some people who absolutely can't eat breakfast before they work out because they know they'll hurl. Not me. I usually wake up between six and seven a.m. My kids are my alarm clock. In the morning, Isaiah likes to come into my room and say, "Mommy, the sun is up. Let's cuddle"—which is just about the best way to wake up that I can think of! I get breakfast for my kids, I get breakfast for myself, I have my coffee, and then and only then can I function like a human. My favorite time to work out is around nine a.m. By then, I'm fully awake and ready to go.

But this schedule might be different, depending on the day. If I have a show at night and end up not going to bed until one a.m. or later, I'll still do my morning routine in the usual order, but I may be moving a bit more slowly. Everything might get pushed back a bit, so I end up working out in the early afternoon.

And sometimes I miss my morning workout and have to do it at the end of the day, but that's always a lot harder when I feel like I have a whole day's worth of food in my system. If I end up working out later, I might choose to go for a walk rather than trying to lift weights.

It's always better to be flexible than to think that if you miss your workout at the exact time you planned, you can't do it at all.

Do It When You Can, Because Sometimes You Can't

Do I always work out, no matter what? Come flood or famine or hell-fire? Oh my gosh, no. There are certainly days when I *don't* get a chance to work out. Some weeks are just nutty. I'm on a plane for hours or I'm on the road and don't get a chance to stop or I'm up at three a.m. to do a morning talk show and then I'm doing appearances all day. I'm not going to work out on days like that. That's why I always exercise *when I can.*

Even if I don't feel like it, if I have the time, I will make myself do it. If I have seven days where I can work out, I'll work out every one of those seven days (rotating what I do each day). I have to do this because the next week, I might only be able to exercise for two out of seven days. My schedule is so random and so crazy that it's unavoidable, and I know yours is, too.

Maybe you have to go into work early and work late. Maybe your kid gets sick and you have to drop everything else. Maybe you have unexpected guests or there's a hurricane or you have to spend the whole

day dealing with fixing a broken pipe or whatever it is. Life is full of surprises. Take your opportunities when they come. I always say, work out on the days you can because of all the days you can't.

Make a Plan

Finally, a plan is critical, especially for an obsessive planner like me. Maybe you already have one with a trainer, but if you don't, make planning part of the fun. One of my favorite things to do is to plan my workout while I'm having breakfast. I get out my journal and make a game plan of everything I'm going to do. If I'm doing the workout that I'm going to show you in the next chapter, I'll plan what all my cards will be

your fitness plan, organized

Whether you already exercise or not, try making a fitness plan in your journal. It doesn't have to be perfect. Brainstorm ideas for how you can be more active during your day. Think of reasons why exercise would improve your life and make a list. Are you setting an example for someone? Write about what kind of impression you want to make. Do you have a step counter or a smartwatch? Do you want to start using it to pay more attention to your steps, or do you think you would use one and it would be worth purchasing? Think about all the different kinds of exercise you might want to try. Make up sample fitness plans and think about how you would execute them. Don't limit yourself. You aren't committing to anything. These are just ideas. You might even go for a walk first. While you're walking, think about what you want to write in your journal. You'll get your circulation moving and your creativity flowing. Think outside the box!

(you'll see what I mean). Then, when I'm ready to work out, I take my journal to my home gym with me so I can execute my plan. This gives me a great feeling of accomplishment. I planned something good, and then I did it, and it's not even noon yet!

What you choose to do for exercise could, of course, be anything. There are a million ways to exercise and everybody has to find what they love. I like running. I know that's not for everyone (my hubby hates to run). I didn't always love running so much, but now, especially when it's hot outside, I like to run until I get completely sweaty and disgusting.

When I get back home, I feel like I've sweated out a pound of toxins and I feel better. Then, for the rest of the day, I have this kind of mellow vibe. I feel good and clear and creative and ideas just come to me.

That's another good thing about running. The rhythm and the regularity and the solitude without having to think about what you are doing is the perfect environment for coming up with ideas. I've solved a lot of problems and come up with a lot of creative solutions and even thought of songwriting ideas when I was running. What some people accomplish through meditation, I accomplish through running. It's a way to make a blank space in your mind, and anything can appear in that space. Walking works, too.

But you need more than cardio. Back in the days when that was all I did, I often overdid it and would have to pay for it later with injuries or exhaustion. Good balanced workouts should involve cardio along with some kind of flexibility or mobility training (like stretching) and some kind of resistance training (like with weights or bands) that covers all the major muscle groups. Again, this is where a trainer can help. My trainer Eve taught me how important it is to balance my workout, and she is always coming up with new ways for me to do this.

The bottom line is that overall and in every way, exercise makes you better. It gives you clarity . . . and feel-good endorphins! It makes you feel happier. It makes you a better parent, partner, friend . . . it makes you better at everything you do. It makes you stronger and gives you more energy. It makes everything you do easier. It helps you breathe better (important for singing!) and gets your heart in shape for whatever comes your way.

When you've worked out, you can feel like you've accomplished something in your day, even if nothing else gets done. There's no reason not to do it, as long as you start where you are, and just push yourself a little more each time. It doesn't have to be complicated. Even if it's just a walk, it will improve your day. And although you can work out any time that is best for you, I know that for me, if I've done my workout early, then I feel like I'm already winning before lunch.

5

PLAY ON

The Fit52 Workout

There are a lot of ways I like to work out. I like to run, I like to use weight machines, I like to do calisthenic-type exercises like push-ups and sit-ups and burpees, and I always like to change it up to keep things interesting. My trainer Eve has created a lot of different workouts for me over the years. She has notebooks full of Carrie workouts (or so she tells me!). My all-time favorite is one that we have officially named the Fit52 Workout. I love it because it requires only a deck of cards and you can do it with a few very simple, inexpensive pieces of equipment. And it takes my Fit52 concept to a whole new place.

This workout is based on a fitness game that Eve introduced me to years ago. It's one of those things that has been around for a long time in the fitness world, and people have a lot of different ways of adapting it to what they want to do. I immediately loved the way it changed up my routine and was something that I could do very easily on my own. Over the years, Eve and I have continued to refine it to make it even more flexible and adjustable—so that with modifications, it can be done by almost anyone, anywhere, anytime. This ingenious workout uses a standard deck of 52 cards, which, as you'll soon see, allows the workout to be different

The suit determines the exercise. The number determines the reps.

WHY YOU SHOULD BE LIFTING WEIGHTS

No other form of exercise can change your physique like weight training can. You can burn more calories during a cardio session, but weight training will result in an increased calorie burn long after your workout is over. This happens because lifting weights increases muscle mass, so it increases your metabolic rate. A properly programmed workout routine should include both cardio and weight lifting.

But exercise isn't just about burning calories. Weight training has more functional carryover to everyday life. We tend to lose strength as we age, and weight training can keep us strong, mobile, active, and in the game for as long as possible. You'll get the most bang for your buck with gross motor or compound movements that work many muscles at once, and there are a few foundational exercises that should be part of every workout because they have the most carryover to everyday living—for example, if you have to squat down or bend over to pick up your child, or put an awkward roller bag into the overhead bin on a flight. These are:

› Squats
› Deadlifts
› Overhead presses
› Chest presses
› Pull-ups or back rows

As you will see, the Fit52 Workout incorporates all these foundational exercises, but even when you aren't doing this particular workout, I recommend making these basic exercises part of your workout plan. It won't take long before you start feeling your whole life getting physically easier.

every time, with every exercise a surprise. Which exercise you'll do next, and how many reps you'll do, are all the luck of the draw.

I also like the idea of using a deck of 52 cards because there are 52 weeks in the year—52 clean-slate chances to score a healthy, fit week all year long and for every single year of your life. Those 52 weeks can add up to significant changes in your health, your body, and your well-being, and it all starts with a simple deck of cards.

In this chapter, Eve and I will show you exactly how you can do Fit52 at home. At first it may sound complex, but really, it couldn't be easier, once you get the hang of it. All you need are a deck of cards and the equipment listed on pages 92–93. And it's fun! Let's go through it step by step.

Fit52 Workout Basics

First, an overview:

1. The Fit52 Workout is a plan that assigns certain exercises to each suit in a deck of cards:

UPPER BODY   LOWER BODY   CORE   CARDIO

Every time you work out, you'll be doing exercises for each of these areas.

2. There are 52 playing cards in a standard deck. First you'll divide the deck in half. During the first half of your workout (Set #1), you'll go through the first half of the deck. During the second half of your workout (Set #2), you'll go through the second half of the deck.

3. For each suit, you'll get two exercises: one for Set #1, and one for Set #2. So you'll have two upper body exercises, two lower body exercises, two core exercises, and two cardio exercises—eight total exercises for each workout.

4. You will work through each half of the deck by drawing the cards one at a time. The suit of each card that you draw determines which type of exercise you will do (upper body, lower body, core, or cardio). The number on each card that you draw determines how

IF YOU'RE JUST GETTING STARTED

If you haven't worked out for a while (or ever!), doing one set of exercises with half the deck, for a 30-minute workout, may be enough for you until you build the strength and endurance for a 60-minute workout. If this sounds like you, I advise doing only Set #1 for all six days, then moving to Set #2 the following week. If you were to do Set #1 one day, then Set #2 the next day, you would be working the same set of muscles two days in a row. It's good to rest those muscle groups in order to recover properly, especially if you feel really sore.

many reps you will do. For example, in your first set, if you draw a 6 of spades, you will do 6 reps of the first cardio exercise. If you draw a 7 of diamonds next, you will do 7 reps of your first upper body exercise. Note that the lowest number of reps you can draw is 2. If you draw a jack, that's 11 reps. Queen is 12 reps. King is 13 reps. Ace is 14 reps, the most you will do with any single draw.

5.   During Set #1 (first half of the deck), you'll do the first of each pair of exercises, and the exercise you do will correspond with which suit you draw. Example: If you draw a heart, you will do the first lower body exercise. During Set #2 (second half of the deck), you will do the second of each pair of exercises, and the exercise you do will again correspond with which suit you draw. Example: If you draw a club, you will do the second core exercise.

6.   Each workout takes approximately an hour—30 minutes for the Set #1 exercises, and 30 minutes for the Set #2 exercises. If you have only 30 minutes total to work out, do the Set #1 exercises for six days, then do the Set #2 exercises for the six days after that, so you take twelve days to get through all the exercises. That's totally fine—go at your own pace or according to your own schedule. You can take even longer if you alternate the Fit52 Workout with other workouts you like to do.

JOKERS WILD!

If you have a pair of jokers in your deck of cards, you can make these "wild cards" and assign any exercise to them—but it should be one that's challenging for you. What I like to do is assign one minute of forearm plank (think top of a push-up, but on your forearms instead of on your hands). This is a great full-body exercise, but especially beneficial for strengthening your core. Keep your body in a straight line from the crown of your head to your heels. If you can't quite make it the full minute, try starting with 30 seconds and work your way up.

Because there are many cards of each suit, you will do each exercise multiple times, but you will never know how many reps you'll do or what order you will do the exercises in until you draw your next card. That's the fun part!

The other fun part: You can do this workout exactly as written, or you can substitute any exercises for the suits, making this workout ultimately adaptable. At the gym? Assign a weight machine to each suit. In a hotel room? Pick a basic exercise for each suit: push-ups, sit-ups, squats, and burpees, for example. At the playground? Pick a different playground exercise for each suit.

Now let's look at how it works in practice. Here's what you will do during each workout:

1. Let's say it's Monday. You will start with Day #1, which consists of a pair of complementary upper body, lower body, core, and cardio exercises. Take note of what those exercises are. (They start on page 100.) Be sure you know how to do them by consulting the instructions. (It won't take long for you to learn them all and not have to look anymore.)

2. Get out any equipment you will need for your Day #1 exercises. Now you're ready to go!

3. Do the warm-up described starting on page 94.

4. Shuffle the deck and divide it in half. Put one half in front of you and set the other half aside for when you get to your second set.

5. Draw a card. The suit determines which exercise you will do. If you draw a diamond, you will do the first upper body exercise for Day #1. If you draw a 10 of diamonds, you will do 10 reps.

6. Draw another card. If you draw a spade, you will do the first cardio exercise for Day #1. If you draw a 4 of spades, you will do 4 reps.

7. Draw another card. Uh-oh, it's another diamond, this time an 8 of diamonds. That means you're going to do the same upper body exercise again, this time for 8 reps.

8. Draw another card. This time it's a 3 of clubs. Do your first core exercise for Day #1, and do 3 reps.

9. Draw another card. Oh no, another diamond! This time a queen. Back to that same upper body exercise, but this time you do 12 reps. Are your arms getting tired? Great! That means you're building muscle!

10. Draw another card. It's a 7 of spades. Do the first cardio exercise for Day #1, and do 7 reps.

11. Keep going until you've gotten through all the cards in the first half of the deck.

12. Now it's time for the second half of the deck, and Set #2. Proceed just as you did with the first half of the deck, but switch to the Set #2 exercise for Day #1.

13. Once you've gotten through the whole deck, do the cool-down starting on page 131.

14. Congratulate yourself on a workout well done! Now you can go on with your day knowing you've done your workout and are feeling great.

15. Do Day #2 tomorrow!

WORKOUT EQUIPMENT BASICS

For every workout, before each set, I will cue you about which pieces of workout equipment to have available, but here is your workout equipment basics list. This includes every piece of equipment mentioned in this chapter.

› **BOX, BENCH, OR AEROBIC STEP:** You could get one or all of these—Carrie prefers wooden boxes for exercises like box jumps, but she also uses benches and steps. Weight benches are good, but any bench will do. Aerobic steps are lower, and many have adjustable risers. The height of what you use depends on the exercise and your fitness level. One of the things I have purchased for my clients and for my home gym is called the Reebok Deck. You can buy it online. It's so versatile—it has an adjustable back, so you can use it as an incline bench, and it has attachments for resistance bands, but it is low enough that you can also use it as an adjustable-height step. When Carrie saw mine, she bought one, too!

› **DUMBBELLS (LIGHT, MEDIUM, AND HEAVY):** Dumbbells are probably the piece of fitness equipment people are most likely to have. If you don't have any, find them at a sporting goods store or discount store. Choose dumbbells that are light, medium, and heavy for you—try

before you buy. But don't go too easy on yourself. There must be resistance and effort involved in order to gain strength and to shape muscles. If you pick up a set and you can easily do 20 or more reps, that's too light. Even your lightest dumbbells need to provide some level of challenge if you want to see results. You might be able to go heavier than you think, and remember that you will gain strength quickly. Buy dumbbells individually, or in sets.

› **RESISTANCE BANDS (LIGHT, MEDIUM, AND HEAVY):** These flexible tube-shaped bands are stretchy, have handles, and offer different levels of resistance. If you can find a set with a variety of sizes, handles you can clip on or off, and a door anchor to hold the band (very handy and will give you a lot more exercise options), that would be your best bet. All bands will tell you the weight equivalency for the different bands (e.g., 10 pounds or "medium resistance"), so you will have a better idea of which one to choose for any given exercise.

› **MINI BANDS (MEDIUM AND HEAVY):** These are like giant circular rubber bands that are most commonly used around the legs or ankles, to provide resistance for lateral movements.

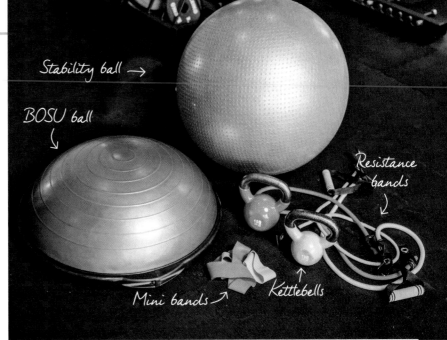

Stability ball →

BOSU ball

Resistance bands

Mini bands ↗

Kettlebells

› **STABILITY BALL:** Technically called a Swiss ball, this is a large inflatable ball that helps build core stability. It's good for a variety of exercises that use just your body weight (like crunches and hamstring curls). You can even use it instead of a bench for exercises like the seated shoulder press or dumbbell bench press. It is very versatile.

These items can also be used in the Fit52 Workout as options, but are not essential:

› **MEDICINE BALL:** These weighted balls are about the size of a volleyball and are available in different weights—mine is 8 pounds. These are great for ab/core exercises, partner work, or even in place of dumbbells.

› **KETTLEBELLS (MEDIUM AND HEAVY):** These heavy cast-iron flat-bottomed weights with handles are good for many different exercises, the most common being the kettlebell swing.

› **BOSU:** (Carrie loves this one!) Like a stability ball cut in half and stuck to a flat platform, a BOSU provides an unstable surface for improving balance while doing various movements.

› **BARBELL:** If you go to a gym, you don't need this at home, but some people like to have one to add variety and more exercise options. It is a bar that can hold plates on either end to increase the weight.

› **EXERCISE MAT:** Not a must, but nice to have when you are doing an exercise on the floor.

Your Fit52 Workout

Now let's look at the exercises you'll actually be doing. Eve has carefully selected these exercises to complement each other so you'll get a complete full-body workout each day. Over the course of six 60-minute workouts (or twelve 30-minute workouts), you will cover them all.

Note that in Appendix 2 there are modify-down and modify-up options, for when these exercises are a little too strenuous or a little too easy for you on any given day. Every day is different, and everyone is in a different place on their fitness path, so this gives you a little more flexibility to adapt any exercise to your current needs.

Ready to get Fit52? Here we go!

EVE'S FIT52 DYNAMIC WARM-UP

There are two kinds of stretching: dynamic and static. *Dynamic stretching* is more active. You stretch your muscles during movement, rather than holding the stretch for a period of time, as you would do in *static stretching*. As a general rule, dynamic stretching is best for warming up, and static stretching is best for cooling down. Here's a good basic dynamic stretching warm-up that you can do before any exercise session.

You may have heard that all you really need to do to warm up is to jump on the treadmill or elliptical trainer or take a short jog and break a light sweat. However, how you warm up is related to how you plan to work out. Therefore, warming up with cardio really just prepares your body for . . . more cardio. The purpose of a dynamic warm-up is not just to raise your core temperature (although that's part of it), but to improve your power, strength, and performance when you begin your actual workout. Don't get me wrong—I love me some cardio. And if you love it, go for it. But in addition to your cardio, you will get more benefit if you add dynamic stretching to your warm-up routine. The benefits of dynamic stretching include:

› Increased blood flow to your muscles

› Increased efficiency of your body's cooling mechanisms

› Better focus during your workout

› Decreased likelihood of injury

› Priming of your central nervous system (CNS)

› Improved mobility, stability, balance, and range of motion (ROM)

› Greater power output

Here is the basic process I recommend. Spend **30 seconds** doing each of these exercises, and move as quickly as you can from one to the next, for a total warm-up of about 6 minutes.

(Note that many smartwatches and fitness trackers, not to mention most smartphones, have functional timers on them, and there are also a lot of free timer apps that can be useful when timing these warm-ups.)

1. **HIGH KNEES:** Jog or walk in place while lifting your knees as high as you can.

2. **ALTERNATING KNEE HUGGERS:** Stand on one leg and lift the opposite knee. Hug it in close to your chest. Draw circles in the air with your toes to warm up your ankles. Take a beat or two before switching legs. Do each side twice.

3. **LOW SQUAT WITH ALTERNATING HIP OPENERS:** Squat as low as you can, then, as you come up, swing your leg up and out, as if you're swinging it over an invisible chair (you can keep your knees bent). Squat again and repeat with the other leg.

Butt back. Knees don't go past toes.

4. **ALTERNATING REVERSE LUNGE WITH OVERHEAD REACH OR TORSO TWIST:** Step backward with one leg, lowering yourself into a lunge, as you reach both arms straight overhead. Come back to standing, then repeat with the other leg. For the Torso Twist variation, as you lunge, hold your arms out in front of you and twist your torso and arms in the opposite direction of your back (lunging) leg. Return to standing, then repeat with the other leg and opposing twist.

5. **BUTT KICKERS:** Jog (or walk) in place, trying to kick your rear with each foot when it is bent behind you.

6. **STANDING QUAD STRETCH:** Stand on one leg and hold your foot behind you to stretch your quad muscles, shifting your hips forward for a deeper stretch. Release your foot and step forward. Repeat with the other leg.

7. **BODY WEIGHT GOOD MORNINGS:** From a standing position, feet shoulder-width apart, put your hands behind your head, elbows extended out wide. With a slight bend in your knees, push your hips back and "take a bow," hinging at the hips and keeping your spine straight and your core tight. Pause for a beat when your torso is as close to parallel to the floor as possible, then return to standing.

Can't reach the floor? Slightly bend your knees.

8. **INCHWORMS (WITH OPTIONAL PUSH-UP):** From a standing position, bend from the hips until your hands reach the floor. If you can't quite reach the floor, bend your knees just enough to get there. Walk your hands out in front of you until you are in a plank position like the top of a push-up—in fact, for extra credit, you could throw in a push-up here. Hold for a breath or two, keeping your ab muscles engaged. Walk your hands back to your feet, keeping your legs as straight as possible and taking your time to feel the stretch in your hamstrings. Return to standing. Repeat.

9. **ALTERNATING SLOW OUTSIDE MOUNTAIN CLIMBERS:** Get into plank position. Keeping your abdominal muscles tight, bring one knee out to the side, as close to your triceps muscle (the back of your upper arm) as possible. Move your leg back to return to plank position, then repeat on the other side.

10. **ALTERNATING LIZARD LUNGE WITH ROTATION:** Start in a plank position. Take a big step forward with one leg, placing your foot outside your hand on the same side, with your knee bent at 90 degrees. You are now in a low runner's lunge. Reach the hand closest to your bent leg up to the sky while keeping the other hand on the floor. Twist your torso toward your bent knee. Stay for a beat or two. Return your extended hand back to the floor. Step back into plank position and repeat on the other side.

11. **UP/DOWN DOGS:** You yoga folks will know this one. Start in plank position and lower your hips while raising your head and chest. Look slightly upward, but don't collapse your neck backward. Try to keep as much length as you can between your shoulders and your ears. Keep your arms straight and your hips low. This is Up Dog. Next, move your hips up and back as high as you can, keeping your head between your upper arms. Your heels should

be as close to the ground as possible. This is Down Dog. Move between these two positions—hips up, head down; hips down, head up—with control, keeping your core engaged.

12. **FIVE FAST FEET AND JUMP:** With your feet a little wider than hip-width apart and your knees slightly bent, take five tiny fast running steps in place (moving your right foot then your left foot equals one step). Think of a football drill. Then jump as high as you can. Land soft. Repeat. (To make this more challenging, you can do a tuck jump: While jumping, tuck both knees up to your chest.)

eve says

DUMBBELL GUIDANCE

In general, use heavier dumbbells to work larger muscle groups like those in the legs and back. These muscles can typically handle more weight. You may need to use medium weights when performing a lower body unilateral exercise like a Bulgarian Split Squat because it requires more balance. Many of my female clients use medium weights for their chests and shoulders, but you would be surprised how quickly they progress to a heavier set.

Light weights are great for the smaller muscle groups like your biceps and triceps, and exercises like the Lateral Raise. They can also be useful for those who are new to weight lifting and need to build strength from the ground up. But these people are likely to progress quickly to heavier weights also.

REMEMBER: If you can do 20 reps with ease, that weight is too light for any of the exercises in this book.

DAY #1 EXERCISES

EQUIPMENT LIST FOR SET #1

› **DUMBBELLS** (since these exercises focus on the lower body, use weights on the heavier side)
› **MAT** (optional)

EQUIPMENT LIST FOR SET #2

› **BENCH, STEP, OR CHAIR**
› **LOW STEP** (or a stair step)
› **DUMBBELLS** (the same ones you used for Set #1)

eve says

Your Day #1 exercises will use your whole body, but your legs will be the primary focus—in particular the Heart (lower body) exercises. I would like you to challenge yourself with these exercises, and I encourage you to go as heavy as possible with your weights, as long as you can maintain good form and control. Leg muscles are larger and generally stronger than the upper body and core muscles, so they are good to train first. For your Diamond (upper body) exercises, we'll work two complementary pushing muscle groups: chest and triceps (the backs of your arms). For your Heart (lower body) exercises, we'll work the quads (the muscles in the front of your thighs) and your glutes (your backside). Your Club (core) and Spade (cardio) exercises will also activate your leg muscles. Get ready for a great workout and an awesome kickoff to your week of fitness!

(UPPER BODY) ◆

PUSH-UPS

1. Get into plank position, with your shoulders over your wrists.

2. Bend your elbows, pointing them back toward your hips, lowering your body with a straight spine and a tight core. Go as far down as you can without touching the floor. Keep the tension. Don't relax at the bottom.

3. Straighten your arms and raise your body back up, keeping your spine straight and your neck in line with your spine. Your body should make a straight line from the crown of your head to your tailbone during this entire exercise.

4. Do the number of reps on your card.

TRICEPS BENCH DIPS

1. Sit in a chair or on a bench. Put your palms on the chair or bench on either side of your hips.

2. Slide forward off the bench or chair. Keep your knees bent and your feet on the floor in front of you. Your hips (or backside) should always be under your shoulders, so stay close to the bench or chair.

3. Bend your elbows and lower yourself down until your upper arms are parallel to the floor, elbows pointing behind you (don't splay them out to the sides).

4. Straighten your arms and squeeze your triceps to raise yourself back up to the starting position.

5. Do the number of reps on your card.

SET #1 (FIRST 30 MINUTES)

DOUBLE SUITCASE SQUATS

1. Holding a heavy dumbbell in each hand, stand with your feet about shoulder-width apart and your arms hanging at your sides, like you are holding two suitcases.

2. Squat down slowly with control, so your legs form a 90-degree angle, or slightly lower, if you can.

3. Keeping your weight in your heels, stand up straight again.

4. Do the number of reps on your card.

SET #2 (SECOND 30 MINUTES)

STEP UPS

1. Holding a heavy dumbbell in each hand, stand facing a step or bench, both feet close to the step. Put one foot on the step or bench and lean forward very slightly—only enough to put your weight on the upper foot.

2. Maintaining good posture, drive off the leg that is on the step or bench, to stand up fully on top of the step or bench. (If this is too difficult, you don't have to use the dumbbells.)

3. Lower yourself back down, keeping the same foot on the step or bench.

4. Repeat using the same leg for the number of reps on your card. Then do the same number of reps on the other side.

Keep these slow and controlled.

SET #1 (FIRST 30 MINUTES)

REVERSE CRUNCHES WITH LEG DROP

1. Lie on your back, with your hands close to your sides, palms facedown. Keeping your legs straight, lift your legs a few inches above the ground. Tuck your pelvis to keep your lower back on the floor.

2. Using your abs (rather than momentum), draw your knees in so they are bent at 90 degrees and directly above your hips, then straighten your legs and raise your hips up, as if you are trying to make a footprint on the ceiling. Lower your hips back down, and slowly lower your legs back to the floor without arching your back.

3. Do the number of reps on your card.

SET #2 (SECOND 30 MINUTES)

PLANK AROUND-THE-WORLDS

1. From a plank position (the top of a push-up), keeping your body straight, extend your right arm in front of you to shoulder height, then return your hand to the ground. Repeat with your left arm.

2. Lift up your left foot so your leg is at hip height or slightly higher (but without any curve or arch in your lower back), keeping your body straight. Don't twist or reach all the way to the ceiling—keep your hips and shoulders as square to the floor as possible.

3. Return your foot to the ground, then repeat with your right foot. All the way "around" is one rep.

4. Do the number of reps on your card.

Try not to touch the floor with your heels!

SET #1 (FIRST 30 MINUTES)

STAR JUMPS OR STAR JACKS

1. Stand with your feet close together. Squat as low as you can, still keeping your chest up and your heels on the ground. Wrap your arms loosely around your shins.

2. Jump up, reaching your arms and legs out to make a star shape. Land softly with feet together and come back into the squat.

3. Do the number of reps on your card.

SET #2 (SECOND 30 MINUTES)

JUMP LUNGES

1. Stand with your feet hip-width apart and bring one leg in front of you, the other behind you. Bend both legs at a 90-degree angle and lower yourself into a lunge.

2. From this position, jump up and switch your legs in the air to land with the opposite foot forward.

3. Make sure to keep your back straight and land with soft knees to absorb impact.

4. Jump back to the original lunge position. This is one rep. Do the number of reps on your card.

DAY #2 EXERCISES

EQUIPMENT LIST FOR SET #1

› **RESISTANCE BAND** (heavy) with handles (a door anchor or a pull-up bar is helpful to hold your band for Lat Pull-Downs)

EQUIPMENT LIST FOR SET #2

› **DUMBBELLS** (heavy for Biceps Curls, light for Sit-Ups with Cross Punches)

› **MINI BAND**

› **MAT** (optional), **BENCH OR CHAIR**

eve says

For Day #2, we will focus on your upper body. After yesterday, you'll probably be glad to give your lower body a bit of a break. Your Diamond exercises will complement each other using your pulling muscles: back and biceps. Today is the day I encourage you to lift as heavy as possible for the Diamond exercises. The Heart exercises will work the smaller muscles in your legs and glutes. The focus is on three things: 1) the gluteus medius (one of the three gluteal muscles, commonly known in the industry as the "side butt"); 2) your abductors (the muscles that help you push your thighs apart); and 3) your adductors (the muscles that help you squeeze your thighs together). The Club exercises include arm work to round out the upper body focus day, and the Spade exercises will work laterally (side to side), using many of the same working muscles you use in your Heart exercises.

Try to reset and shove shoulders down before each pull-down.

SET #1 (FIRST 30 MINUTES)

LAT PULL-DOWNS

1. Loop your resistance band with handles through a door anchor, over a pull-up bar, or in any other secure overhead position.

2. Take hold of the handles and kneel down on one or both knees. (You can also sit completely on the floor, if that is more comfortable or the band is too long.) Raise your arms overhead. The band should be straight with slight tension in this position.

3. Keeping good posture, lean back slightly and bring your shoulders down "into your back pockets." This is your starting position. Pull the band down by bringing your elbows down to the side of your body. When the resistance band handles are about shoulder height, this is the bottom of the rep. Squeeze your shoulder blades together and raise your arms back up.

4. Do the number of reps on your card.

SET #2 (SECOND 30 MINUTES)

BICEPS CURLS

1. Hold a dumbbell in each hand. With your hands at your sides, turn your palms forward.

2. Keeping your upper arms against your sides and moving your lower arms only, bend at the elbows without rotating your wrists to lift the weights up to your chest.

3. Lower the weights back to the starting position.

4. Do the number of reps on your card.

SET #1 (FIRST 30 MINUTES)

ALTERNATING CURTSY LUNGES

1. Stand up straight, with your core tight and your feet hip-width apart. You can hold your hands in front of your chest or place them on your hips or wherever is comfortable.

2. Step back with your right foot, bringing it behind you at an angle and past your left foot. Keep equal weight on both feet, back straight and hips square as you bend both knees into a lunge. Return to starting position.

3. Repeat with the left foot to complete one rep. As an alternative, you could do all reps on one side, then do all the reps on the other side.

4. Do the number of reps on your card.

SET #2 (SECOND 30 MINUTES)

BANDED SQUAT TAP-OUTS

1. Stand and put a circular (mini) band around your ankles. Squat down to about 45 degrees.

2. From the squat position, tap your right foot out to the right side and back in.

3. Staying in the squat, tap your left foot out to the left side and back in, to complete 1 rep.

4. Do the number of reps on your card.

(CORE) ♣

SET #1 (FIRST 30 MINUTES)

SUPER PLANKS OR PLANK UP-DOWNS

1. Get into a forearm plank (like the top of a push-up but on your forearms instead of your hands) with your body straight.

2. Put your right hand on the floor directly under your shoulder exactly where your elbow was and push yourself up on one side, then put your left hand on the floor and push yourself fully up. You are now at the top of a push-up.

3. Lower your right forearm back to the ground, then your left.

4. If you feel yourself shifting from side to side or need more stability, bring your feet into a wider stance.

5. Repeat the whole sequence on the other side, starting with your left arm, to complete 1 rep.

6. Do the number of reps on your card.

SET #2 (SECOND 30 MINUTES)

SIT-UPS WITH CROSS PUNCHES

1. Lie on your back with your knees bent and your feet flat on the floor. Hold a dumbbell in each hand at your chest.

2. Do a sit-up, twisting slightly to the right on the way up and punch with your left hand across your body at a diagonal (holding the dumbbell), then twist in the other direction and punch with the right hand.

3. Lower back down and repeat on the other side, twisting to the left and punching with your right hand (holding the dumbbell), then twist in the other direction and punch with your left. Lower back down.

4. Do the number of reps on your card.

SET #1 (FIRST 30 MINUTES)

SKATERS

1. Stand with your feet about shoulder-width apart, your knees slightly bent, and your back straight, with a slight forward lean.

2. Transfer all your weight to the right leg and bring your left leg behind you at an angle, crossing your midline (like a curtsy lunge without putting the foot back down). Swing your left arm in front of you, as if you were skating.

3. Drive off the right leg and take a lateral hop to the left, to land on your left leg with your right leg back behind you at an angle as you swing your right arm in front of you. Immediately leap to the right again with the same motion on the opposite side.

4. Right and left is 1 rep.

5. Do the number of reps on your card.

SET #2 (SECOND 30 MINUTES)

LOG HOPS

1. Place both hands on the end of the bench on either side, with both legs together extended behind you. Keep your head up and your back straight. Squeeze the bench to engage the muscles in your upper body. Your arms should be straight, but your elbows should not be locked.

2. Bend your knees, engage your core, and jump both feet to the side, as if you are jumping over an imaginary log.

3. Immediately jump your feet to the other side. Do your best not to double bounce. Right and left is 1 rep.

4. Do the number of reps on your card.

HOW YOUR MUSCLES MOVE

Muscles move in two primary ways: concentrically and eccentrically. It's important to work both in order to move and perform your best. When you lift something, like a weight, your muscles shorten and make a concentric contraction. Think of a biceps curl: You hold the weight at the bottom, then bend your elbow, and your biceps muscles make a concentric contraction to lift the weight up toward your body.

An eccentric contraction is the opposite motion—the lengthening of the muscles—and it allows you to lower the weight back down again with control. Whether you are exercising or just going about your everyday life, I bet you can notice when your muscles contract concentrically (like when you're lifting a baby out of a crib or standing up from a chair), and when they contract eccentrically (such as when you're putting a bag of groceries down on the kitchen counter or relaxing into a warm bath). Becoming aware of these muscle actions is just another way to refine your body awareness, which includes movement awareness. Being aware of how you move is especially important for remaining mobile, healthy, and injury-free throughout your life.

DAY #3 EXERCISES

EQUIPMENT LIST FOR SET #1

› **STABILITY BALL**
› **MAT** (optional—you might want to use a mat since several of these exercises require lying on the floor)
› **STEP OR LOW BENCH** (if you have a BOSU, you could use it for the Up and Overs)

EQUIPMENT LIST FOR SET #2

› **RESISTANCE BANDS WITH HANDLES** (a door anchor is useful here)
› **HEAVY DUMBBELLS** (if you have a kettlebell, you could use it instead of dumbbells for the Romanian Deadlifts)

eve says

Day #3 is another lower body focus day, but we'll also be lighting up your core and going hard with cardio. Your Diamond exercises will include shoulders and chest, your Heart exercises will be all about the hamstrings (with an engaged core), and both your Club and Spade exercises will elevate your heart rate. Do your best to go all out with these! You'll give your heart and lungs a great workout today.

Special Note About Deadlifts

The Romanian Deadlifts in Set #2 seem simple enough. You just bend over and lift up a weight, right? The truth is, this exercise is actually quite technical, and when it is performed incorrectly, it can result in back strain. I purposefully start you out with Hamstring Roll-Outs in the first set to prime or wake up your hamstring muscles and your glutes for the deadlifts in the second set. Isolating your hamstring muscles in the first set elevates your mind-muscle connection to this area. This will help you to keep good form and focus on your hamstrings instead of recruiting your lower back for the heavy lifting. Keep that in mind when you get there: Let your hamstrings do the work.

◆ (UPPER BODY)

SET #1 (FIRST 30 MINUTES)

DIVEBOMBERS

1. Put your hands on the floor and walk forward, keeping your hips up, so your body forms an upside-down V.

2. Bending your elbows but keeping your legs straight, lower your upper body almost to the floor. Imagine a line drawn right between your thumbs. Leading with your forehead, aim to touch the center of that line with your forehead, your chin, and then your chest. Right before your chest touches the ground, swoop it up through your arms, raising your head so you are looking up, in an Up Dog position.

3. Without stopping, draw your hips up and back, keeping your arms straight, to return to your starting upside-down V position.

4. Do the number of reps on your card.

SET #2 (SECOND 30 MINUTES)

CHEST FLYS

1. Loop your resistance band around a pole, pull-up bar, or other stable object at or above chest height, or through a door anchor at the top of the door. With your back to the band, take hold of the handles with both hands. Move forward or backward to extend the band fully but not tightly. Take a natural step forward with one leg and hold your arms out to your sides, palms facing each other with your elbows slightly bent, at chest height.

2. Fly the handles in toward each other like you are "hugging a tree" until your hands almost meet in front of you. Keep your back straight, your shoulders down, and a slight bend in your elbows.

3. Return your arms to your sides. Do not go so far that your arms are behind your body.

4. Do the number of reps on your card.

Divebombers

Think forehead, chin, and chest—
like a plane swooping down and
then back up again.

SET #1 (FIRST 30 MINUTES)

HAMSTRING ROLL-OUTS

1. Lie on the floor and put your heels on a stability ball with your knees bent 90 degrees, your arms down by your sides at about a 45-degree angle (to help stabilize), and your palms facedown on the floor.

2. Lift your hips up, keeping your core tight. Your shoulders and head remain on the floor.

3. Keeping your feet on the ball and your hips high, slowly straighten your legs, pushing the ball away from you. When you reach full extension, bend your knees and curl the ball back toward your hips with your feet.

4. Do the number of reps on your card.

SET #2 (SECOND 30 MINUTES)

ROMANIAN DEADLIFTS

1. Hold a heavy dumbbell in each hand, in front of your hips, with your feet about hip-width apart in a comfortable stance and your knees slightly bent in a fixed position. Keep your chest up, shoulders back, and core tight.

2. With your back and arms straight, hinge at the hips and slide them back as you lower the dumbbells toward the floor. Stop when you feel a good stretch in your hamstrings, about mid-shin. Do not relax at the bottom of the movement. Keep the tension and your leg muscles active.

3. Stand up straight again, using your hamstrings to pull you up and squeeze your glutes at the top.

4. Do the number of reps on your card.

SET #1 (FIRST 30 MINUTES)

BICYCLES

1. Lie on your back on the floor. Put your hands behind your head, elbows out. Tighten your core and lift your straight legs off the floor about 30 degrees, while also lifting your head and lower back slightly off the floor.

2. Bend your right knee toward your chest and twist so your left elbow moves toward your bent knee. Don't pull on your neck.

3. Straighten your right knee as you bend your left knee, bringing it toward your chest and twisting so your right elbow moves toward your bent knee.

4. Do the number of reps on your card.

SET #2 (SECOND 30 MINUTES)

MOUNTAIN CLIMBERS

1. Get into plank position.

2. Keeping your palms firmly planted on the floor, pull your right knee in toward your chest, while your left leg remains straight and extended. Jump back with your right foot as you pull your left knee in toward your chest.

3. Quickly jump back with your left foot while pulling your right knee in toward your chest, as if you are running up a mountain.

4. Do the number of reps on your card.

Right and left equal one rep.
1,1... 2, 2...

SET #1 (FIRST 30 MINUTES)

UP AND OVERS

1. Stand sideways on a step or low bench (or a BOSU), then step off to the side with your right leg. One foot will be on the step and one on the floor.

2. Jump up and land with your right foot on the step and your left foot on the ground on the opposite side of the step.

3. Quickly jump again and land with your left foot on the step and your right foot on the ground.

4. Do the number of reps on your card.

SET #2 (SECOND 30 MINUTES)

REVERSE LUNGES WITH HOP

1. From standing, step back into a reverse lunge by bringing your right leg behind you and lowering your knee toward the floor.

2. Jump up and bring your back leg forward, driving your knee up in front of you as you jump. Come back down into the lunge on the same side.

3. Do the number of reps on your card on one side, then repeat on the other side.

DAY #4 EXERCISES

EQUIPMENT LIST FOR SET #1

› **DUMBBELLS** (medium or heavy, or optional medicine ball; use as heavy as possible for Shoulder Presses and medium to heavy for Sumo Squats with Upright Row)

› **BENCH OR CHAIR** (optional, if you want to sit during Shoulder Press)

› **JUMP ROPE**

› **MAT** (optional)

EQUIPMENT LIST FOR SET #2

› **DUMBBELLS** (light or medium for Lateral Raises and as heavy as possible for Thrusters)

› **MEDICINE BALL** (optional)

› **MAT** (optional)

CHOOSING YOUR JUMP ROPE

There are many types of jump ropes available. Personally, I like a nylon rope. The length is also important for maximum fitness benefit. If it's too short, you are more likely to trip on it. If it's too long, you will have to bring your arms too far away from your body, swinging your arms and using your shoulders too much. All the twirling motion should come from your wrists. To get the right length, stand on the rope with one foot and bring the handles up to your armpits. The ends of the rope should reach in the range from 1 inch above to 1 inch below your armpits when the rope is tight.

eve says

Today it's all about your shoulders. Every single exercise—Diamond, Heart, Club, and Spade—will have shoulder engagement. When you jump rope, focus on using your shoulders to stabilize the rope. In the second set, when you do the Frog Jumps, use a medicine ball if you want even more shoulder strengthening.

SET #1 (FIRST 30 MINUTES)

SHOULDER PRESSES

1. Either stand or sit on a bench or chair, holding a dumbbell in each hand at your shoulder, palms facing forward. Keep your back straight and your core tight.

2. Raise both dumbbells straight overhead, arms straight and fully extended and biceps close to your ears. (There should be a perfect line from your wrists to your shoulders; think about stacking "bone on bone.") Lower the dumbbells back to your shoulders.

3. Do the number of reps on your card.

SUMO SQUATS WITH UPRIGHT ROW

1. Holding a dumbbell in each hand in front of your body, stand with your legs wider than shoulder-width apart, toes pointed out.

2. With your chest up tall, sit back and squat down low, bringing the dumbbells toward the floor between your legs. Make sure to keep your shoulders back and spine straight.

3. As you stand, raise the dumbbells up toward your chin, elbows out and raised in a V. This should be one fluid motion, with no pause between the squat and the upright row.

4. Squat back down, as you bring the dumbbells toward the floor to the starting position.

5. Do the number of reps on your card.

SET #2 (SECOND 30 MINUTES)

LATERAL RAISES

1. Stand holding a dumbbell in each hand at your sides.

2. Raise both arms out to the sides to shoulder height, with your arms straight, palms facing down. If you feel any tension in your neck, or you see yourself "shrugging" (relying on your trapezius muscles), lower the weight. Avoid using momentum to bring the weight up. Keep good form and control.

3. Lower your arms back down to your sides.

4. Do the number of reps on your card.

THRUSTERS

1. Hold a dumbbell in each hand at your shoulders, with your elbows down, palms facing each other. Stand with your feet about shoulder-width apart.

2. With your chest up and back straight, squat down and try to get your elbows close to your knees. Keep your core engaged to stabilize the weight and avoid falling forward.

3. Drive through your heels and explode up to standing. As you come up, raise the dumbbells above your head, keeping your palms facing each other and straightening your arms at the top. The power should all come from the leg drive, and your arms should just go along for the ride.

4. Squat back down, bringing the dumbbells back to your shoulders.

5. Do the number of reps on your card.

(CORE)

SET #1 (FIRST 30 MINUTES)

SIT-UP AND REACH

1. Lie down on the floor with your knees bent, feet and knees apart. Hold one dumbbell or medicine ball in front of your chest with your arms straight. Tighten your core.

2. Perform a full sit-up and reach your arms up toward the ceiling, keeping them straight. At the top of the sit-up, make sure to have a straight spine and "peek through the window" (as your arms frame your face, biceps by your ears).

3. Slowly and with control, lower yourself back down, keeping your arms raised.

4. Do the number of reps on your card.

SET #2 (SECOND 30 MINUTES)

PLANK SHOULDER TAPS

1. Get into plank position, with your hands firmly on the floor and your core tight.

2. Lift up your right hand and quickly touch the inside of your left shoulder, then return to the starting position. Try not to move anything but your arm.

3. Lift up your left hand and quickly touch the inside of your right shoulder, then return to the starting position.

4. Right and left is 1 rep.

5. Do the number of reps on your card.

Try to keep your hips square to the floor at all times.

SET #1 (FIRST 30 MINUTES)

JUMP ROPE X10

(10 jumps per rep, so a 2 of spades would be 20 jumps, and an ace of spaces would be 140 jumps)

1. Hold the jump rope so your hands are just above your hips with your elbows slightly bent and tucked in close to your body.

2. Twirl the rope using your wrists only, and jump over it with both feet. Keep your jump as low as possible and land on the balls of your feet.

3. Find your rhythm and jump over the rope as fast as you can without a double bounce.

4. Do the number of reps on your card.

SET #2 (SECOND 30 MINUTES)

FROG JUMPS WITH OVERHEAD REACH

1. Stand with your feet wide apart, toes turned out, heels on the ground, arms in front of you, hanging down (or hold a medicine ball in front of you).

2. Squat down and lightly touch the floor between your feet with your fingertips (or the medicine ball).

3. Jump up from the squatting position and reach your arms (or the medicine ball) straight up overhead.

4. Land softly back down into the squat and immediately jump again.

5. Do the number of reps on your card.

DAY #5 EXERCISES

EQUIPMENT LIST FOR SET #1

› **RESISTANCE BAND** (medium or heavy). Even though it is lower focus day, you can use a heavy resistance band for Low Rows. You may find that the medium resistance band feels too light for this particular exercise. Your back is a large muscle group, so we tend to be stronger here.

› **DUMBBELLS** (one heavy or medium dumbbell for Goblet Squats—it is lower focus day, so go as heavy as you can for this exercise)

› **BOX OR STEP**

EQUIPMENT LIST FOR SET #2

› **MAT** (optional)

› **BENCH**

› **DUMBBELLS** (medium or heavy). Bulgarian Split Squats are a very advanced move. Even if you are a seasoned exerciser, it is perfectly fine to start with medium weights until you master form.

---

eve says

WEIGHTY ADVICE

Aim for choosing weights that feel heavy (but not impossible) for any exercise, especially for those foundational exercises that use the larger muscle groups and gross motor movements (exercises like Lateral Raises and Chest Flys will require lighter weights than exercises like squats and deadlifts). As the workout continues, if your form starts to break down or you get too tired, you can always drop to a lighter weight. Or go heavy for the lower-numbered cards (2, 3, 4, etc.), and drop to medium for the higher numbers (9, 10, queen, etc.). The goal is to increase your strength so you will be able to do all the reps with the heaviest weight that you can. When your heavy weights get too light (and they will, if you keep at it), then it's time to go out and buy heavier dumbbells!

eve says

Back to your lower body with a focus on your core today. You'll also be upping your cardio game with more advanced Spade exercises. (If these are too advanced, check Appendix 2 for "Modify Down" options.) The Diamond exercises work the mid-back, lower back, and core. The Heart exercises focus on your quads, glutes and core. Your legs are involved in both Club exercises, and in Set #2, your ab exercise specifically targets the obliques (the muscles along the sides of your torso). For your Spade exercises, you'll do burpees. They pretty much work everything.

◆ (UPPER BODY)

SET #1 (FIRST 30 MINUTES)

LOW ROWS

1. Secure a resistance band in a door anchor, or around a pole or another sturdy object slightly higher than hip level. Facing the anchor, hold the handles and walk backward to take out the slack in the band. Get into an athletic stance—knees slightly bent, back straight, core tight— and bring your shoulder blades down and back, as if aiming for your "back pockets."

2. With your palms facing each other, draw the handles straight back toward your body, aiming for the bottom of your rib cage, keeping your elbows in. Squeeze your shoulder blades down and back at the end of the motion.

3. Release the band with control as you straighten your arms again.

4. Do the number of reps on your card.

SET #2 (SECOND 30 MINUTES)

SUPERMANS

1. Lie flat on the floor on your stomach, with your legs extended behind you and your arms extended straight out in front of you.

2. Using your lower back, lift your legs and arms off the ground. Keep your neck in line and the crown of your head reaching long in front of you. Squeeze your glutes at the top.

3. Hold for a beat. Feel the contraction before you lower your legs and arms back down to the floor.

4. Do the number of reps on your card.

(LOWER BODY)

GOBLET SQUATS

1. Holding a single dumbbell in front of your chest with both hands, stand with your feet wider than shoulder-width apart.

2. Squat as low as you can, keeping the dumbbell in front of your chest.

3. Stand up straight again.

4. Do the number of reps on your card.

BULGARIAN SPLIT SQUATS

1. Holding a dumbbell in each hand, at your sides, stand with your back toward a bench. Take a step forward with your left foot and bring your right leg behind you to rest the top of your foot on the bench. You may have to adjust your front foot forward or back to find proper alignment.

2. Keeping your chest up and spine straight, slowly squat with your standing leg and drop the knee of your back leg straight down toward the floor, hovering a few inches above it. Your front knee should be directly over your ankle. Drive through the heel of your standing leg to return to the starting position.

3. Do the number of reps on your card with one leg, then repeat with the other leg.

(CORE)

CRAB TOE TOUCHES

1. Sit on the floor with your knees bent, your feet on the floor, your hands behind your hips, aligned with your shoulders. Your palms should be flat on the floor, fingertips facing your backside.

2. Lift up your hips so your body is elevated off the floor.

3. Extend your right leg straight up and lift your left arm up to reach your right foot at the same time. Lower your foot and hand back to the floor.

4. Repeat on the other side. (Right and left is 1 rep.)

5. Do the number of reps on your card.

RUSSIAN TWISTS

1. Sit with your knees bent and your feet on the floor. Hold a single dumbbell in both hands right below your chest. Keeping your chest up and shoulders down, lean back slightly to engage your core.

2. If desired, raise your knees to lift your feet up off the floor, keeping them together. Tighten your abs as you balance on your sit bones.

3. Keeping the dumbbell close to your body, twist right to left in an arching motion so the end of your dumbbell reaches your hip. Make sure to keep your head straight, chest open, and spine long.

4. Right and left is 1 rep.

5. Do the number of reps on your card.

SET #1 (FIRST 30 MINUTES)

BOX JUMPS

1. Stand in front of a sturdy box or bench.

2. Bend your knees, hinge your hips, and swing your arms back. Drive with your hips, swing your arms forward, and explode off the balls of your feet to jump up onto the box with both feet.

3. Land with soft knees, making sure not to collapse them in. Straighten your knees fully to stand at the top. Pause for a moment before you jump back down to the ground. Land softly and repeat.

4. Do the number of reps on your card.

SET #2 (SECOND 30 MINUTES)

BURPEES

1. Stand with your feet about shoulder-width apart.

2. Bend your knees, hinge at your waist, and bring your hips down and back until your hands reach the floor.

3. Plant your palms on the floor and immediately jump your feet back behind you into plank position. Do one push-up.

4. Jump your legs forward again so your feet land about shoulder-width apart, heels on the ground. Transfer your weight back into a low squat position. Stand up and jump at the top, raising your arms overhead.

5. Do the number of reps on your card.

DAY #6 EXERCISES

EQUIPMENT LIST FOR SET #1

› **DUMBBELLS** (medium or heavy for Alternating Floor Press, depending on fitness level; medium or heavy for Walking Lunges). People still working on chest strength may have to go lighter with floor presses.

› **STABILITY BALL**

EQUIPMENT LIST FOR SET #2

› **DUMBBELLS** (medium or heavy for Renegade Rows; light or medium for Triple Crushes). Because Renegade Rows are an advanced exercise, you may want to start out with a medium weight. Note: Always keep the same weight throughout the entire exercise. Even if you can squat, curl, and press heavier, the triceps extension will be the deciding factor for weights you choose.

eve says

Day #6 will be your toughest workout of the week—or month, or however long it takes you to get through all the exercises in this six-day plan. No hurry if you're building your fitness. Do your thing, work your program, and meet yourself where you are. The Fit52 concept of living healthy and fit every week means that some days, you'll push yourself a little harder than other days. This is definitely a push-yourself workout, so buyer beware! For your Diamond exercises, you'll do more upper body push-pull work as you focus on the muscles in your chest and back. Your Heart exercises will engage everything lower body: quads, glutes, hamstrings, and calves. For your Club exercises, you'll work all your ab muscles, and for Spades, you'll do some serious jumping exercises, focusing on length in Set #1 and height in Set #2. Good luck, and give it your all! (Your next workout goes back to the first pair of cards you draw, so you can look forward to that—it will seem easier each time you go through the entire six days.)

(UPPER BODY) ◆

ALTERNATING FLOOR PRESSES, NEUTRAL GRIP

1. Lie on your back on the floor with your knees bent and your feet flat. It is important to drive your shoulder blades down as your upper back and head rest on the floor. Hold a dumbbell in each hand and bend your elbows to 90 degrees. Rest your upper arms on the floor beside you, palms facing each other.

2. Keeping your elbows tucked close to your body and bent roughly 45 degrees, raise the right dumbbells up, keeping your arm straight and rotating your palm to face your feet. Lower the arm back down to the starting position.

3. Repeat with your left arm. Pressing up with right then left equals one rep.

4. Do the number of reps on your card.

RENEGADE ROWS

1. Get into plank position, holding a dumbbell in each hand. As you hold the dumbbells on the floor, maintain proper alignment from your shoulders to your wrists, keeping your wrists as straight as possible. (Your knuckles should be facing the floor as much as possible.)

2. Engage your core and transfer your weight into your left arm. Bend your right elbow and raise the dumbbell up toward your rib cage, keeping it close in to your body. Keep your hips and shoulders square to the floor. If you find yourself rocking and rolling to each side, widen your stance with your feet to help stabilize and keep your body in a perfect plank position.

3. Lower your right arm back to the floor and place it directly under your shoulder.

4. Repeat on the left side (right and left is 1 rep).

5. Do the number of reps on your card.

Don't rock those hips! Squeeze shoulder blades at the top!

SET #1 (FIRST 30 MINUTES)

WALKING LUNGES

1. Holding a dumbbell in each hand, arms down at your sides, stand with your feet shoulder-width apart, keeping your chest up and back straight.

2. Lunge your right leg forward, lowering your back knee as close to the floor as you can. Both knees should be bent at 90 degrees.

3. Drive off your right leg and step your left foot forward to meet your right. Stand up fully.

4. Repeat on the other side (left and right is 1 rep).

5. Do the number of reps on your card.

SET #2 (SECOND 30 MINUTES)

TRIPLE CRUSHES

1. Holding a dumbbell in each hand at your shoulders, palms facing each other, stand with your feet wider than shoulder-width apart, toes pointed slightly out in a wide squat stance.

2. With your chest up and back straight, perform a squat, and at the same time, lower the dumbbells in between your legs, with your elbows resting lightly inside your knees.

3. At the bottom of the squat, perform a bicep curl by bringing the dumbbells up to your shoulders. Do not lower the dumbbells back down. Keeping your core tight and your weight in your heels, stand straight up.

4. Press both weights straight up over your shoulders, palms facing in, keeping your upper arms close to your ears.

5. Bend both elbows, lowering the dumbbells behind your head. Straighten your elbows to complete the triceps extension.

6. Lower the weights back down to your shoulders to the starting position.

7. Do the number of reps on your card.

SET #1 (FIRST 30 MINUTES)

BALL PASSES WITH STABILITY BALL

1. Lie on your back and place a stability ball between your feet, with your legs straight up in the air, squeezing your inner thighs together. Your head and shoulders should be resting on the floor and your arms reaching long overhead.

2. Crunch up and reach forward to grab the ball with both hands.

3. Lower the ball behind your head toward the floor as you lower your straight legs to a 45-degree angle to the floor. Make sure to keep your lower back connected to the floor.

4. Lift the ball back up and forward as you raise your legs back up toward your hips. Transfer the ball from your hands to between your feet.

5. Lower the ball to a 45-degree angle (it is fine if it touches the floor) as you bring your upper half back down to the floor.

6. Do the number of reps on your card.

SET #2 (SECOND 30 MINUTES)

SIDE PLANK HIP DROPS

1. Lie on your side, propping yourself up on your elbow directly under your shoulder, your forearm on the floor. Your legs should be stacked on top of each other.

2. Lift your hips into the air so your body forms one straight line from your head to your feet—this is side plank position.

3. Lower your hips to the floor, then raise them back up again.

4. Do the number of reps on your card on one side, then repeat on the other side.

Just tap the floor with your hips—don't rest there.

SET #1 (FIRST 30 MINUTES)

BROAD JUMP BACKPEDALS

1. Stand with your legs about shoulder-width apart and bend your knees slightly.

2. Lean forward, swing your arms back, and use that power to jump forward as far as you can, landing softly with both feet at the same time.

3. Staying low, take small steps backward to your starting position, then jump again.

4. Do the number of reps on your card.

SET #2 (SECOND 30 MINUTES)

SQUAT TO TUCK JUMPS

1. Stand with your feet about shoulder-width apart.

2. Squat down, then jump up as high as you can from the squat, tucking your knees into your chest.

3. Land with soft knees, absorbing the impact, and repeat immediately.

4. Do the number of reps on your card.

EVE'S FIT52 STATIC STRETCH COOL-DOWN

Cooling down after an intense workout should not be an afterthought. I understand the temptation: You're done with your workout and you just want to get going. I'm guilty of it, too, having run right out of the gym on occasions, seconds after my last set. But skipping your cool-down can mean missing the opportunity to optimize your health and fitness level, as well as your future performance. Here are some other great reasons to take the time for a cool-down:

› Cooling down allows your heart rate and breathing rate to return to normal.

› It increases your flexibility and range of motion (ROM).

› It can help to prevent future injury.

› It helps with overall recovery from the workout you just did.

› It helps with mental focus, relaxation, and calming the central nervous system (the parasympathetic state, or the "rest and digest" state).

In other words, it's a useful and pleasant transition back to your "real life."

Do these static stretching exercises right after your workout when your muscles are still warm. These are not for warming up. (Imagine stretching a cold rubber band—it's more likely to snap. Ouch!) Hold each position for at least 20 to 30 seconds, then flow immediately into the next position, as directed.

First, walk for 2 minutes (if your heart rate is still elevated). You could walk on a treadmill, outside, or just around your house or the gym. Then do these stretches.

1. **RUNNER'S STRETCH (SEATED HAMSTRING STRETCH):** Sit on your mat with your right leg straight and your left leg bent, with your left foot against your right inner thigh. Sit up tall and turn your torso toward your straight leg, then bend at the waist and reach for your right foot. Hold. Keep your spine straight and go down only as far as you can without rounding your back. The goal is to get the center of your chest touching the top of your thigh. Move to the next stretch (don't do the other side yet).

2. **SEATED SPINAL TWIST:** From the position you are already in, cross your left leg over your right leg. Twist so your right elbow is resting on the outside of your left knee. Sit up tall with a long spine. Stretch and hold, then move immediately to the next exercise.

3. **PIGEON STRETCH:** Shift your left leg behind you and bend your right leg in front of you at a 90-degree angle so your shin is horizontal in front of your body. Keep your hips square. Sink into the position, feeling the stretch in

your hips. Walk your hands in front of you and rest your torso on your front leg, stretching as deeply as you can. You could rest your forehead on the floor. Come out carefully by swinging your back leg to the front.

4. **REPEAT STRETCHES 1 THROUGH 3 ON THE OTHER SIDE.**

5. **LIE DOWN ON YOUR BACK, EXTENDING YOUR LEGS. TAKE A FEW BREATHS FOR A NICE FULL-BODY STRETCH.**

6. **KNEE HUG:** From your supine position, keep your left extended leg long and hug your right knee into your chest. Hold. Flow directly into the next stretch.

7. **LYING HAMSTRING STRETCH:** Still lying on your back, keep your left leg long and extend your right leg straight up into the air. Gently pull on the back of your thigh or calf, drawing your leg closer to your body. Hold, then flow right into the next stretch.

8. **SUPINE SCORPION:** Still lying on your back, extend your arms into a T, keeping your shoulder blades on the floor. Raise your right leg straight up again, then, without bending your knee, let it fall across your body to the left side. Breathe into the spinal twist, then return to the starting position and extend both legs long. Stretch your arms overhead for another full-body stretch.

9. **HUG YOUR LEFT KNEE IN, AND REPEAT EXERCISES 6 THROUGH 8 ON THE OTHER SIDE.**

10. **ROLL ONTO YOUR STOMACH.**

11. **CHILD'S POSE:** Get up on your hands and knees, bring your big toes together to touch, and sink back, resting your hips close to your heels and your body between your knees. Bend forward to rest your forehead on the mat, arms extended long in front of you, palms grounded on the floor. Walk both hands to the right, hold,

and breathe as you stretch the left side of your body. Walk both hands to the left, hold, and breathe as you stretch the right side of your body. Walk your hands back to center.

12. **THREAD THE NEEDLE:** From Child's Pose, "thread" your right arm under your chest and under your left arm. Reach your right arm as far to the left as you can to stretch your shoulder. Hold, then pull your right arm back underneath you and return to starting position. Repeat on the other side.

13. **PRONE SCORPION:** Lie back down on your stomach with your legs behind you, your arms out to your sides, and your head resting on the mat, looking to the right. Bend your right knee so your foot is raised, then lift up your knee and, keeping your leg bent, try to touch your toes to the floor on the outside of your left leg.  Bring your leg back and repeat on the other side.

14. **UP DOG:** You did Up Dog and Down Dog in your warm-up. Get into the Up Dog position by lying on your stomach, putting your hands under your shoulders, and lifting your upper body. Your hips and thighs should lift slightly off the floor. Open your chest. Keep your shoulders away from your ears by pressing firmly into the mat. Stretch and hold.

15. **DOWN DOG:** From Up Dog, curl your toes under and lift your hips up to make an inverted V with your body. Keep your head down between your arms and sink your chest closer to your thighs and your heels closer to the ground. Hold and breathe. You can also

pedal your feet, right and left, for an extra hamstring/calf stretch while you are holding this position.

16. **ROLL UP SLOWLY AND SHOULDER STRETCH:** From the Down Dog position, walk your hands back to your feet, then slowly roll up to standing. Once standing, cross one arm straight across your body. With your opposite hand, apply gentle pressure on your upper arm, pressing toward yourself, to stretch out your shoulder. Repeat on the other side. Roll your shoulders back a few times, take one more deep breath in, and notice how your body and mind feel after working so hard and getting it done!

TRY THE FIT52 APP

If you'd like an additional resource to make the Fit52 Workout even more easy and fun, check out the fit52 app! The app can be downloaded from the App Store.

THE JOURNAL OF YOU

your workout progress

As you learn the Fit52 Workout, keep track of your progress in your journal. Are there certain exercises you love? Exercises that challenge you? Are you noticing that the exercises are getting easier as you build strength? Were you sore at first? This kind of self-feedback can be really useful later when you look back and see how far you've come. It's also a really good way to keep your brain engaged in what you're doing. The more you notice and focus on your workout, the better your form will be and the faster you will progress.

Your Fit Pregnancy

I wrote much of this book while pregnant with baby Jacob. Pregnancy is a game-changer in the world of working out. With Isaiah, I was able to work out throughout my entire pregnancy, but with Jacob, I had various physical reasons that made working out more difficult. But I always did my best to keep at it! I recommend staying active while you're pregnant, if you're feeling up to it. However, exercising when pregnant isn't the same as exercising when you're not. First of all, it is extremely important to talk to your doctor about any physical activity you want to do. Get the medical okay before you do anything strenuous!

Also, respect your current fitness level. If you haven't been exercising, during your pregnancy is not the time to start training for a marathon (or even a 5K). Keep going with your current level of fitness to the extent you can. The only exception is if you haven't been exercising *at all*. In that case, check with your doctor to see if you can start doing more walking. Walking is almost always a good idea.

Some research shows that when moms exercise during pregnancy, they have an easier labor and healthier babies, and their kids end up being fitter later.

That's awesome! So do what you can, but also keep these things in mind:

› Always, always get your doctor's approval for any exercise!
› Stay well hydrated. Drink lots of water.
› If you get tired, stop. This is no time to push yourself.
› If you were doing it before, you may be able to keep doing it (whatever "it" is), especially in your first trimester. But if anything ever feels uncomfortable, take it off your exercise list until after the baby arrives.
› Do not do exercises that require you to lie on your back or on your stomach.
› Do not do exercises that work or strain your abdominal area in any way.
› As your belly gets larger, protect your lower back. You have a different center of gravity now, and your back may not be prepared for that change in weight on the front side.
› Your balance is different now, too, so be careful. Be aware that you could fall.
› Always, always, always listen to your body. Do what it tells you. If you have energy, do what is medically approved. If you're tired, rest.

› Breathe! It's not good to hold your breath when you work out. Keep your breath steady and notice if you start holding your breath. Keep breathing!

Keeping all these things in mind, I'll say again that exercising during pregnancy is good for you! Just be smart about it and err on the side of caution. During pregnancy, I tried to exercise on most days, but I also stopped whenever I was tired, and I was extra careful. And did I mention that, first and foremost, you should check with your doctor to make sure you can stay on the exercise train? Please do!

That's baby Jacob in there!

YOUR BODY IS AN ADAPTATION MACHINE

When it comes to exercise, one of the key pieces of advice I give my clients is: "Stay consistently inconsistent." Your body adapts to whatever you're doing, whether it's cardio or weight lifting, in 4 to 6 weeks. If you continue to do the same exercises with the same amount of weight and at the same intensity, eventually your progress will stall and you'll hit a plateau. Exercise—any exercise—is always beneficial, in terms of cardiovascular health, mobility, better mood, and bone density, but if you want to lose fat, gain muscle, get stronger, and burn calories, you're going to want to do something different.

Here's why. Our bodies are wired to move in the most efficient way possible to conserve energy and calories. If you're an athlete running a marathon, conserving energy is a great thing, but if your goal is to burn calories, not so much. As soon as your body gets the message that whatever exercise you're doing is the new normal, it adjusts. The trick is to stay one step ahead of a plateau by switching it up every month or two. This will also keep things fresh so you don't get bored.

If you've been doing the Fit52 Workout exclusively for 4 to 6 weeks, try swapping out different exercises or different types of cardio for the exercises and cardio in this chapter. You could include exercises that use different equipment you have at home, like a pull-up bar or a treadmill. Or you can even take this workout to the gym and use different machines there. Get creative!

When it comes to weight lifting, changing the amount of weight and the number of reps is important to ensure you continue to progress and get stronger. This is another way to adapt the Fit52 Workout—you can always increase or decrease the weights, depending on your goals, and you can choose the number of reps instead of letting the cards do it. For example, every time you draw a diamond, you could lift the heaviest weight possible but only do 6 reps. Or every time you draw a heart, choose a lighter weight and do 15 reps. For an extra challenge, you could even do something like doubling the rep number you get on each card. The possibilities are endless.

How else could you change up your program? You could mix up your week to include a few days at the gym (maybe do Carrie's leg workout in the next chapter), or do Fit52 a few times a week, and other workouts, classes, or activities on the other days. The important thing about being consistently inconsistent is the *consistent* part. Find a routine that fits into your lifestyle and that you enjoy, so you want to keep at it.

6

LEGS

How I Got 'Em and What You Can Do for Yours

very chapter in this book is named after one of my songs, except this one. I'm borrowing a song title from ZZ Top because the one fitness-related question I get asked more than any other is, "How did you get your legs?"

I've had people tell me they keep a picture of my legs on their refrigerator as inspiration. It's kind of embarrassing to hear that people like my legs so much, but I love the feeling of strength in my base. If that also comes with the added bonus of being aesthetically pleasing, then . . . sweet!

So, since people want to know, I thought it might be nice to devote an entire chapter to one (or two) of my favorite body parts to work out. The Fit52 Workout has a strong lower body component that covers the legs, but that's not the only thing I do. I also have leg workouts that are pretty advanced. On some days, I devote my entire workout to legs. I will say that this workout is definitely not for beginners. If you're already very fit and you want to try it, then go for it. If you're just getting started with fitness, then it's probably best to stick with the Fit52 Workout, walking or jogging, and other more basic fitness activities until you feel like you have built some good cardiovascular and leg strength. Either way, check it out as a workout option or a goal.

Catcher's Legs

It all started on the softball field. I played softball for nine years, starting in grade school, and my position was catcher. That meant I was constantly squatting and standing back up again—up and down, up and down. I think that was probably what started developing the muscles in my legs. Obviously, at that young age, I wasn't thinking much more about my legs than what I needed them to do for me.

But my legs have always been on the strong side, and the more I learned about fitness, the more I was able to take advantage of that. When I started to work out in a more regimented way, I felt like there was some kind of muscle memory going on from my catcher days. My legs recognized those squats! And I kept up with that focus because I wanted to maintain my leg strength. I like having strong legs. I appreciate them every day. I'm proud of the work I've put into my legs, and I'm proud of what they can do for me.

You don't have to have been a catcher to get strong, great-looking legs. Start now! It's never too late to build muscle tone. You may not have the same muscle memory as I do, but you can start new muscle memories by working those legs, and as they get stronger, you'll discover that everything gets easier—climbing stairs, running across the street, carrying heavy things (like children)—and as you get older, you'll be less likely to lose your mobility. I plan to be up and walking around well into my nineties! My strong legs are useful to me right now, but my leg workouts are also an insurance policy for the future.

Everyone has different areas where they are naturally strong, and others they need to work a little more. I have really strong quads (thigh muscles) and calves, but I have to constantly work my hamstrings (the backs of my thighs) and my rear, which tend to be less strong by comparison. Leg strength has to be balanced for the best function.

My trainer Eve put this leg workout together, and I often use many of its moves. You'll notice that unlike the Fit52 Workout, this workout uses some weight machines. I have these in my home gym (and in my mobile gym), but you should be able to find all this equipment at any well-stocked gym. All the advice in the previous chapter still applies here—keep in mind the importance of your warm-up, your cool-down, and being consistently inconsistent by switching periodically between strength, muscle building, and endurance phases.

Are you ready to get your own legs in shape? Let's go work out!

THE THREE PHASES OF STRENGTH TRAINING

There are three different phases that combine different levels of weight and different reps to accomplish specific goals. The three phases I typically identify for my clients are:

1. **STRENGTH PHASE:** In this phase, you use heavy weights with low reps. Do not go so heavy that you cannot maintain form and control over the weight, but do go heavy enough that you can only do 1 to 6 perfectly executed reps. This phase also has the longest rest period. You should rest for at least 90 seconds between sets.

2. **MUSCLE-BUILDING PHASE:** This phase develops and shapes muscles. Another word for this is hypertrophy. The idea here is to do more moderate weight that allows you to do 8 to 12 reps, but heavy enough that the last two reps are very difficult (but still controlled). The rest period between sets for this phase is about 1 minute.

3. **ENDURANCE PHASE:** This phase is about building endurance with lighter weights and higher reps. Typically you would do 12 to 15 reps or more with a weight that is challenging but not so heavy that you cannot do all the reps with good form. The rest period between these sets is shortest—just 30 seconds.

When I program workouts for my clients (and myself), I cycle through these phases to keep challenging the body. This can also help break through a strength or weight loss plateau.

As you get more and more familiar with the Fit52 Workout, you will see how you can adjust your weight and reps to cycle through these phases. This also applies to any weight lifting exercises you incorporate into your regular fitness routine, such as the leg workout in this chapter. If you have been working out for several weeks or even months with light to medium weights in a higher rep range for muscle building, it may be time to increase the weight and do lower reps to move into a strength phase, or vice versa. Just keep it consistently inconsistent, and you will progress.

PLAYLIST FOR WEIGHT LIFTING

When I lift weights, I like to listen to super intense music. The louder the guitars, the more I seem to be able to bench/squat/press/curl etc. Add a scream-y lead singer and I'm set! Everyone has their own preferences, though. I once knew someone who would listen to jazz standards when he was in the gym. I tried really hard not to judge, but I figured that's why my biceps were bigger than his! Just joking (sort of). Mike likes to listen to music that is more on the inspirational side when he's in the gym. My point is, everyone knows what motivates them. Here is an example of what I might be listening to when I'm pumping iron!

> "The Violence"—Rise Against
> "Go to War"—Nothing More
> "BURN IT"—fever 333
> "Waking Lions"—Pop Evil
> "Betray and Degrade"—Seether
> "Into the Fire"—Asking Alexandria
> "Kickstart My Heart"—Mötley Crüe (This song makes it onto all of my workout playlists, if you haven't noticed)
> "Enemies"—Shinedown
> "You're Going Down"—Sick Puppies
> "Big Bad Wolf"—In This Moment
> "Na Na Na (Na Na Na Na Na Na Na Na Na)"—My Chemical Romance
> "My Own Summer (Shove It)"—Deftones
> "Coming Home"—Falling in Reverse
> "Bang Your Head (Metal Health)"—Quiet Riot
> "Welcome to the Jungle"—Guns N' Roses
> "Not Falling"—Mudvayne
> "Born for Greatness"—Papa Roach
> "Bad Company"—Five Finger Death Punch

"Sabotage"—Beastie Boys
"When Legends Rise"—Godsmack
"Ace of Spades"—Motörhead
"Bully"—Shinedown
"Fuel"—Metallica
"Duality"—Slipknot
"Bulls on Parade"—Rage Against the Machine
"Do You Really Want It?"—Nothing More
"Coming Undone"—Korn
"Master of Puppets"—Metallica
"Sing"—My Chemical Romance
"Paradise City"—Guns N' Roses

eve says

WHAT IS A "PUMP"?

"Pump" is a fitness term that refers to that feeling of tightness under your skin as your muscles swell. When you lift a lot of reps, especially in a fixed position (think of biceps curls), blood shuttles into your muscles faster than it can be released, causing temporary swelling and increased size. At the same time, during strenuous exercise, metabolic by-products like lactic acid accumulate in your muscle cells. Your body will try to equalize this concentration by increasing the flow of water into your muscle cells, and this can also cause swelling on a cellular level.

eve says

LEG WORKOUT GUIDELINES

Before you jump into the leg workout, I want to prepare you for what's coming and give you some guidance. First of all, in general, it's important to do the heaviest and/or the most technical or difficult exercises at the beginning of a workout when you're still fresh. This will help you to maintain good form, so you get the most out of the exercise, and it may help avoid injury. If your form starts to break down and you can no longer control the weight, that is the cue that the set is over—drop the weight on the next set so you can perform the allotted number of reps. Keep with the "two reps shy of failure" mentality.

Also, always choose the appropriate amount of weight for the prescribed number of reps. This may take a bit of experimentation, but that experimentation will heighten your body awareness. Be honest and listen to your body. Give 100 percent of what your body has to offer each day. That is all you can ask of yourself. Each day may look different. But I stress the "be honest" part. This takes work and self-awareness. I have had clients who think they're listening to their bodies, but they're really just making excuses. Then

there are the hard chargers who get the workout in because they physically can, but it is doing more damage than making progress because they put themselves at risk of overtraining, or they don't address an underlying injury. Don't forget that rest and recovery are just as important as the workouts themselves.

This chapter consist of six supersets, or groups of exercises: A, B, and C. The A exercises are the easiest, getting you ready for the B exercises, which are harder. The C exercises have a cardio component, so adding those too makes these supersets the most challenging. Ahead of the first two supersets, you will also get two additional priming exercises that help to prime your central nervous system for better form and more lifting power (we call these CNS Primers).

For many people just beginning a fitness routine, sticking with the CNS Primers and the A exercises in this workout may be enough. As your fitness level increases, you may choose to add the additional exercises in each group. Doing the entire workout as written is for those with higher fitness levels, like

Carrie. Please remember that Carrie is an advanced lifter. If this level of fitness is your goal and you can't get there today, keep it up! Remember, exercise is just practice, like playing a sport, an instrument, or singing. The more you do it, the better you get!

This particular workout is an example of a muscle building/shaping (or hypertrophy) phase, with moderate weight in the 8-to-12-reps range. (For a refresher on the phases, go back to page 145.) If you do this workout for four to six weeks, remember you should switch it up by changing phases—increasing the weight and decreasing the reps, or decreasing the weight and increasing the reps. Aim for 10 reps on the major lifts, but if that is too much for you, take it down in weight or reps. If you are lifting a challenging weight and only get 8 reps in (with 2 reps shy of failure), that is just fine. If you get 12 reps, awesome! However, I would challenge my clients to increase the weight and see if they can get 8 to 10.

Here is phase-specific guidance for you:

› **FOR BEGINNERS AND THOSE DOING THE STRENGTH PHASE (HIGHER WEIGHT, LOWER REPS):** Focus on the priming exercises (1. and 2.) and the A-level exercises in each superset. Rest for 90 seconds or longer if you need to between sets.

› **FOR THOSE DOING THE MUSCLE-BUILDING/SHAPE (HYPERTROPHY) PHASE (MODERATE WEIGHT, 8 TO 12 REPS):** Perform the priming exercises, along with the **A- and B-level** exercises, with the option to include or omit the **C-level** exercise, depending on your goals and fitness level. Rest for 60 seconds between supersets.

› **FOR THOSE DOING THE ENDURANCE PHASE (LOWER WEIGHT, HIGHER REPS):** Perform the workout as prescribed, adding the **C-level** exercises if your fitness level allows. This is particularly beneficial in the endurance phase. Keep your reps high and the rest period as short as you can (aim for no more than 30 seconds), and work on getting a good "pump."

Carrie's Leg Workout

I'm not gonna lie—this workout is hard. I've been doing the Fit52 Workout for a long time, and I've worked my way up to this. Maybe you're just curious to know what my leg workout looks like, but you don't necessarily want to do it yet. That's great. However, if you do decide to try it, be sure to modify what I do according to your own strength and fitness levels. Work through these exercises in order, following the above instructions, and adjust the weight and reps for your own purposes. If you aren't sure how, I would advise booking even just one session with a trainer, to help you figure out how you can do this workout in a way that will benefit you. If you're an experienced fitness person, you may be able to do this workout with few, if any, modifications. Be sure that you know your limits, but at the same time, don't shy away from your potential.

Note that every exercise includes the weight that I would typically use, but again, don't take this as gospel. Definitely choose the weight and reps that are right for you, your goals, and your fitness level right now.

WARM-UP

Before you begin, do the warm-up for the Fit52 Workout beginning on page 94.

CNS PRIMER #1: *1 set*

Primer exercises get your muscles ready to move with proper form and also wake up your central nervous system (CNS) so it can fire more rapidly for more difficult activities. This one is a "dress rehearsal" for the Dumbbell Front Squat:

DUMBBELL BOX SQUATS: *10 reps with a 20-pound dumbbell*

1. Stand in front of a box, bench, or chair tall enough to keep your legs bent at 90 degrees when you sit on it. Hold a single dumbbell in both hands, horizontally against your chest at about shoulder height.

2. Slowly squat until you are sitting on the box or bench. Don't just tap or fully relax and sit back when you make contact. Maintain good posture, keep your core tight, and drive through your heels to return to standing. Repeat.

Rest for 60 seconds. (For this light primer, you may not need to rest for the full minute.)

SUPERSET #1: *Do 3 to 4 sets.*

EXPLOSIVE TUCK JUMPS: *5 reps*

This exercise will recruit more muscle fibers and help them to fire more quickly. This will lead to more power and help you lift heavier weights for squats and their variations.

1. With your arms out in front of you, jump up, lifting both your knees as high as you can. Think of an exploding action when you jump.

2. Land with soft knees and immediately jump again. These 5 reps should be continuous.

DUMBBELL FRONT SQUATS: *10 reps*

1. Stand with your feet about shoulder-width apart.

2. Hold a 25- to 30-pound dumbbell in each hand. Raise them up so the dumbbells just touch the fronts of your shoulders with your elbows tucked in at your sides.

3. Slowly squat down, using the same form you did with the Dumbbells Box Squats. Try to get down as close as you can to a 90-degree angle. If you can maintain proper form and even go a little lower, awesome! Drive through your heels and return to standing. Repeat.

Rest for 60 seconds.

HIGH BOX JUMPS: *30 seconds*

1. Stand in front of a box or bench that is between 12 and 24 inches tall.

2. Bend your knees, hinge your hips, and swing your arms back.

3. Drive with your hips and swing your arms forward, then explode off the balls of your feet onto the box, landing with both feet.

4. Land with soft knees, making sure not to collapse them in. Straighten your legs fully to stand at the top. Pause.

5. Jump back down (you will be jumping backward), land soft, and keep your knees aligned. Repeat.

Rest for 60 seconds.

CNS PRIMER #2: *1 set*

This exercise wakes up your glutes and hamstrings, preparing you for the next group of exercises.

DUMBBELL HIP THRUST: *10 reps with a 20-pound dumbbell, or 20 reps without a weight*

1. Sit on the floor with your back against a bench. Shift to lie down with your upper back on the bench, just below your shoulder blades. Your feet stay on the floor, hip-width apart, right under your knees.

2. Hold a single dumbbell over your hips, just below your hip bones. Keep your core tight and your chin slightly tucked.

3. Drive through your heels to push your rear end up off the floor until your thighs and shins are roughly at a 90-degree angle. Squeeze your glutes at the top.

4. Lower your hips back down with control. Depending on the height of your bench, your glutes may or may not touch the ground. Either is fine. Repeat.

Rest for 30 to 60 seconds.

SUPERSET #2: *Do 3 to 4 sets*

EXPLOSIVE BUTT KICKS: *5 reps*

1. Stand with your feet about shoulder-width apart. With your chest up and your back straight, swing your arms behind you, bend your knees, and hinge at the hips as if you were getting ready to dive into a pool.

2. Using the power of your arms and forward hip drive, propel yourself off the ground. When you jump, bring both feet up behind you, as if you are kicking your own backside.

3. Land back in the starting position and repeat.

DUMBBELL ROMANIAN DEADLIFTS: *10 reps with two 30- to 35-pound dumbbells*

1. Hold a dumbbell in each hand, in front of your hips. Your feet should be about hip-width apart in a comfortable stance, knees slightly bent in a fixed position. Keep your chest up, shoulders back, core tight.

2. With your back and arms straight, hinge at the hips and slide your hips back as you lower the dumbbells toward the floor. Stop when you feel a good stretch in your hamstrings. Do not relax at the bottom of the movement—keep the tension and keep your leg muscles active.

3. Stand up straight again, using your hamstrings to pull you up. Squeeze your glutes at the top.

Rest for 60 seconds.

HAMSTRING CURLS ON STABILITY BALL: *20 reps*

This exercise doesn't immediately appear to have a cardio component, but it's actually pretty strenuous, so it should get your heart rate up.

1. Lie on the floor and put your heels on a stability ball with your knees bent at a 90-degree angle. Arms are down by your sides at about a 45-degree angle to help stabilize you. Your palms should face the floor.

2. Lift your hips up, keeping your core tight. Your shoulders and head should remain on the floor.

3. Keeping your feet on the ball and your hips high, slowly straighten your legs, pushing the ball away from you. When you reach full extension, bend your knees and curl the ball back toward your hips with your feet.

Always keep your hips up and locked in.

Rest for 60 seconds.

SUPERSET #3: *Do 4 sets*

For High Box Step-Ups and Step-Up Jumps, alternate each leg. For the Dumbbell Walking Lunges, doing both sides counts as one rep (Carrie and I call this a "2fer").

DUMBBELL WALKING LUNGES: *10 reps with 20- to 25-pound dumbbells*

1. Start with your feet shoulder-width apart, chest up, back straight. Hold a dumbbell in each hand, arms down at your sides.

2. Lunge your right leg forward, lowering your back knee as close to the floor as you can, until both knees are bent at 90-degree angles.

3. Drive off your right leg and step your left foot forward to meet your right. Stand up fully. Repeat on the other side (right and left equal 1 rep).

Rest for 60 seconds (or preferably less).

HIGH BOX STEP-UPS (RIGHT LEG ON SETS #1 AND #3, LEFT LEG ON SETS #2 AND #4): *12 reps per leg, with a 15- to 20-pound dumbbell in each hand*

1. Stand facing a bench or box holding two heavy dumbbells. Both feet should be close to the box. Put one foot on the bench or box, with just a slight lean forward—only enough to put your weight on the upper foot.

2. Maintaining good posture, drive off the leg that is on the bench or box, to stand up fully at the top—let that leg do the work. (If this is too difficult, you don't have to use the dumbbells.)

3. Lower yourself back down, slowly and with control, keeping the same foot on the bench or box.

4. Repeat using the same leg for all reps. You will do the opposite leg in the next set.

Immediately move to the next exercise—there should be no break between High Box Step-Ups and Step-Up Jumps

STEP-UP JUMPS (RIGHT LEG ON SETS #1 AND #3, LEFT LEG ON SETS #2 AND #4): *10 reps with body weight only. If you are advanced, use the same dumbbells you used in the last exercise.*

1. Stand facing a bench or box. Put one foot on the box. Your knee should be bent at a 90-degree angle. (This exercise and equipment is set up the same way as the High Box Step-Ups.)

Try to catch a little air!

2. Bend your standing leg slightly, drive off the leg that is on the bench or box, and jump straight up. The foot on the bench or box should leave its surface and "get some air."

3. Land with the same foot on the bench or box and the same foot on the floor, in the starting position.

4. Immediately jump up again into the next rep. You will do the opposite leg in the next set.

Rest for 60 seconds, or as long as you need to get ready for Superset #4.

SUPERSET #4: 3 sets

LEG PRESS: 10 reps

This exercise uses a leg press machine. The weight for the leg press machine is very equipment-specific, so you may have to experiment to determine what weight works for you. With some machines, you press the plate away with your feet. In others, the plate stays stationary and you push yourself and the seat backward. Remember that for this workout, we are using moderate to heavy weights. You should go heavy enough that 8 to 10 reps are difficult, but not impossible.

1. Sit in the seat of the leg press machine with your back resting against the pad. Place your feet on the center of the plate or slightly higher, about hip-width apart (much like you are setting up for a squat). You may need to adjust the seat or the plate to put you in a comfortable position with your knees close to your body, but not so close that you feel squished. You may then need to adjust your feet again so your knees are bent at a 90-degree angle.

2. With your spine straight and core tight, drive through your heels to push the plate away from your body. Keep the movement slow and controlled. Do not lock your knees at the top—keep them slightly bent.

3. Return to the starting position, slowly and with control.

Rest for 30 to 60 seconds.

BODYWEIGHT SQUATS: *10 reps Set #1, 20 reps Set #2, 30 reps Set #3*

1. Stand with hips about shoulder-width apart, or a little wider.

2. Keeping your chest up and your back straight, sink your hips back, drop your rear end, and bend your knees as if you are sitting in a chair. Try to get your knees bent to about 90 degrees.

3. Drive through your heels to stand up completely.

Move immediately to Jump Squats without resting.

JUMP SQUATS: *10 reps*

1. Set up exactly like you did for Bodyweight Squats, with your feet hip-width apart.

2. Keeping your chest up and your back straight, sink your hips back, drop your rear end, and bend your knees as if you are sitting in a chair. Squat as low as you can.

3. Jump up from the squat position, landing as lightly as you can, and immediately go into another squat. Repeat.

Rest for 60 seconds.

SUPERSET #5: *Do 3 sets*

Again, rest as little as possible between the exercises—just enough to transition from one exercise to the next. If you can, wait until the end of the superset to rest.

ELEVATED SUMO DEADLIFT ON TWO AEROBIC STEPS (OR BENCHES, OR IF YOU DON'T HAVE OTHER OPTIONS, ON THE FLOOR): *10 reps with one 50-pound dumbbell*

1. Stand with one foot on each of two steps or benches, with your feet about two to three feet apart, toes turned out. Hold a single dumbbell in both hands, hanging in front of you.

2. With your back straight, shoulders back, and core tight, hinge at the waist and slide your hips back behind you as you lower the dumbbell toward the floor. Because you are elevated, you should be able to achieve a greater range of motion. The bottom of the dumbbell can go past the top of the steps.

3. Drive through your heels and fire up your glutes and hamstrings to stand up straight again. Repeat.

Rest as little as possible between Elevated Sumo Deadlift and Elevated Sumo Squat.

ELEVATED SUMO SQUAT: *12 reps at the same weight as the previous exercise, or drop down to 40 pounds, if that helps you get to 12 reps.*

1. From the same position you started in for the previous exercise, holding the dumbbell in front of you, keep your chest up and squat down, lowering the dumbbell toward the floor, past the benches.

2. Push through your heels to stand.

Chest up, shoulders back—let your legs do all the work!

No rest!

POP SQUATS ON LOW BENCH: *30 seconds*

1. Start in a squat positon straddling a low bench with one foot on each side, the narrow way.

2. Jump up onto the bench with both feet while staying in a low squat.

3. Jump back off to the starting position and repeat.

Rest for 60 seconds.

SUPERSET #6: *Do 4 sets total—2 right, 2 left (alternate legs on each set)*

ECCENTRIC LATERAL BOX STEP DOWN (RIGHT LEG, SETS #1 AND #3, LEFT LEG SETS #2 AND #4): *10 reps*

1. Stand on a box. Move your right foot out to the side of the box, and squat with your left leg, to lower your right foot to the ground. The goal here is to lower slowly with control. Lightly tap your toe (or your heel if you are more advanced) to the floor.

2. Straighten your left leg to stand back up on the box.

3. Repeat the entire set with one leg before switching to the opposite leg for Set #2, etc.

Rest as little as possible between Eccentric Lateral Box Step Down and Curtsy Lunge over Bench.

HOW WIDE?

When doing squats, how wide apart should your feet be? You may have heard the old "shoulder-width apart" refrain, but the truth is that everyone is built differently, with different muscle lengths, insertion points, skeletal structure, ankle and hip mobility, and flexibility. When you do squats, your feet should be roughly shoulder-width apart, although some people may feel more comfortable or more stable with their feet set slightly wider than this. Your toes should point forward, but again, because of individual factors, some people may feel better with their feet slightly turned out. However, this is not a toes-out squat like a sumo squat or a plié. If you keep your knees tracking directly over your toes as you squat and you don't buckle your knees or splay them outward, that is a good indication of proper form.

CURTSY LUNGE OVER BENCH (RIGHT LEG SETS #1 AND #3, LEFT LEG SETS #2 AND #4): *10 reps, body weight only (no weights)*

1. Stand on a bench lengthwise and get into a low, narrow squat position, feet and knees together. Transfer your weight to your right leg and bring your left leg back behind you into a "curtsy" position, until your left toe touches lightly on the floor.

2. Staying low, use the strength in your right leg to bring your left leg up and off to the opposite side of the bench. Tap your toe lightly on the ground. The challenge is to work on balance and core stability.

3. Do the first set using the same leg. Switch to the opposite leg for the next set.

Rest for 30 seconds, if needed.

UP AND OVERS: *30 seconds*

1. Stand sideways on a step or low bench. Step off to the side with your right leg. One foot will be on the step and one foot will be on the floor.

2. Jump and land with your right foot on the step or bench and your left foot on the ground on the opposite side of the step or bench.

3. Quickly jump again and land with your left foot on the step or bench and your right foot on the ground.

4. Keep going as quickly as you can for 30 seconds.

COOL-DOWN

Use the cool-down for the Fit52 Workout (see pages 131–35).

your favorite body part

I think it's important to love *all* your body parts, but maybe you do have a favorite. My legs are probably my favorite body part. What's yours? Is there something you get complimented on a lot, or that you're particularly proud of? Maybe you haven't thought about it before. Use this chance to think about what your favorite part of your body is and why: What does it do for you? In what ways can you rely on it? Are there ways to maintain it?

7

THE CHAMPION

Extracurricular Fitness for Wherever You Are

f working out is fitness, then being active in your "regular" life is extracurricular fitness. Moving more and finding opportunities to use your lungs and your muscles doesn't have to be or even feel like a workout, but it can be a workout nevertheless. In reality, most people won't have time to work out every single day. There are many days when I just don't have the time. Even though I have a workout room at home, there are literally days when I don't have time to go in there and spend even 30 minutes exercising. On the road, there are days when I'm booked from early morning to late at night, and there's no time to hang out in my mobile gym. So what do I do? I get moving every chance I get.

The ways that you can move more in your daily life may not always be obvious. Extracurricular fitness can take a bit of imagination. So in this chapter, I want to help you think outside the box a little. Whatever you are doing, I bet there are ways to do it more actively. These are some of the ways that I stay active when I can't officially work out, along with some additional ideas that may work for you and your lifestyle, even if they aren't applicable to mine (like, I don't work in an office, but I still have those sedentary days, so I have included ideas for staying active when you have a job that requires a lot of sitting).

Let's get creative so that you never have an excuse for a completely inactive day. Every active thing you do makes you a little bit fitter. One of my favorite inspirational sayings is "Be stronger than yesterday."

When the Weather Is Nice

First of all, let's talk about the weather. Why waste a beautiful day sitting on the couch? And for that matter, why waste a beautiful day in an indoor gym? Depending on where you live, you may have plenty of bad-weather days, so good weather is a great excuse to get outside and be active in the fresh air and sunshine.

Just feeling that warm sun or that cool breeze, seeing the green of the trees and the blue of the sky, hearing birds singing or kids playing, can be enough to energize you and make you want to move. So do it! Go for a walk, go for a bike ride, go to the park to play basketball. These are all workouts that aren't workouts. They're just living, moving, being active, and spending time with your partner, your kids, your dog, your friends, or some well-deserved alone time with your headphones in and your favorite songs playing. Some other ideas:

› **FIND YOUR INNER CHILD.** Don't just watch your kids play tag or red rover or capture the flag. Join in. Young kids still think their parents are cool enough to play with, but that won't last long, so get it while you can! Some other fun things to do outside with kids are to make your own obstacle course, give each other "challenges" (like, "Touch every tree in the yard and run back to me and I'll time you. Now it's my turn.") Set up a zipline (be safe!). Learn how to hula-hoop. Have a water balloon fight. Have a three-legged race. Climb a tree (carefully!). Get some sidewalk chalk and play hopscotch or jump rope.

› **WALK YOUR DOG.** Dogs need exercise, too! You can both get more fit and healthier if you go on walks together, and knowing your dog needs a walk is like having an exercise buddy—you'll be more likely to get out there and do it. Canine accountability!

› **HAVE A BEACH DAY.** You don't have to live on the coast. Most communities at least have a lake nearby with a beach. Pack up some healthy snacks and walk along the beach. Go for a swim or play water polo with your family or friends. You could also rent a canoe or a kayak (great arm workouts) or even one of those paddle boats (a great leg workout) and get out on the surface of the lake. Wear sunscreen!

› **GO GREEN.** If you live somewhere that has hiking trails, check those out. Some cities have cool bike paths through natural areas. Nature is therapy. I've heard that just looking at the color green relieves stress.

› **PICK UP TRASH.** Teach kids about caring for their community by having a trash pick-up day. Get gloves and trash bags and head to a local park. See who can fill their bag up the fullest.

› **YOU-PICK.** If you live near a you-pick farm, you can take family or a group of friends to pick strawberries, blueberries, apples, or whatever else is available. You'll get exercise and healthy food to bring home with you.

› **GO CAMPING.** Setting up a tent, unloading the gear, building a fire, and hiking around the area are all active outdoor activities that can change your perspective about comfort and make you feel more connected to nature.

› **PLAY TENNIS.** You don't have to be good at it. Grab a racquet and a can of tennis balls and hit some balls back and forth with a friend or family member.

› **PLAY OTHER CASUAL SPORTS.** Set up an informal game of baseball, softball, or even Wiffle ball. What about kickball, basketball, or volleyball? Or go old school with a game of badminton or croquet. So much better than watching TV or sitting in front of the computer. You don't even need to keep score (unless you're competitive like me!).

› **GO TO THE POOL.** Swimming is such a great way to exercise! You literally use every part of your body to move yourself through the water. Plus, it's fun! And in my book, if you have an outdoor pool available to you, that's even better. So lather up with some sunscreen and swim some laps or take a water aerobics class.

› SNOW DAY! Snowy cold days can also be beautiful if you bundle up. You don't need to be a little kid to have fun building a snowman or a snow fort or an igloo, or to ride a sled down a hill. While you're at it, make some snow angels. Who cares what the neighbors think? Cross-country skiing is another really great winter fitness activity.

FUN-THEMED PLAYLIST FOR ANY WORKOUT

I love putting together themed playlists. I once made a five-hour-long playlist for a friend's baby shower, where all the songs could loosely be tied to something baby-related—it was epic! Of course, nothing is literal, but hopefully these fitness-related songs will make you smile while you're sweating it out in the gym . . . or anywhere else!

"Body Talks"—The Struts
"Physical"—Olivia Newton-John
"Work Hard Play Hard"—Wiz Khalifa
"Rock That Body"—The Black Eyed Peas
"Stronger"—Kanye West
"Jump"—Van Halen
"Runaway Baby"—Bruno Mars
"Get Low"—Lil Jon & the East Side Boyz (feat. Ying Yang Twins)
"Sexy and I Know It"—LMFAO
"Back That Azz Up"—Juvenile (feat. Mannie Fresh and Lil Wayne)
"I'm Gonna Be (500 Miles)"—The Proclaimers
"Stronger (What Doesn't Kill You)"—Kelly Clarkson
"Iron Man"—Black Sabbath
"My Body"—Young the Giant
"Work"—Rihanna (feat. Drake)

"Low"—Flo Rida (feat. T-Pain)
"Push It"—Salt-N-Pepa
"Rock Your Body"—Justin Timberlake
"Push It"—Static-X
"Heavy"—Collective Soul
"Pump It"—The Black Eyed Peas
"1, 2 Step"—Ciara (feat. Missy Elliott)
"Run"—Foo Fighters
"Sweat (A La La La La Long)"—Inner Circle
"I Ran (So Far Away)"—A Flock of Seagulls
"Work from Home"—Fifth Harmony (feat. Ty Dolla $ign)
"Twist and Shout"—The Beatles
"Jump"—Kris Kross
"Your Body"—Pretty Ricky
"U Can't Touch This"—MC Hammer

Walking

Walking is something that is awesome to do on a beautiful day, but that you can really do on any day—and you should. I believe walking is really important. Our bodies are made to walk. So many things feel better after a good brisk walk in good weather. I try to take a walk on every nice day if I possibly can, even if I only have 20 minutes—but an hour-long walk is *the best*. It's like rebooting your brain so you feel good again. Some people make walking the primary part of their workout. This is especially good if you're just starting out. Walking is low-impact, and almost anyone can do it. You can start slow and work up to a faster walk as you get more in shape. This is great training to get you ready for more advanced workouts. If you can take a walk on most days, you are moving in the right direction.

When walking gets too easy, you can start trying new things, like doing lunges up hills, or even running a little. But listen to your body and progress at your own speed—not too fast, but not too slow. Push yourself just enough to be right on the edge of your comfort zone, and you will see results. And on those bad-weather days? If you have access to a treadmill or you can walk inside somewhere (like a mall), you can keep up with your walking program, rain or shine. (But "shine" is always nicest.)

And while you're at it, you can always throw in some other exercises. When I go on walks with my trainer, we intersperse our walk with calisthenics. We make goals, like every time we get to a stop sign, we have to stop and do 20 squats. Every time we hit a crosswalk, we have to do lunges until the little man on the traffic light says it's safe to cross the street. Every time we hit a green space, it's 20 burpees. Make up your own goals like this to give yourself a more complete workout, and don't be afraid of what people think. Who cares? You're getting healthy, and that's what matters.

On the Playground

If you're like me, you may end up at the playground fairly often. Most parents sit around on the benches and watch their kids play. But why should your kids get to have all the fun? You can do some pretty cool exercises on playground equipment. I have been known to use those monkey bars for pull-ups. Sometimes I hang from them and do leg lifts. If the playground has a bench or a curb, you can do step-ups, jump-ups, or dips. Even swinging can be a workout. If nothing else, you can always jog in circles or do lunges around the play area while you keep your eyes on your kids.

At the Office

I don't work in an office and I don't want you to get fired because I told you to work out at your desk, but there are some things you can do on sedentary days that hopefully would not be a problem at any kind of office job. I might set it up first by telling anybody around me, "Hey, look, guys, don't think I'm weird but I might be doing a few lunges or squats or curls while I'm on the phone. Don't judge me!" If you treat the subject with humor, most people probably won't mind. Of course, if you don't work in that kind of office, feel free to completely ignore this advice! But when I have to spend a long day sitting, like during songwriting sessions or when I'm stuck on the tour bus, these are some of the things I might do:

› **DO ISOMETRICS.** Even just sitting in a chair, you can squeeze your muscles as tight as you can and then let them go. Do "reps" like this: Squeeze those booty muscles, or tense up your thigh muscles or your biceps. Hold the squeeze for 10, 20, 30 seconds, or squeeze and release in pulses. You can get a workout, and nobody will ever know!

› **STAND UP EVERY 30 TO 60 MINUTES.** You may not be able to stand up for long, but exercise your calves by going up on your toes and back down 20 times, lift your knees high, do some arm circles, take a good stretch. Depending on your setup, you could also do some push-ups against the wall and a few squats in front of your chair. Or just stand up and sit down 20 times. Look around your environment to see what else you could do. Whatever it is, you'll be physically and mentally refreshed, so you can be more efficient. Some people set a timer on their watches to remind them when to stand up and stretch.

› **TAKE WALK BREAKS.** If you can, spend your coffee breaks or even your lunch break walking, and walk outside, if possible. This can make a big difference, breaking up a long day of sitting with actual movement. Maybe one of your work colleagues would like to come along. Or offer to get everyone coffee and use that as an excuse to walk even more. Everyone will love you—it's a win-win.

› **FIND MORE REASONS TO WALK.** Whenever you have a good reason, don't delay—get up and move. If you need to ask a colleague something, walk over and ask rather than sending a text message or email. If you need a photocopy or you need to fax something (if you're old school like that), do it yourself rather than asking someone else. Then, when you really need to get something done while sitting, focus in and be efficient and just do it, rather than letting yourself get distracted by random computer tasks that aren't really necessary but add hours of sitting to your day.

› **TAKE THE STAIRS.** If you work in a building with more than one floor, don't use the elevator. Take those stairs! (As long as you don't work on the twentieth floor—although how strong would you be if you walked up nineteen flights of stairs every day?) Or get off the elevator a couple of flights early and walk the rest. Climbing stairs is even better exercise than walking. If you have to go up and down a lot during the day, you can actually get a pretty good workout.

› **DRINK LOTS OF WATER SO YOU HAVE TO GET UP AND WALK TO THE BATHROOM A LOT.** Just kidding! (Sort of . . .) When you're in the bathroom, do some stretches.

› **WHENEVER YOU'RE ON THE PHONE, WALK AROUND.** I don't know about you, but I can't sit still and talk on the phone. If I'm ever on a long chat with someone, I love for my body to be doing something that I don't really have to think about, like organizing things or cleaning up the space around me. It's the perfect opportunity to multitask—just make sure you're not moving so much that you're out of breath while you're trying to close that big deal!

> › **STANDING DESK?** I've heard some offices encourage this and might even provide them for employees who ask. Even if you have to purchase one, a standing desk is a great way to stand more and sit less. The adjustable ones let you stand when you want and sit when you need to, so those may be the best option. I don't have one, but it sounds like a good idea to me.

> › **BIKE OR ELLIPTICAL PEDALS.** There are little pedal-only trainers that can fit right under a desk! Some are more like bike pedals and some are more like elliptical trainer pedals. I have one on the tour bus so that when I'm sitting, I can keep my legs moving.

On the Road

Vacations are great, but they don't have to mean taking a vacation from exercising. You'll feel so much better when traveling if you keep moving. You'll be less bloated, retain less water, have better digestion and more energy, look better, and be in a better mood. You'll also feel more fit for vacation activities. Instead of sitting in a beach chair for hours, you might be more inclined to keep the activity going with a walk or a swim or a game of beach volleyball.

But this is easier said than done. Whenever I'm on the road, I get this feeling like, hey, I'm in a hotel, so I must be on vacation. Time to kick back! I have to remind myself I'm traveling *for work* and I have to stay on it. Now that I have my mobile gym, I admit I don't have to be quite as creative about working out on the road, but I well remember the days when I had to figure out ways to stay active while traveling. Here are some of the things I did:

> › **USE THE HOTEL GYM,** unless it is just not usable. Some of them are nice, and some . . . well, not so much. But many of them have elliptical trainers, treadmills, or exercise bicycles, along with

some basic weight lifting equipment. Even if you just walk on the treadmill for 30 minutes, you'll feel better. I like to bring my workout playlists to keep me motivated. Otherwise, some of those little workout rooms can be pretty unpleasant if you're just walking away on the treadmill and looking at a gray wall in a tiny room or a TV that doesn't really work.

› USE THE HOTEL POOL. Some are too small for lap swimming, but you might be able to get some laps in, especially if the pool isn't too crowded.

› WALK THE CITY. If your hotel isn't in a pedestrian-friendly area, ask the concierge or the desk clerk about good places to walk or hike. They should be able to tell you where to go, and if you're lucky, they'll even drive you. Or you could cab it or take an Uber or Lyft, of course. Depending on where you are, you could have a great time walking through the city, seeing the sights, or wandering through a cool natural area in a part of the country (or world) you've never seen before.

› USE YOUR HOTEL ROOM AS A GYM. You can get a pretty good workout right there in your room with a little creativity. Use a chair to do triceps dips. There are a lot of things you can do with just a chair. Do walking lunges around the room, then do some squats. You could try push-ups and sit-ups on the floor (maybe put down a blanket or unroll a mat if you brought one with you—see "Exercise Equipment for the Road" on page 180). Use your ab roller on the floor. Honestly, if you warm up with a little stretching, do a good set of burpees, or step outside to jump rope, then do some sit-ups, push-ups, triceps dips, and squats, you'll be ahead of the game. Stretch out when you're done, take a shower, and you're ready for whatever your trip has in store for you.

Exercise Equipment for the Road

Everything on this list should fit in your suitcase, and the benefits you'll get from exercising while traveling will far outweigh the inconvenience of any space these things take up. Here are the things I always brought with me, pre–mobile gym:

› **RESISTANCE BANDS** in a variety of resistance levels. I like the ones with handles. There are hundreds of different exercises you can do with resistance bands. You can look up different routines online and pick your favorites. You probably already have these if you're doing the Fit52 Workout (which is also good to do on the road).

› **PORTABLE AB ROLLER.** Basically a wheel with handles, this little gadget provides an intense core workout. You get in push-up position, then roll the wheel forward and backward, using your core to control the movements. Break it down, pack it up, and hit the road.

› **JUMP ROPE.** If you have a place to step outside, you can get a good cardio workout in just a few minutes.

› **MAT.** You never know what kind of surfaces you might have to work out on. If you bring your own mat, and maybe a few wipes to keep it clean,

you might feel better about doing those sit-ups and push-ups on the hotel room floor.

› **DECK OF CARDS.** You can come up with your own travel-friendly version of the Fit52 Workout, based on what equipment you packed and what is available in your hotel room or hotel gym. You could also do an entire Fit52 Workout with no equipment at all—just assign equipment-free moves for each suit.

Jesus, take the ab wheel!

This crushes my abs! Just roll out as far as you can and keep the tension in your abs, not in your lower back.

And as long as you're committing to health on the road, keep your eating on track, too. It is all too easy to think: *I'm on a trip! I can order room service!* Or, *Hey, we're right next door to an Arby's . . . sweet* (those curly fries *are* delicious)! But nothing puts on weight and saps energy like a week (or more) of room service and fast food. I know a lot of people who travel for work and have this problem, and I share it—a week of room-service veggie burgers with all the toppings, pasta, and flatbread pizzas is no way to eat right.

Now whenever I go somewhere, I go to the grocery store, or do grocery delivery to wherever I'm staying (which is more and more available these days). I get enough food to last me for the time I will be there so I never have to rely on going out. I can go to restaurants every once in a while instead of for every meal. Restaurant portions are huge, and the food is full of salt and fat. It all tastes good, but it's not good for you every day. If nothing else, I can always find a big salad at a grocery store. More health-oriented stores like Whole Foods have the healthiest salads. For more on road food and what I always bring with me, see pages 48–51.

At Home

On those days when you have a lot to do around the house (and if you're like me, there's *always* lots of stuff to do around the house), multitask those household chores by making them into exercise. Cleaning can be pretty strenuous, but you can make it even more workoutlike with a few adjustments. Here are some of the things I do:

1. **USE THE STAIRS MORE.** Some people save up a batch of things to take up or down the stairs, but sometimes it's healthier to be less efficient. Every time you see something that should go up or down, take it up or down. One thing at a time. You can get a lot of good cardio going up and down your own stairs all day long. You could

your extracurricular fitness inspiration

We all do a lot of the same things—we clean, we work, we play, we exercise. But your life also has unique qualities that mine doesn't. Brainstorm some ideas for extracurricular fitness that work with how you live, where you spend your time, what you have in your home, and what you do for work. Make a list in your journal. Whenever you need inspiration to get moving more, you can go back to this list. Keep it fresh by adding to it whenever you think of something new.

also do 20 step-ups on the bottom step every time before going up the stairs. If you're relatively coordinated, you can also hop up the stairs. Do little squats with every jump and feel the burn!

2. **JOG IT.** I already mentioned that sometimes I jog around my own house from room to room. I might look silly, but I can get in a lot of steps that way. And you know what they say: Don't sit when you can stand, don't stand when you can walk, and don't walk when you can run! Okay, maybe they don't say that exactly. But it's what I try to do.

3. **ELBOW GREASE.** You could douse your surfaces in high-powered toxic cleaners, or you could use good old-fashioned elbow grease and scrub. Scrubbing your own kitchen or bathroom floor or tub by hand may not be the most pleasant thing you do in a day, but it

will definitely give your arms a good workout. Scrub and scrub and scrub harder, and you may even be able to count it as cardio.

4. **LIFT HEAVY THINGS.** Every time I have to lift or move something heavy, I don't just move it. I turn it into a weight-lifting exercise. Full bottle of laundry detergent? Gallon of milk? Sack of potatoes? Do some biceps curls. Moving the couch to vacuum under it? See if you can lift it. (But don't hurt yourself!)

5. **SPEED IT UP.** If you vacuum, sweep, mop, dust, or wash windows faster, you can get your heart rate up.

6. **TURN UP THE VOLUME.** Crank up the music while you're getting stuff done! Music always gives me a little more spring in my step, and if I can dance my way through my household chores, it only makes the time fly by faster!

I guess my point is obvious: Move more, even when you're not officially "working out"! I hope that you'll want to borrow some of my own nonworkout-workout ideas from this chapter, and that the concept of extracurricular fitness will spark even more ideas for you. There are always ways to move more. What's stopping you? Why not take a break from reading this and go do some jumping jacks or squats right now? You won't regret it.

PART THREE

undo it

BALANCING FOOD INDULGENCE AND FOOD SENSE

8

UN-
APOLOGIZE

The Pleasure Principle

here have been times in my life when I took food for granted. There have been times in my life when I overindulged. There have been times in my life (as you've read) when I didn't let myself eat enough. Finally, I've found a happy balance—a balance between using food as good fuel to power my life and enjoying the experience of delicious food and the way it brings people together and makes people happy. I believe food should be appreciated for both practical and pleasurable reasons. A lot of discipline, a little indulgence—it's a good recipe for life, not just food.

This is my food philosophy. I call it the Pleasure Principle (gotta thank the gorgeous Janet Jackson for the inspiration . . . and I guess Dr. Sigmund Freud as well). Being a relatively moderate person who likes balance and order, I appreciate what food does for me as fuel, but I also appreciate what it does for me when it comes to pleasure. Some of the best moments happen around a table with friends or family gathered to share a meal. The tricky part is finding that line between sensible restriction and sensible indulgence. I wouldn't call myself a strict eater, but I would say that I'm all about being a disciplined eater, so when I really want to loosen it up and enjoy myself, I can afford to do that.

What I am *not* about is deprivation. Instead, I love figuring out healthier ways to make foods that I like. This is how to make healthy eating sustainable. If your eating plan is too strict, you probably won't stick to it, and you certainly won't enjoy it. At least, that's how I am. But turning your favorite foods into healthier versions? That's the best of both worlds: You get to eat the foods you love, but you also get to reach your health and fitness goals. That's the Pleasure Principle.

The way I put this theory into practice isn't complicated at all. It's really very simple. I only have to remember three things, and I can tell you those three things in less than a minute. They are:

1. **EAT MOSTLY FOODS THAT GOD MADE.** I try to eat mostly foods in their natural form—things like fresh vegetables, fresh fruit, whole

grains, or the occasional egg. Not obsessively. Just most of the time. That's the good stuff!

2. **MAKE HEALTHY SWAPS FOR YOUR FAVORITE INDULGENCES.** Swap out junky ingredients for healthier ingredients so you can still enjoy your favorite foods without the bad effects. You'd be surprised at how healthy you can make a meal and still have it taste like good ol' down-home comfort food.

3. **BE ACCOUNTABLE FOR WHAT YOU EAT AND HOW YOU LIVE.** Do you really know what and how much you're eating? Do you really know what's in your food? Have you decided how you want to live and how you want to feel? Being accountable means being honest with yourself, making conscious choices, and following through.

That's it. That's my whole nutritional strategy, and it works really well to keep me on track, fuel my physical needs, and also give me the pleasure and enjoyment I crave from food. Do you want to know a little more about how I actually implement these strategies in my life, and how you can implement them in yours? Let's look at them one at a time.

Eat Mostly Foods That God Made

What do I mean when I say "foods that God made"? I mean real, natural food in its whole form, the way it grows in the garden, orchard, or field. When I imagine food God made, I think of fresh ripe vegetables, juicy whole fruits, toasty whole grains, protein-rich beans and legumes, and things made from them like tofu, oatmeal, or a beautiful tray of roasted vegetables. I also think of fresh eggs from healthy chickens, and every

Meet Nutritionist (and My Friend) Cara Clark

I met Cara Clark in college. We were both mass communication majors with an emphasis on broadcast journalism, so we had a lot of the same classes and ran into each other quite a bit. Cara was one year behind me and came to Northeastern State University from Ohio to play on the basketball team. I always thought she was so cool and such a sweet person . . . and obviously gorgeous! Cara went on to become a certified sports and clinical nutritionist and she's been doing that work for eleven years. She founded Cara Clark Nutrition and Fitness in 2008, but now she focuses mainly on nutrition to support people's fitness goals. She approaches health by looking at each person's big picture, and she believes that real food nutrition is at the root of all well-being. She says our brains have to work with our bodies, and she focuses on the effects of nutrition at the cellular level. So cool. She has taught me a lot about the dangers of fad diets and how the diet industry is more about profit than health, so I trust her guidance. And she's the mom of four beautiful little girls, so she knows what it's like to juggle everything life-

related, just like the rest of us! I asked her to weigh in on various topics in this chapter, so look for her "Cara Says" boxes. She's the professional when it comes to nutrition, so she knows a lot more than I do! You can find out more about her at caraclarknutrition.com.

now and then some cheese from the milk of a happy goat or a contented cow, as foods God made. These are the foods that the earth naturally yields up to us to keep us nourished and sustained, and also the foods that make me feel strong and healthy, like I can accomplish anything. (You may choose to add some animal foods to this list, but if you do, they should be organic and pasture-raised, in their most natural form.)

But notice that I did say "mostly." Let's be honest—God didn't make pizza, and pizza is awesome now and then. I don't eat it every day, but I do eat it. (See chapter 10 for more about how to manage foods like pizza.) God didn't make protein bars and protein powder, either, but I look for brands that come from natural ingredients. I do eat packaged food because I'm so busy (I have more to say about this throughout this chapter). But I do my best to eat mostly whole food, and that's what counts.

BELIEVE AND FOLLOW THROUGH!

Believing in whatever diet method you decide to follow is just as important as following the right one for you. The reason there are so many dietary arguments out there is that often, our individual belief systems are attached to how we decide to eat. Carrie has nailed both of these—she strongly believes in eating "as vegan as possible" (for herself), and she follows through. I believe this is one of the major reasons for her success in achieving great health and fitness. She is one of the most consistent people I've ever been around. Consistency and belief will contribute not only to good results from your dietary choices, but also to good fitness results. Find what works for you . . . and then commit!

It shouldn't be hard to eat what's good for you, but then again, I know it can get confusing. Even if you know *what* foods to eat, you may still be unsure *how* to eat them. Should you be counting calories, or carbs, or sugar grams, or protein grams? Should you be eating low-carb, or keto? Should you go vegetarian or vegan? Should you cut out all sugar, or all fat, or all carbs? Should you eat a Mediterranean diet? All these questions may still occur to you even if you've chosen a basic, simple dietary strategy, because even if you're eating mostly whole foods, you may question whether you should eat *all* the available whole foods—or if there are some you should avoid.

The fact is, there's a lot of information out there—so much information that it's really hard to know what's true. You can probably find a study to justify just about anything you want to eat, or don't want to eat. You can find a study that says you should eat nothing but bacon for the rest of your life—*eat bacon daily!* And you can find a study that says bacon causes cancer—*never eat bacon!* We're not just living in the information age. We're living in the *extreme* information age, and it can feel like circuitry overload.

The only way I have found to keep from getting confused or doubting myself is to keep it simple and use common sense. Take all the studies you read with a grain of salt. If a diet or a way of life sounds too good to be true, it probably is. I actually read about an ice cream diet once . . . what? If it sounds too weird, I'm not going to do it. I'm definitely not a believer in fad diets (in my younger days, I did a few of them and got nowhere). We've all heard the statistics about how diets don't work. They don't work because they are temporary, and/or because they are too extreme. You might lose weight on your super-low-carb or super-low-fat or super-low-calorie diet, but as soon as you end the diet, you and I both know you're going to gain it all back, and maybe even then some.

The only way to change your health is to change your lifestyle in ways that you can accept. That are sustainable for you. That make you think, *Sure, I could do this forever. It's not so bad. In fact, I kind of like it.* The changes you make for your health shouldn't be too restrictive. They should still allow you to participate fully in life.

I think the best way to tell if something you are doing is sustainable is to ask yourself, "Will I still be doing this a year from now?" If the answer is no, if you're miserable from not eating carbs, miserable about no gluten, no dairy, no sugar, no wine, whatever it is, and it's torture, then no, you're not going to be doing it a year from now. You're probably not going to be doing it a month from now. If you can't do the things you want to do because they might not fit with your "plan," if you avoid seeing friends and you fear holidays because they might interfere with your diet goals, you're making yourself and everyone else around you miserable. That's just no way to live. It's like when I wasn't eating enough. Eventually, my body rebelled, and at certain points I'd fall off the wagon and make really bad food decisions. *Not sustainable.*

Instead, listen to your own body and your own mind. What feels right to you? What sounds sensible to you? What is sustainable for you?

cara says

WHAT YOU SHOULD KNOW ABOUT MACROS

You've probably heard of "macros," but you may not be sure how to use them for your benefit. First, a definition: "Macros" is short for "macronutrients," the three main nutritional components of food; they are protein, carbohydrates (carbs), and fat. If you use an app like MyFitnessPal, you can see how your meals and your entire day of eating break down into macronutrients. You might even get a nice pie chart to show what percentage of your daily calories come from protein, carbohydrates, and fat.

But what does it all mean, and why does it matter? The main thing to know is that you need some of each of these nutrients. We all need some protein, some carbohydrates, and some fat, and I do not recommend any diet that completely removes any one of these. However, most diets do allow you to achieve a balance of all the macronutrients. For example, Carrie doesn't eat meat, but she has no problem getting enough protein from plant sources. She also gets enough fat and enough carbohydrates.

Next, let's consider what "enough" means. In general, I teach that

macronutrients should be balanced in the following ratios:

> › 50% carbs
> › 20% protein
> › 30% fat

That being said, humans are omnivorous. We can survive on many different diets, and this ratio is very flexible. You can still maintain a healthy lifestyle if you vary these ratios so you are getting anywhere from:

> › 40 to 65% carbs
> › 10 to 30% protein
> › 10 to 40% fat

In other words, you could be fine eating 65% carbs and just 10% fat if you get 25% protein. A lot of vegans have diets that are higher in carbs and lower in fat. Or, you could eat 30% protein and 40% fat and only get 30% of your calories from carbs. A lot of low-carb and Paleo people are closer to this ratio. Then again, you could be vegan and get a full 30% of your calories from fat because you eat a lot of avocados, nuts, and olive oil. Carrie has found a good balance that works for her, of 45% carbs, 30% fat, and 25% protein. Or you could be following a Paleo diet and get 65% of your calories from carbs because you eat lots of naturally starchy vegetables like sweet potatoes and plenty of fruit and keep your animal products very lean.

As you can see, there are no hard-and-fast rules. Some of my professional-athlete clients eat a higher-carb diet to fuel their intense physical activity. My clients with insulin resistance often do better on a diet with less than 50% carbs and more fat and protein. Go with the ratio that you feel best on and that gives you healthy results, like blood sugar and cholesterol levels and blood pressure readings that are all in the normal range according to your doctor. Everyone is different.

My only "rules" are to combine some carbs with fat and protein at every meal and every snack, and to include a minimum of five different plant foods of different colors every day. If people choose to incorporate animal protein, I suggest thinking about it as more of a side than a main dish, but this is up to each person. I teach that vegans, vegetarians, flexitarians (people who eat mostly vegetarian), people following a Paleo diet or Mediterranean diet or any other balanced diet, and regular old omnivores (people who eat anything) can all make good choices, and each of these eating styles can be nourishing and healthful.

Finally, consistency is always key when it comes to a healthy diet. That means making good choices most of the time, week after week, throughout the years. What isn't going to work is jumping on every trendy diet that pops up on Pinterest. Instead, stick with a nutrient-dense, colorful, fiber-rich diet with a balance of carbs, protein, and fat. Eat when you're hungry and stop eating when you're getting full. And enjoy good whole food. Following these main points 80 percent of the time will keep your body fit and healthy, and your macros (whether you keep track of them or not) should fall right into place.

If you aren't going to do it, it's not going to work. You can't cut out all carbs or all protein or all fat. It doesn't make sense. Any good dietitian or nutritionist will tell you that we need a good balance of all these macronutrients, along with a range of micronutrients like vitamins and minerals. Getting them isn't all that hard, if you just pay attention and put in a little effort.

For some reason, people always want to know what I eat, and maybe now you're wondering what I eat when I'm seeking out whole foods. But the truth is, I don't eat a million different interesting things on a weekly basis. I thought about this for a while and came up with the twelve foods I eat the most. I try to be a creative eater, but really, I tend to stick to the same old reliables, and these are my favorites. They are mostly whole foods, or things made with whole foods, with just a few exceptions.

The 12 Things I Eat the Most

1. **STIR-FRIES:** This is definitely one of my go-to dinners. I buy either broccoli slaw or bags of raw, ready-to-eat mixed vegetables like broccoli, cauliflower, and carrots. I throw them in a pan with a little water. I add some protein, such as vegan "chicken" or "beef," and then I add either a little cooked brown rice or quinoa. I sprinkle on some soy sauce or Liquid Aminos (a soy sauce–like product made by Bragg) and call it done! It's barely even a recipe. It's super quick and simple and really filling.

2. **AVOCADOS:** I probably eat at least half an avocado every day. Avocado toast is one of my favorite breakfasts. Avocados are a super-trendy food right now, and for good reason. Fresh avocado mashed onto some good sprouted or seed bread (such as Ezekiel bread or Dave's Killer Bread) has the good kind of fat and helps

keep me full for hours. Sometimes I'll even throw an avocado in my snack bag (I generally carry a small lunch-size cooler bag with me everywhere I go, for when hunger hits). I'll cut it in half, remove the pit, sprinkle with a little salt and pepper, and scoop it out with a spoon. So simple and yummy!

3. **BERRIES:** I eat a ton of blueberries, strawberries, and raspberries, either fresh on my plate in the morning with breakfast, or frozen in my smoothie later in the day. They are so sweet and good, but they don't have any added sugar and they have a lot of vitamins, so I know they're good for me.

4. **SMOOTHIES:** Speaking of berries, I absolutely love smoothies for a snack or for lunch (I've included recipes on page 204 and throughout chapter 9). They're quick and adaptable because you can put any fresh or frozen berries in them, and any other healthy ingredients. I'm usually headed somewhere around lunchtime, like a meeting or a playdate with my son, so I often whip up a smoothie to drink on the way. If I've got to grab lunch on the go, this is a delicious and surprisingly filling way to do it.

5. **BRUSSELS SPROUTS:** I know that some people have less-than-fond childhood memories of Brussels sprouts, because back in the day, people usually boiled them into a bitter mush. But when they're cooked right, they're one of my favorite side dishes ever! I keep it simple, and either sauté them in a little olive oil with some salt and pepper and maybe a little Mrs. Dash seasoning, or I toss those same ingredients on a baking sheet and roast them in the oven. If I can find Brussels sprouts shredded at the store, I even like them raw in a salad-type dish. I would definitely encourage you to give veggies that you didn't like as a child another chance. Not only are many vegetables better when cooked by a different method than boiling, but palates change, and adults are less sensitive to certain tastes than kids are. You may like the taste of something now that

you didn't like when you were growing up. Keep an open mind, and you never know what goodness you might rediscover!

6. **ROASTED VEGGIES:** I roast so many veggies, it's crazy! I probably roast veggies more than I do any other kind of cooking, and roasted vegetables are my favorite thing to eat. My dinners usually consist of some sort of meatless protein (like meat substitutes from Gardein, MorningStar Farms, etc.) and a plate full of roasted veggies. I don't really use a recipe—I'll just toss whatever fresh veggies I have in a little bit of olive oil and season them with whatever I've got nearby, like salt and pepper or garlic or some sort of seasoning blend. I put them on a baking sheet and roast them in the oven at 375°F until they're just starting to get crispy. Fresh veggie goodness! I think roasted veggies are one of the best ways to keep your diet simple. They are always a smart choice, and they're really great at filling me up.

7. **A GOOD OLD-FASHIONED SANDWICH:** This might sound a little boring, but I eat a lot of sandwiches. There's just something about a sandwich that feels like lunch, and I find it comforting and satisfying. I make them with Ezekiel bread or Dave's Killer Bread, some Tofurky slices (of course, you can use lean deli meat instead if that's your thing), tomato slices, avocado, red onion slices, raw spinach, and some mustard. This is another way to keep it simple and fill yourself up with good fuel for the rest of the day.

8. **DARK CHOCOLATE:** This is my go-to dessert—of course it would be something that doesn't require cooking. My issue with making your own dessert is that you end up with an entire pie or cake or a whole batch of cookies you'll be eating for days every time you walk through the kitchen. But with dark chocolate, I can eat two or three squares and I'm done. I buy dark chocolate that is around 85% cacao. If I can find individually wrapped chocolates with a high cacao percentage (Ghirardelli makes some), I'll keep those in

my purse or lunch bag. It's a good little treat that satisfies my need for something sweet following a meal, and it's actually good for me! If you're a milk chocolate eater, trust me, you can eventually get used to this much healthier substitute. Dark chocolate is what real chocolate is all about.

9. **EGGS:** I used to avoid eggs most of the time because I didn't approve of the way egg-laying hens are treated in factory-farm situations. I'd seen a lot about this in various documentaries and read about it in articles, and it bothered me enough that I decided eggs were off my list. But then . . . we got our own chickens! They are sweet and happy little pets, and we very much enjoy getting fresh eggs from them every day. This certainly isn't an option for everyone, but I know of lots of little family farms in our area that sell fresh eggs. Maybe you have neighbors near you who keep chickens and might sell you some of their eggs. Local farmers' markets also often have fresh local eggs (and while you're at it, you can fill up your bag with some fresh local seasonal fruits and veggies). Whatever way you can manage it, if you can get your hands on some fresh organic eggs (and you feel comfortable eating them), go for it! Eggs are an amazing source of complete protein and I use them in some of my favorite recipes.

10. **TOFU SCRAMBLE:** I am more of a savory breakfast person than a sweet breakfast person, and this is my all-time favorite thing to eat in the morning before I work out. I included a recipe for tofu scramble on page 230, but basically, I sauté onions, bell peppers, and spinach with a crumbled-up quarter of a block of firm or extra-firm tofu. When the tofu starts to brown, I top it all with some salsa, and voilà! It's great with toast for breakfast, but I would eat this for any meal (and have).

11. **SOUP:** This is another easy grab, whether you're looking for something quick at home or at a restaurant. Just look for vegetable-

EAT YOUR CHOCOLATE!

Dark chocolate is super high in antioxidants—it has as many antioxidants as tea! This is my personal favorite benefit, although I could probably write an entire chapter on the many benefits of dark chocolate. Just stick to Carrie's advice and choose the forms closest to how they occur in nature, which means choosing the least-processed forms (like raw cacao powder and cacao nibs), or dark chocolate bars with a minimum of 60% cacao (the higher the cacao percentage, the better).

based brothy soups, not cheesy or creamy soups, which have a gazillion calories and a ton of fat and pretty much zero nutritional value. Nothing beats a hot bowl of good veggie soup, in my opinion, and the more veggies, the better. If there are beans or chickpeas thrown in for good measure, sign me up! The only thing to watch out for is the sodium. Most packaged soups are loaded down with salt, so when you're picking some out from the store, don't forget to read those labels and compare (most major soup brands have lower-sodium versions of their popular flavors).

12. **BROCCOLI SLAW:** So versatile! From making "spaghetti" without the pasta to using it in salads or quiches or stir-fries (is it frys or fries? I'm never sure), broccoli slaw is a definite staple in my diet. Mike loves this as a spaghetti replacement—I just cook it in a pan with a little water until it softens but isn't mushy and top it with some low-sugar spaghetti sauce. I often add onions, garlic, and some "ground beef" (Boca is my go-to meatless ground beef substitute.) It's another quick-and-easy side, or can be a meal if you make enough of it.

What I Eat (and Don't Eat) When I'm Expecting

I was pregnant when I was writing much of this book, so I thought I would take a minute to tell you about how I eat when I'm expecting. I originally wanted to make a list of pregnancy foods for you to read about, but it's hard (or downright impossible, actually) for me to tell you what you should and shouldn't eat while you're pregnant. Every body and every pregnancy are completely different. All I can do is tell you a little bit about what I did.

To be honest, I don't really eat much differently when I'm pregnant than when I'm not. However, I'm a firm believer in those pesky pregnancy cravings—I do think they mean something, but I think a lot of us go about satisfying them in a less-than-healthy way. For instance, when I was pregnant with Isaiah, I wanted pumpkin . . . lots and lots of pumpkin. It would've been really easy for me to get my fix with some naughty (but certainly yummy) pumpkin pie or some sort of pumpkin-spiced sugary drink from the nearest coffee shop. Instead, I tried to think about *why* I might be craving pumpkin, because, let's be honest,

who craves that much pumpkin? It was weird.

So . . . I googled. As it turns out, pumpkin is an amazing source of beta-carotene, which gets converted to vitamin A in the body. It also has a decent amount of vitamin C and other good antioxidants, as well as lots of fiber to help keep me (and baby) full. So, I decided to believe my cravings. I needed pumpkin! But I didn't need sugar. I made myself a sort of pumpkin "pudding" with things like cocoa powder, maple syrup, vanilla, and even some protein powder for good measure. It did the trick to kill my pumpkin craving in a healthy way. (The recipe is on page 250.)

When I was pregnant with Jacob, I wasn't really craving pumpkin as much, so I figure that I must have been doing a better job of covering my nutritional bases. My point is, follow your body and whatever it is telling you to do, but try to think about the *why* behind it and make decisions accordingly. Try to find a way to satisfy even your weirdest cravings with something that nourishes you.

WHAT A NUTRITIONIST EATS

People often want to know what nutritionists eat. Here is an example of my typical day, including how I plan it out:

GOALS

Food: 1,600 calories (55% carbs, 15% fat, 30% protein)
Water: 80+ ounces
Focus: Keep my body healthy and strong by fueling it with real, powerful food. Maintain weight and energy.

SCHEDULE

5:30 a.m.: *Wake up and drink 16 ounces of water with lemon. Take probiotics.*
5:45 a.m.: *Two shots of espresso with Nutpods creamer*
7:30 a.m.: *Have breakfast and take vitamins (women's multi, buffered vitamin C, and Skin Savior) with 8 ounces of water*

Breakfast:

Note: I'm not a vegetarian, but I try to eat plant-based for about 80 percent of my meals. This means I will typically have some meat or seafood at dinner, but not usually any at other meals or in snacks.
Egg scramble made with 2 eggs, onions, bell peppers, and spinach, topped with ¼ avocado and 2 tablespoons salsa
2 Cuties (mandarin oranges)

10:00 a.m.: *Work out and drink 20 ounces of water*
10:30 a.m.: *Have a snack and drink 8 ounces of water*

Snack: Green Smoothie

In a high-speed blender, blend together:
2 cups dark greens (spinach, kale, spring greens, collard greens, beet greens, turnip greens, etc., or a mix)
1 cup unsweetened coconut milk or another nondairy milk
½ cup frozen mixed berries
½ frozen banana
1 scoop collagen peptides
2 tablespoons hemp seeds
1 teaspoon camu camu powder
Zest of ½ lemon
Juice of 1 lemon
Ice, when I want it frostier
1:30 p.m.: *Have lunch and drink 12 ounces of water*

Lunch: Fermented Salad

In a large bowl, combine the following, and toss until well mixed. Serve just after mixing.
2 cups mixed greens
½ cup cooked quinoa (or whatever grain I have already cooked)
¼ cup prepared hummus
¼ cup shredded carrot
¼ cup pickled onion
¼ cup sauerkraut

4:00 p.m.: Have a snack and drink 8 ounces of water

Snack: Adult Ants on a Log

2 tablespoons natural almond butter (no-sugar-added)

4 celery stalks

Pumpkin pie spice (no-sugar-added), for sprinkling

1/4 cup chopped unsweetened dried cherries or fresh blueberries

Spread the almond butter into the celery stalks, sprinkle with pumpkin pie spice, and press the dried cherries or fresh blueberries into the almond butter in a line along the whole length of the celery stalk.

7:00 p.m.: Have dinner and drink 8 ounces of water

Dinner: Asian Lettuce Wraps

Serves 4 to 6

For the sauce:

1/3 cup plus 1 tablespoon coconut aminos (a coconut-derived sauce similar to soy sauce)

3 tablespoons natural almond butter (no-sugar-added)

1 tablespoon raw honey or pure maple syrup

2 teaspoons toasted sesame oil

1/4 to 1/2 teaspoon sriracha

For the filling:

1 pound lean ground chicken or turkey breast (or, for a vegetarian version, 1 3/4 cups seasoned steamed lentils, 1 cup finely diced mushrooms, and 1/4 cup chopped walnuts)

1 red bell pepper, chopped

1 cup chopped purple cabbage

1 cup shredded carrots

1 cup finely chopped broccoli

8 scallions, chopped

1/2 cup celery

1/2 cup chopped jicama

For serving:

8 to 12 lettuce leaves (Bibb, Boston, and romaine work well), depending on how many people you are serving

1/2 cup unsalted cashew pieces

Toasted sesame seeds or hemp seeds

Make the sauce: Combine all the ingredients for the sauce in a blender and blend until smooth. Set aside.

Make the filling: In a large nonstick skillet, brown the ground chicken or turkey over medium-high heat, breaking up the pieces into medium-size chunks. (If you are making the vegetarian version, warm up the lentil mixture in the skillet.) Add the bell pepper, cabbage, carrots, broccoli, scallions, celery, jicama, and sauce to the meat or lentil mixture. Cook, stirring occasionally, for a few minutes, until the scallions and bell pepper are softened. Keep warm.

To serve: Spoon about 1/3 cup of the filling onto each lettuce leaf. Sprinkle chopped cashews and toasted sesame seeds over the top, fold or roll up the lettuce leaf, and enjoy!

Evening Snack

1 ounce of dark chocolate, or a glass of red wine 2 or 3 nights per week

Now that you know the foods I eat, you might be wondering about my typical day. Usually, I start the day with some water and black coffee. Then I have some kind of egg white or tofu scramble for breakfast, along with some Ezekiel toast and maybe some berries. Then I exercise. Lunch is typically a sandwich of some sort. For an afternoon snack, I might have a green smoothie or a protein bar. Dinner is more often than not a little piece of Gardein vegan "chicken" and a whole mess of roasted vegetables. Some dark chocolate or a glass of red wine to unwind later ends my eating day.

Make Healthy Swaps

For the second part of the Pleasure Principle, let's talk about my secret weapon for enjoying foods that taste indulgent but are much less naughty than they could be: the swap. I'll admit that I'm a disciplined eater. That is just the way I am. But I'm also all about treats. If you love pizza like I do, or macaroni and cheese, or a big burger piled high with toppings, or anything chocolate, you can make swaps to turn these favorite foods into good nutritional investments rather than empty-calorie overindulgences you regret later. Here's how I think about this.

There are some indulgences I don't care that much about, and some indulgences that I couldn't live without. For me, I'm not a big dessert person, but I have a hard time resisting salty, crunchy snacks. Maybe you're the opposite. Think about those indulgences you sometimes have but don't care that much about, and think about the indulgences you absolutely love.

For example, if you sometimes eat potato chips even though you wouldn't die without them, then maybe you won't care that much about skipping the potato chips when you're trying to eat healthier. But what if you really, really love ice cream, and life without ice cream would feel like living alone in the middle of a barren landscape with nobody to love you? In that case, you need to figure out a way that you can have ice cream sometimes without derailing your health goals. To you, ice cream is *important*, so if I or anybody else tells you "No more ice cream for you!" then you are not going to listen. You're going to have that ice cream. "No ice cream" isn't sustainable for you.

But you know what else isn't sustainable if you want to be healthy? Eating a pint of chocolate peanut butter ice cream every night. That's not good for anybody (except maybe the ice cream company). So how do you have your ice cream and eat it, too? Well, these are the kinds of things I might think of doing. They are all different versions of swapping:

> **BRAND SWAP.** Look for brands that have a lot less sugar and fat than the brand you usually buy. Some might not taste good to you. Some might taste just okay at first but taste better and better the more you get used to them. And then you might just hit on the perfect one, that is a compromise between all or nothing. One example might be Halo Top, a brand of ice cream that is much lower in fat, calories, and sugar. Do some experimenting. Have a taste test. The ice cream section of the store has a lot of choices, and the healthier, lower-fat, lower-sugar, or vegan choices are often all grouped together in one area.

> **SWAP THE DEFINITION.** You say ice cream, I say sorbet. Sorbet isn't exactly ice cream, but it's close. A creamy coconut sorbet with a tablespoon of chopped peanuts and a drizzle of chocolate syrup might totally ease your craving for ice cream, with a lot fewer calories and a lot less fat.

> **THE DIY SWAP.** If you're a kitchen whiz, you might want to make your own ice cream. Experiment with recipes that use better ingredients, like almond milk and real maple syrup and natural peanut butter, or frozen bananas and almond butter and raw cacao. For one example, see Cara's Nicecream recipe on page 278.

> › **SWAP THE BASE, KEEP THE FLAVORS.** Are there other foods that aren't ice cream but that might give you the same deep soul satisfaction? Again, if peanut butter and chocolate is your thing (and I'm just using this as an example), what if you stirred 2 tablespoons of peanut butter and 1 tablespoon of dark chocolate chips into your morning oatmeal? What if you mashed up that peanut butter and those chocolate chips with a banana? You could even freeze it before eating it. Or maybe you don't even need the ice cream part at all, and would be perfectly happy with a square or two of dark chocolate spread with some peanut butter. Take little bites and savor it as the wonderful treat that it is. You won't know what else might satisfy you until you try.

> › **SWAP BIG PORTIONS FOR SMALLER ONES.** If you've determined that ice cream and only ice cream is what you need, then think about your portion size. If it's way too easy for you to polish off the whole pint (or even half the pint) during one episode of your favorite show, remind yourself that a serving of ice cream is ½ cup. A half cup of ice cream is not a nutritional disaster. Measure it out, put it in a cute little bowl, and put the rest of the ice cream *away*. (Never eat out of the carton!) Then make it an occasion. Sit down and really focus on how good it is. Enjoy every bite. Experience that ice cream fully. You might find out that if you do this, you won't need it quite so often.

> › **DO IT LESS OFTEN.** Spread those ice cream indulgences apart. Try not to eat it every day. If you have any food every day, you miss out on a lot of variety and other foods you could try. I'll admit that I tend to eat the same things every day, but I only do this with healthy foods. I try to keep special foods like ice cream, cake, and cookies for special occasions only, like holidays or celebrations. The more you practice *not* having your favorite indulgence every day, the more natural that will feel, and the more special these treats will be when you do decide to eat them.

About Food Issues and Bad Eating Habits

Sometimes people mistake bad eating habits for a way to have fun or to feel pleasure. Really, these aren't the same at all. Pleasure is about feeling good, celebrating life, and enjoying yourself in your own skin and with the people you love. If you're using food like a drug, to muffle emotions or fill some hole in your life, that is not "pleasure." One of my favorite quotes is, "Food is the most widely abused antianxiety drug in America, and exercise is the most potent yet underutilized antidepressant."* I really believe this. I'm obviously not a therapist, let alone a weight loss coach, so I'm not going to give you any advice other than to say that if food has become a crutch for you, there are a lot of really great people who can help you get past that. Pleasure means enjoying food for what it is and how it can enhance your life, rather than relying on it for things it was never meant to do for you, like help you calm down or cheer you up or fix your loneliness or keep you from looking at things in your life that you don't want to see.

*Fitness author Bill Phillips said this.

Okay, enough with the ice cream. Another example that is probably even more relevant for my life (and maybe for yours) is a nice glass of wine. I love to have a glass of wine in the evening after dinner. I put the kids to bed and then it's my unwind time. Sometimes Mike and I relax on the couch and enjoy our wine while watching some mindless TV. That's one of those things that gives me a lot of pleasure, so I'm not going to give it up. But I have to make allowances for it, or those empty calories can really add up.

I make up for it by planning and balancing. On the nights when I plan to have a glass of wine, or when I just know I'm going to want one, then I'll choose not to have dessert. If there's a can't-miss dessert and I decide to enjoy it, then I won't have the wine. See what I mean? It's really about juggling and making decisions: What do you really want, and how can you make that fit into your plan? For example, if I know that later in the week, I'm going to a party or some big holiday celebration where there will be a ton of great food, I may skip the treats for a few days in preparation. Balancing in this way will make you proud of yourself later, but it won't make you feel deprived. You're fitting your pleasure into your life in a smart way that *you* control, instead of in a random, out-of-control way that might make you feel bad later (bad as in regretful, but also bad as in *oh no, now I have a food hangover!*). It's all about balance.

But finding that balance is tricky. I know it is. This is one of the reasons I keep a food journal—it helps me to balance what I'm doing now with what I know I'll be doing later. It's a planning tool for me. If I know I'll be going out for dinner that night, I know I better make good choices at breakfast, and I can map that all out. I like this kind of accountability, but I also like being able to plan out what I'm doing so it all fits together—a lot of discipline, a little indulgence.

So what foods require swaps in my book? There are certain foods I never eat, or almost never eat, because I don't like how they make me feel, and/or I know they aren't good for me. But that doesn't mean I deprive myself. Instead, I skip the things I don't care about and make healthy swaps for the things I love. This, again, is the Pleasure Principle at work—indulgence without all the health fallout.

10 FOODS I TRY TO AVOID AND THE HEALTHY SWAPS I USE INSTEAD

1. **MEAT:** Obviously. Again, that's just my choice and what's best for me, but I've never felt like my health or nutrition is lacking because I skip meat. I've never been told I'm protein deficient or anemic, and I've never felt like the fuel I've chosen for myself has let me down!

   HEALTHY SWAPS: Vegan protein sources that can stand in for meat. I've already mentioned many of these, such as Gardein "chicken" and Boca "ground beef." Other good options are tofu and beans or legumes like chickpeas or lentils.

2. **SUGARY DRINKS:** I don't drink my calories. Well . . . let me revise that statement. Other than red wine, I don't drink my calories. You can't see me right now, but I'm smiling as I write this because I wasn't always this way, and the thought makes me nostalgic. When I was just a kid, we always had bottles and cans of pop lying around (yes, I call it pop), and since I'm from the South, we drank sweet tea (although I'll give my mom credit for not completely overloading it with sugar). There was also a period in my life when I enjoyed those super-sweet whipped-cream-topped frappé mocha whatevers from the coffee shop . . . that is, until I learned that they basically have as many calories in them as an entire meal *should* have, as well as, like, two days' worth of sugar—no thanks!

   HEALTHY SWAP: Now that I'm a little older and a little wiser, I really only drink three things (other than smoothies, which are more like a meal to me):

   › Water . . . oh so much water . . .
   › Black coffee (coffee actually contains a lot of antioxidants so it can be good for you in moderation if it doesn't make you jittery—just don't "junk it up" with sugar and cream, although a bit of unsweetened almond milk is a nice addition sometimes)
   › Red wine, as I said before
   By not drinking my calories, I make sure I get to use food as my fuel, not useless liquid sugar that will only make my blood sugar spike and then later crash and won't do anything to fill me up.

3. **"DIET" DRINKS WITH ASPARTAME:** Just because I'm not drinking sugary drinks doesn't mean I'm advocating for drinking their diet counterparts. No way. Back in high school and pretty much all through college, I drank a diet pop with my breakfast every day, unless it was one of those sad mornings when I didn't have any in the fridge. When that happened, there was a good chance I was going to get a terrible headache. Once I started noticing this

pattern, I became concerned that the diet drinks (or my addiction to them) could actually be causing the headaches. I started looking things up on the internet and found a lot of disturbing information regarding aspartame, the most popular artificial sweetener in diet drinks. I'm no doctor and have done no laboratory studies of any kind on this subject, but I will tell you that once I stopped drinking things containing aspartame, those headaches were drastically reduced. Take that for what it's worth!

HEALTHY SWAP: Sparkling water has all the fizz and none of the bad stuff. The flavored ones are fine, as long as they don't contain sweetener or artificial sweetener.

4. **FRUIT JUICES:** Are you sensing a theme? I feel like I'm on a bit of a "what not to drink" tangent here, but fruit juice is a trap that so many people fall into, thinking they're being healthy when they could actually be sabotaging their entire diet. I like juice bars just as much as the next gal, but when I go in, I usually opt for juices that are green, with no or hardly any fruit. Maybe there's some apple or beet in there, but that's as far as I'll go. I definitely don't get the ones with mango or banana or any other high-sugar fruits. When you drink these super-sweet juices, you're getting all the concentrated sugar but none of the fiber from the whole fruits and/or vegetables. You're also getting a lot more fruit sugar in one serving of juice than you'd get in a serving of whole fruit. Fruit is good, but it's far better to eat it than to drink it.

   HEALTHY SWAP: The whole fruit instead of the fruit juice. The fruit is the package the juice came in, and I think it's all meant to go together.

5. **USELESS STARCHY FOODS:** I'm mainly talking about white bread and pretzels and pasta and sugary treats that have no nutritional value. Read those labels, people! If it doesn't have any protein or

OTHER BEVERAGE OPTIONS

For more variety in your beverages, I would also recommend herbal teas and kombucha, which is a fermented tea drink that tastes a little like a mild fruity vinegar (an acquired taste, maybe, but many people love it and it has probiotics in it, which are good for healthy digestion).

---

fiber or (hopefully good) fats, chances are, it's just plain pointless. Pure starch won't do anything to fill you up or keep you going, and it could make you even hungrier.

HEALTHY SWAP: If I'm going to have grain, I make sure it's the whole grain. I swap Ezekiel bread for white bread, and roasted chickpeas or whole-grain crackers for pretzels, and when it comes to pasta, I'm most likely to use broccoli slaw instead. If you're going to have pasta, there are many different varieties out there made from whole grains like quinoa or brown rice, and many are also gluten-free (if that matters to you). I don't know what on earth it is we're doing to our food that is making so many people gluten-intolerant. Some people say that nobody can easily digest gluten very well. If you don't seem to have a problem with gluten, then choosing to eat it is up to you, of course. I try to avoid it most of the time, just because it seems to me that anything causing that many health problems for that many people must not be a good thing to eat all the time.

ABOUT GLUTEN

Gluten, one of the main proteins in wheat and similar grains, can be inflammatory for some people, and gluten-filled products also tend to be highly processed. In my family, we try to be mostly naturally gluten-free. In other words, we eat foods that simply do not naturally contain gluten, such as potatoes, or flours made from almonds or chickpeas (pasta made with chickpea flour is great). An added bonus: All these foods are naturally more nutritionally dense than foods with processed wheat flour. But sprouted whole grains, which can be found in some of the breads mentioned in this book, have great nutrients to offer. Sprouting the grains makes the vitamins and minerals more bioavailable (ready for your body to use) and breaks down their starches, making them easier to digest. If you do not have celiac disease and you don't think gluten is a problem for you, try sprouted grains to see how you tolerate them.

6. **EGGPLANT:** I have absolutely no nutritional reasoning behind never wanting to eat this food. I just can't stand eggplant! We all have that one food that makes us gag, and this is mine.

    HEALTHY SWAP: Literally any other vegetable on the planet.

7. **FAST FOOD:** This is one of my "*almost* never" foods, because let's face it, sometimes you're in a bind and you've got to grab *something . . . anything*, or else you'll end up a hangry mess and nobody will want to deal with you (been there).

    HEALTHY SWAP: Of all the fast-food options out there, Subway is probably my favorite because you can find one almost anywhere and you can get a bunch of fresh veggies on whole-grain bread, or just a salad. They even have veggie "patties" and avocado. Some other fast-food restaurants also have salads with good ingredients, and some even have soup. I always do my best to pack my lunch and snacks so I don't have to be put in the position of caving in to the fast-food drive-thru. Generally, every purse, backpack, desk drawer, suitcase, and even my car contains some sort of bar or healthy snack that can, hopefully, tide me over until I get home. Be prepared!

8. **CHIPS:** Chips are a deep, dark rabbit hole that will suck you in until you're basically sticking your head in the bag trying to get those last salty greasy tiny little crumbs into your mouth. I'm always sad when I read the serving size and the nutritional information for chips (potato and corn alike). So many calories and so much fat for so few chips! To me, it's just not worth it, especially because I know that once I start, I'll eat two or three servings at least. These are not a safe food for me!

   HEALTHY SWAP: Sometimes I enjoy some nacho- or ranch-flavored kale chips, or maybe some Mary's Gone Crackers gluten-free seed crackers, if I just have to get my crunchy-snack fix. Also, some roasted chickpeas might satisfy that salty/crunchy craving.

9. **CANDY:** Other than my little bits of super-dark chocolate, I just don't do candy. It's really not my thing, but even if it were, it's nothing but sugar. It's useless. I would rather eat a big plate of real food than a little piece of candy.

   HEALTHY SWAP: A little bit of 85% cacao dark chocolate. That's all I need.

10. **FRIED FOOD:** This is another one that should fall under that *"almost never"* category, because let's be honest—even dirt would taste good if you deep-fried it! But my brain knows that this is definitely

A Simple Plan to Lose Weight and Get Healthier

We all get off track every once in a while ... myself included. I know life throws us all curveballs, and sometimes we find ourselves headed down a path that we know isn't the best for us. Right now, I want to tell you my strategy for getting back on the "fitness train." My number one piece of advice, especially if you have a long way to go from "right now" to "super healthy," is to take it one step at a time. I go through this every year after the holiday season. If I've gone a little overboard and I'm not feeling great, I tell myself, *Okay, Carrie, you've had your fun. It's time to get back on the horse.* But I don't put so much pressure on myself that it feels intimidating and stressful. You don't have to do it all at once or completely overhaul your entire life in one day.

When trying to lose weight, experts say that what you eat can be more critical than how much you exercise* (even though exercise has many other significant benefits). Vigorous exercise can have the effect of making you hungrier, so it makes sense to get your eating in order. You have to be ready to handle that. Make a plan for what you're going to do. Set goals and work toward them. Maybe your goals are very specific, like a calorie count and an organized walking program. Maybe they're simpler, like eating less sugar and more vegetables and trying to move around more. Whatever your goals are, be accountable to yourself about what you're doing, and track your progress. As you begin to get stronger and feel better and lose extra weight that you are tired of carrying around, you'll get more and more motivated. It's a great feeling to notice your own progress.

a cooking method people should avoid. So much grease. So much fat. So unnecessary. Whenever I eat french fries or tempura or any other fried or fritter-type food, I enjoy it for a second and then I *feel* gross . . . and the next morning, I swear my body is just plain angry with me! It might seem right in the moment, but let's all do ourselves a favor and choose better.

Food is step one. Start eating more natural whole foods, especially vegetables. Then start making healthy swaps so you're eating less sugar and fat, and fewer empty calories. Little by little, make shifts that feel doable to you. Next, start walking, if you haven't been exercising. Or just try to move more. As you start to feel better and your eating habits improve, you could add some weights. Adjust as you go, gradually adopting more positive changes as you get stronger and figure it out. But keep it personal to you. This is about *you*, not anybody else.

The stronger you get and the better you feel, the more you can challenge yourself. Walk farther, or even run. Lift heavier weights. Whatever feels right to you. Always continue to eat good food to fuel whatever you're doing, rather than junk that will go against your plan. Keep it all in sync—good food here, more movement there—and you will get the best results. Getting healthy is a big picture. It's never about just one thing. Shift your big picture in manageable ways, and your health and weight will shift, too.

Many studies have demonstrated that what you eat is more influential than exercise for weight loss specifically. Here are a couple of articles that mention some of them: "Exercise or Diet? One Is More Important for Weight Loss," https://www.huffpost.com/entry/diet-or-exercise-for-weight-loss_n_56b39481e4b08069c7a660d0; and "To Lose Weight, Eating Less Is Far More Important Than Exercising More," https://www.nytimes.com/2015/06/16/upshot/to-lose-weight-eating-less-is-far-more-important-than-exercising-more.html.

HEALTHY SWAP: Roast it, sauté it, or bake it. Anything you might fry will be delicious cooked in these other ways, and so much better for you. And no food hangover!

Be Accountable

The final part of the Pleasure Principle is being accountable. I do this in a couple of different ways:

1. **TRACKING.** I track what I eat, and I count calories. I'm a numbers person, so I enjoy it. If that's not you, and you'd rather keep track of what you're eating in your head and make conscious decisions instead of eating compulsively, then more power to you! I do encourage tracking, though, at least in the beginning, because most people aren't fully aware of what they're actually eating and what nutrients or ingredients their meals and snacks contain. I think tracking really helps with accountability.

2. **MY JOURNAL.** As I've told you, I plan out what I'm going to eat so I can balance indulgences with more disciplined choices. I keep it all in my journal. (For an example of how I keep track of things, see Appendix 1 on page 313.) My journal is like my accountability partner because I know that if I eat something, I'll have to write it down and face the music. Sometimes that makes me change my mind about a less-than-healthy choice before I make it. I also have a confession: I buy these fun little stickers to put in my journal for when I do a good job. Picture gold stars or cute animals or little cupcake stickers—ironic that I sometimes give myself a cupcake sticker for not eating a real cupcake. Sometimes Isaiah asks, "Mommy, can I have some stickers?" and I say, "Umm . . . sorry, I think we're fresh out of stickers!" because I need them for my journal. I've learned to buy extra stickers—some for him, some for me!

3. **ACCOUNTABILITY PARTNERS.** Beyond my journal, my husband is a great accountability partner. We are both committed to healthy eating, and we encourage each other to make good choices. Find a

family member or friend who is trying to be healthy, too, and agree to keep each other accountable. You could even compare notes on your progress at the end of each week—knowing someone else is looking might result in better decisions.

4. **A DIETITIAN OR NUTRITIONIST.** I have Cara to consult when I need a professional accountability partner. If you need some professional help, meet with a dietitian or nutritionist to help you make a plan. Health coaches can also hold you accountable with daily or weekly calls, and some counselors even specialize in teaching you ways to be more responsible for your food choices. There is a lot of professional help out there, so I encourage you to find what you need.

your food philosophy

What is *your* food philosophy? Think about what's important to you.

1. What do you do to make good food choices? Do you have any tricks that work?
2. What happens when you don't make good food choices? What are your triggers?
3. Make a list of all the reasons you want to eat better.
4. What food principles do you want to follow, or what kind of eating plan works for you?
5. Write down your plan! (See Appendix 1 on page 313.)

5. **THERE'S AN APP FOR THAT.** So many health apps! I love that so much technology is now health-focused. I use an app called MyFitnessPal because I like how it figures out all my fat, carbs, protein, fiber, and sugar based on the foods I enter. I can look over what I ate and see things like, "Oh, that was a carb-heavy breakfast. I'll go light on the carbs at lunch." I can also track my exercise and see my progress on graphs, but I also use the Fitbit app for that purpose. Apps aren't for everyone. You might prefer just writing it all down. If that helps you, go for it, or find an app you love. As I've mentioned, I use MyFitnessPal *and* I copy everything that I've eaten down into my journal. But that's just me.

6. **THE SCALE?** I really do think that you have to take that number on the scale with a grain of salt. The scale can be a tool to track weight loss, for sure, but it can't tell you how much of that weight is fat vs. muscle. Do I step on the scale from time to time? Of course I do. But I rely more on how I feel in my own skin (and in my own jeans) to assess the progress I'm making.

7. **HONESTY.** This might be the most important part of accountability. It's very easy to look the other way from your own behavior, believe it or not. Don't kid yourself. Consciously acknowledging what you are eating will help you find your balance between discipline and pleasure. I rarely eat a meal or a snack without deciding that it is exactly what I want to eat for my life—whether it's something really healthy that will make me feel good and fuel my day, or something more indulgent that I have planned for.

And there you have it—my eating philosophy. Eat mostly foods God made. Make healthy swaps so you can still enjoy your favorite indulgences and plan out your splurges, balancing them with good choices. Be accountable by recognizing and being honest about what you are actually eating.

9

FOREVER CHANGED

*How to Love Food and
Stay Healthy (with Recipes!)*

I'm not a fancy cook, but I'm a fast cook. As you know, I like to keep it simple. Here's what I might make for myself on a typical day:

> **BREAKFAST:** When I'm making my egg white omelet or tofu scramble, I'll add extra veggies depending on the time I have. Worst case, I'll just throw in a handful of spinach. If I have extra time the night before or in the morning, I'll chop up a bunch of onions and peppers, and I'll add those. I also usually keep quiche in the refrigerator because Mike and I both like it and it's convenient for any meal of the day. I might have a slice of that for breakfast with a piece of toast. Or I might have overnight oats, if I have time to assemble them the night before.

> **LUNCH:** A sandwich on Ezekiel bread (never white bread), piled high with avocado, onions, tomatoes, lettuce, and some vegetarian sandwich "meat," like Yves Veggie Cuisine or Tofurky, for protein. If I have a little more time, I might whip up a stir-fry. If I'm in a real hurry, I'll just make a quick smoothie or microwave a burrito. Sweet Earth burritos are my favorite, and they have a lot of protein.

> **SNACK:** Most of the time, I'll have a protein bar for a snack, or else I'll have roasted chickpeas or fava beans. I'm not going to tell you that you have to roast your own chickpeas (of course you can if you want to). You can find good ones in the store. I might also have a smoothie as my snack, and I make mine pretty much the same every time (see page 238).

> **DINNER:** This meal usually involves roasted vegetables and a protein. The great thing about basing our dinner on simple roasted veggies is that it's easier to make dinner for both Mike and me. We both get the same vegetable sides, but I usually add some sort of vegan protein for me and bake some salmon for him, or else he'll fix some sort of meat for himself on the grill. For other quick dinner options, I might make us a pizza on a tortilla, or cheese quesadillas with black beans, both using veggie cheese (I like Daiya brand), or a stir-fry with vegetables over some brown rice.

My Take on Packaged Foods

Back in the day, people had more time to cook food from scratch. But today, cooking every meal from scratch just isn't realistic for most of us. Back before I had my sweet babies, I used to think I would make my own baby food. I even bought all the washable, reusable storage pouches and accessories to do so. Spoiler alert: I never made my own baby food. The truth is, there are plenty of healthy packaged food options out there. It's not like the old days of TV dinners with a ton of salt. There are microwave burritos and frozen meals you can buy that are full of nutritious ingredients, perfect for a busy evening when you don't have time to cook. Having healthy packaged options may also prevent you from swinging by the fast-food drive-thru on your way home, which in my book is a major win. "Healthy packaged food" may sound like a contradiction, but like so many things in modern life, it's a trade-off. When you're busy, you don't always have time to cook, and sometimes you just don't feel like cooking. You're much more likely to stick with your healthy eating plan if it's easy to sustain. So cook what you can, when you can, and have good options on hand for when you can't.

In this chapter, I share my favorite breakfast, lunch, snack, dinner, and dessert recipes—every one of them is a favorite food I transformed using healthy swaps—and my nutritionist, Cara, will share some of her healthy favorites, too. We'll also both chime in with some cooking tips for speed and simplicity, so you never have to spend more time in the kitchen than is necessary. Cara has useful nutritional info and healthy food facts throughout this chapter, so look out for these opportunities to increase your nutrition knowledge. That can only be a good thing!

I'm not doing anything fancy here, so don't look for recipes with exotic ingredients or gourmet cooking techniques! Healthy versions of simple foods are what I do. I have my go-to list of easy, delicious meals that I make over and over again. If it ain't broke, don't fix it, is what I say. If a recipe has more than ten ingredients, I am not making it. If it involves too many steps or is going to take me forever to make it, forget it. Every time I try a complicated recipe, I can't help thinking, *Why did I just waste all this time?* It's usually no better than something simple, and I don't think it should take 45 minutes to prep a meal, plus however long it takes to cook it. Vegetables, healthy carbs, protein. That's all you need in a meal.

Volume Eating with Veggies

I love those pictures that show you what 1,700 calories of different foods look like. One photo might show a plate with a hamburger, some french fries, and a shake—a whole day's worth of calories you probably ate in one quick meal in your car as you were headed to soccer practice. No thanks! The next plate will be piled high with healthy foods—a huge salad, roasted veggies, beans, rice, fruit, and tofu or vegan "chicken"—you have to eat a whole lot of plant food to match those 1,700 calories! This is how I like to eat because ... well, I like to eat! I want to feel full and satisfied after a meal, and a great, healthy way to do this is by loading up on veggies. I roast vegetables like nobody's business. When my mom, sister, and friends come over and taste my roasted veggies, they ask me, "What did you do? How are these so good?" Honestly, I just toss a bunch of random veggies in a bowl with some olive oil, sprinkle on some Mrs. Dash, and put it all in the oven. That's it. It's easy, and you can eat so much! Just pick your protein to go with it.

The Tools in My Kitchen

I don't use a ton of tools—no fancy gadgets—but these are the basic items that I rely on in my kitchen. Anyone can cook, as long as they have these basics. At the same time, the more you cook, the more you'll develop your own unique cooking style and your list of essential cooking tools for your journey to good health.

› **FOOD SCALE:** Serving sizes are just plain hard to figure out. Different foods are labeled in different ways, and there's nothing more frustrating than trying to figure out how many grams or ounces something is when you're logging your meals. A food scale can help take some of the guesswork out of the equation. It doesn't have to be complicated. I ordered a cheap digital scale from Amazon for around $15.

› **A STURDY ROASTING PAN OR BAKING SHEET:** Since I roast vegetables on a regular basis, I need a good sturdy vessel for my veggies.

› **A GOOD KNIFE AND CUTTING BOARD:** I use these constantly. At least one night a week after the kids have gone to bed, I'll spend a few minutes chopping vegetables to have them ready for the week. I'll always chop up bell peppers and onions because I use them so often in my stir-fries, tofu scrambles, and omelets, among other things. If I can't find prechopped broccoli and cauliflower at the grocery store, I'll buy heads of those as well and chop them up at night to save time.

› **A HIGH-QUALITY BLENDER:** I love making smoothies, but I absolutely can't stand it when my smoothies are full of chunks and seeds and pieces of ice that the blender couldn't take care of. I use a Vitamix—I know these are expensive, but there are many other options out there, so do some research and ask friends for brands they like. If you're planning on making lots of soups and smoothies yourself, I would definitely invest in a good, high-powered blender. I've had mine for years and it gets used *a lot*.

› **OLIVE OIL MISTER/SPRAYER:** I use a lot of extra virgin olive oil (EVOO), but it's easy to use way too much when I'm pouring it out of the bottle. I could end up drowning my food in oil without realizing it. An olive oil sprayer enables me to lightly coat the outside of my veggies before I roast them or to lightly spray some EVOO onto my salad without overdoing it. You can also buy olive oil sprays at the grocery store. Just be sure to read the label and avoid anything that contains strange chemicals, which you really don't want to be spraying onto your food along with your EVOO.

› **SAUTÉ PAN OR SKILLET:** My sauté pan is essential because cooking with it is so quick, and so simple! I envy people who can whip up casseroles and healthy muffins and whatnot at the drop of a hat, but as you've gathered by this point, that's just not me. This is why I mostly roast and sauté everything. I feel like this keeps my food in as close to a natural state as possible. A little heat plus a little oil is perfection, in my opinion!

› **APPLE PEELER/CORER/SLICER:** My mother-in-law bought me this gadget a couple of years ago, and now I'm not sure I could live without it. The one I have is called the Johnny Apple Peeler (there are several versions of this device). It looks kind of crazy, but you stick the apple on some spikes at the end of a metal rod, start cranking the handle, and, like magic, it cores, peels, and slices your apple into spirals. Isaiah loves apples and so do I! I'll either eat an apple with some raw almonds for a snack, or I'll make baked apples drizzled with a little maple syrup and sprinkled with some cinnamon for a healthy dessert (see page 248). This is one of those kitchen tools I never knew I needed, but I'm so glad I have it. Thanks, Karen!

> › **STRAINER:** Don't forget to scrub and rinse your fruits and veggies before you eat them—a colander makes this a lot easier. I've seen some scary reports about pesticides on our foods and what they could be doing to our (and our children's) bodies and minds. I know that it's not possible or affordable for most of us to buy organic produce all the time. So make sure to rinse your produce, especially if you're not buying organic!

> › **STORAGE CONTAINERS:** These are required for packing healthy options to take with you to work. Plan ahead and prep your meals a few days in advance, or if you're making a healthy dinner, simply make double and store the rest for a future grab-and-go meal. Just make sure your containers are microwavable, BPA-free, and leakproof! And, of course, you might want to grab a reusable (or even freezable) lunch tote to carry those healthy lunches in.

> › **SPIRALIZER:** This one is nice to have, but it's not absolutely necessary, in my opinion (my bestie, Ivey, would disagree . . . she uses hers pretty much on a daily basis). I eat lots of zucchini noodles and broccoli slaw, but I can often find these veggies already noodle-ized or shredded at the grocery store. If you have the time and energy to spare, go ahead and go for a spiralizer. If not, be like me and buy straight from the grocery store.

A note on the recipes in this book: The recipes in this book are so customizable and adaptable that the nutritional information won't always be exact—much depends on how you vary the recipes and what ingredients you choose. Please keep this in mind and consider the nutritional information in this book to be a general baseline only.

MY GO-TO BREAKFAST RECIPES

Quick Tofu Scramble

Prep time: 12 minutes
Total time: 15 minutes

Serves 1

1 tablespoon olive oil
½ cup diced yellow onion
½ cup diced bell
    pepper (any color, or a
    combination)
1 cup crumbled or finely
    diced firm or extra-firm
    tofu (about ¼ block)
1 cup tightly packed spinach
    (about 2 ounces)
1½ teaspoons Mrs. Dash
    chipotle seasoning, or any
    other spicy seasoning or
    sauce, such as red pepper
    flakes or chipotle powder,
    or to taste
2 tablespoons any salsa you
    like (optional)
Toast or a light English
    muffin, for serving

My favorite breakfast of all time is tofu scramble. It's simple and quick, it has lots of protein, and it holds me over until lunch. To make this for two people, just double the recipe. As a warning—this does make quite a bit of food, so be prepared to be filled up!

I originally started playing around with this recipe to find a replacement for scrambled eggs. Eggs are a staple in so many people's breakfasts, but as I said before, I have a bit of a problem with most commercially produced eggs. My solution was simple: tofu. Tofu is versatile, and it can become pretty much whatever you want it to be, depending on how you prepare it.

You can make this recipe your own by varying the ingredients. I love chopped onion and bell pepper and spinach in my scramble, but you can throw in any other veggies you might have in the fridge in addition to these, or instead of them. I've used mushrooms or leftover broccoli or Brussels sprouts from dinner the night before. It all just adds to the veggie goodness!

Note: If you make this in a nonstick pan, you won't need to use as much oil.

NUTRITION FACTS
(per serving)

320	calories
21.5 g	fat
14 g	carbs
17 g	protein
5 g	fiber
10 g	sugar

In a medium skillet, heat the oil over medium heat until it starts to shimmer, then add the onion and bell peppers and sauté until they are soft. Reduce the heat to medium-low, add the tofu, and cook, stirring occasionally, until the tofu begins to brown a bit. Add the spinach and Mrs. Dash and cook, stirring, until the spinach is just wilted, 2 to 3 minutes. Put the scramble on a plate and top with the salsa (if using). Enjoy with some sprouted grain toast (such as Ezekiel) or a light English muffin on the side.

Carrie and Mike's Favorite Crustless Quiche

Prep time: 30 minutes
Total time: 1 hour

Serves 8

1 to 2 tablespoons olive oil
1 medium yellow onion, diced
2 cups chopped mushrooms (any kind)
1 medium bell pepper (any color), diced
1½ cups chopped broccoli, broccoli slaw, or shaved Brussels sprouts
2 large eggs
3 egg whites (about ½ cup)
1 cup grated fat-free or reduced-fat cheddar cheese or cheese blend of your choice
1 (3.5-ounce) container Athenos reduced-fat feta cheese
1 tablespoon Mrs. Dash chipotle seasoning or other spicy seasoning or sauce, such as red pepper flakes, chipotle powder, or sriracha, to taste (sometimes I add a few shakes of turmeric—this is optional, so season it to your taste)

Quiche is a crowd-pleaser. The problem with most quiches is that they're usually super crusty, super cheesy, and super not-good-for-you! But . . . they sure are great to have on hand, so I started playing around with traditional quiche recipes, swapping out ingredients and rethinking what might make this timeless treat healthier.

My first step was to nix the crust. Step two was to (you guessed it!) add more veggies. And I thought maybe I could cut down the fat without cutting down the protein by adding some egg whites. So, here's what I came up with.

This is the quiche I make most often, now that we have our own chickens and get our eggs humanely. As you'll see, though, it's more veggies than eggs. Mike and I both enjoy this for breakfast, but really, it's good for breakfast, lunch, dinner, or a snack. It's always in our refrigerator for a quick grab, and it's also good for company.

1. Preheat the oven to 350°F.

2. In a large skillet, heat the olive oil over medium heat. Add the onion and cook, stirring, until translucent, about 5 minutes. Throw in the mushrooms, bell pepper, and broccoli and cook, stirring often, until the vegetables are tender, 7 to 10 minutes.

½ teaspoon sea salt
¼ teaspoon black pepper
Giant handful of spinach
Cooking spray
Olive oil spray
2 tablespoons bread crumbs
(I like gluten-free)

NUTRITION FACTS
(per serving)

144	calories
7 g	fat
7.5 g	carbs
12 g	protein
2 g	fiber
3.75 g	sugar

3. While the veggies cook, put the eggs and egg whites in a bowl and mix with a fork until they are fully combined. Stir in the cheddar and feta and set aside.

4. When the veggies are soft, season with the Mrs. Dash, sea salt, and black pepper. Add the spinach and stir until it's wilted. Turn off the heat and let the veggie mixture cool while you prepare the "crust."

5. Spray a glass pie dish lightly with cooking spray, then coat it lightly with olive oil spray. Shake the bread crumbs over the bottom and then shake and swirl the pie dish until the crumbs cover the bottom evenly.

6. Add the veggie mixture to the egg-cheese mixture and stir to combine, then pour it all into the prepared pie dish.

7. Bake the quiche for about 30 minutes, until it is firm in the center. (The time really depends on the oven—I have a convection oven, so it's faster.) Serve warm, or let the quiche cool for 10 to 15 minutes, cover it, and store it in the refrigerator to enjoy later. It should keep for up to two days.

Any-Flavor Overnight Oats

Prep time: 5 minutes
Total time: 2 to 12 hours

Serves 1

½ cup rolled oats
¾ cup unsweetened vanilla almond milk
½ small apple or peach, cored or pitted and chopped into small pieces
¼ cup blueberries
½ teaspoon pure vanilla extract, or to taste
Dash of apple pie spice (pumpkin pie spice or ground cinnamon are fine alternatives)
1 tablespoon real maple syrup
2 tablespoons sliced or slivered almonds

A few years ago, I noticed that overnight oats were becoming "a thing." I think it's because so many people are looking for easy, healthy, grab-and-go breakfast ideas. Oatmeal has been a staple on breakfast tables for generations—maybe Grandma knew what she was talking about!

Prepare this dish the night before you want to eat it. By morning it will be the perfect texture. It's fun to try different combinations of fruit and nuts in your overnight oats. I like apples and peaches because they stay a little crisp as they soak, but you could try other berries, pears, maybe a few raisins, or whatever fruit you like. Frozen fruit works, too, because by morning, it has defrosted. Sometimes in the winter, I'll add ¼ cup pumpkin puree, shake on some pumpkin pie spice, and use pecans instead of almonds. It's like having pumpkin pie for breakfast!

1. In a container with a lid (like a mason jar), mix together the oats, milk, apple, blueberries, vanilla, and apple pie spice. (You could also mix this in a bowl first, then transfer to a container with a lid, if that's easier for you.) Cover and refrigerate overnight.

419	calories
16 g	fat
49 g	carbs
12 g	protein
9 g	fiber
23 g	sugar

2. The next morning, drizzle the maple syrup over the top and sprinkle with the almonds. Enjoy this cold, right out of the jar, or warm it in the microwave.

Sweet and Salty!

Sugar and salt are acquired tastes, and when you cut back on them, you eventually lose your taste for them. Since I don't typically use much of these in my food (in the name of health) and these recipes are written the way I make them, to you they may taste like they need more salt or sweetener. As you get used to cutting back on these, your palate will adjust and you will become satisfied with much less salt and sugar, but at first, if you need to add more salt or sweetener to any of these recipes, go ahead. I recommend using natural sea salt because of the minerals it contains, and only sweetening with natural sweeteners like maple syrup. Every little upgrade makes a difference for your health.

My Favorite Lunch: Quick-and-Easy 10-Minute Stir-Fry

Prep time: 10 minutes
Total time: 10 minutes

Serves 1 as a main dish or 2 as a side dish

1 serving Gardein Beefless Tips (10 pieces) or your favorite lean protein
Olive oil spray (optional)
¼ cup chopped yellow onion
1 (6-ounce) bag or ½ (12-ounce) bag fresh or frozen vegetable stir-fry mix (any type—I like the one with broccoli, broccoli slaw, and snap peas)
1 cup cooked brown rice (if you don't want to make it from scratch, use Minute Ready to Serve brown rice)
Bragg Liquid Aminos or low-sodium soy sauce
Any other seasonings you like, such as garlic powder, teriyaki sauce, Chinese five-spice powder, or chili sauce

As you well know, I love veggies. What better way to incorporate all kinds of veggies into your diet than a stir-fry? I'm all about getting more food for my calories, and this dish is great because it's super filling and all those veggies mean you get to eat a lot of it. It's one of my favorite lunches, especially after a good long workout.

1. In a small pan, lightly sauté the Beefless Tips over medium heat according to the package instructions, or cook your favorite protein in a bit of olive oil spray—you won't need to use much if you use a nonstick pan. When the protein is almost cooked through, add the onion and cook until it is soft, 4 to 5 minutes.

2. Meanwhile, in a large saucepan, combine the veggies and ¼ cup water. Bring the water to a simmer over medium heat, then cover and cook until tender, about 3 minutes. Turn off the heat.

488 calories
9 g fat
68 g carbs
29 g protein
8 g fiber
7 g sugar

3. Add the protein-onion mixture to the pan with the veggies, then add the rice. Stir in the liquid aminos and any other seasonings you like and cook over low heat until the rice is warmed through. Serve immediately.

what mike likes You could make this with 4 to 6 ounces chicken; just cook it exactly as you would cook the Beefless Tips. Or prepare it as a side dish and serve it with grilled salmon.

SNACK IDEAS

Most of the snack recipes in this chapter come from Cara (those start on page 251). They are all quick and easy, but if you have even less time than that, go for bars (see pages 50–51 for my favorite kinds) or fresh fruit. An apple and a handful of almonds is about as quick as it gets. The only thing I actually make for a snack is a smoothie. Here's my recipe.

Carrie's Purple Power Smoothie

Prep time: 5 minutes
Total time: 5 minutes

Serves 1 as a meal replacement or 2 as a snack

1 cup unsweetened vanilla almond milk
½ cup beet juice
1 cup mixed berries (blueberries, strawberries, and raspberries—I use frozen, but fresh would work, too)
1 tablespoon cacao nibs (optional)
1½ teaspoons MCT oil (optional)
Handful of spinach or kale
1 scoop protein powder
Handful of ice

This is one of my go-to smoothies. If I'm making extra for Isaiah, I skip the beet juice, because he hates beet juice. Also, I'll add greens (like a handful of spinach or kale) if I have them in the fridge. But if I don't happen to have any, I won't worry about it.

If I'm making this for my afternoon snack, I'll probably only use half the cacao nibs (little pieces of the cocoa bean without any sugar—just pure chocolate goodness), or I'll skip them altogether. I'll do the same for the MCT (medium-chain triglyceride) oil. Not everybody likes it, but you might want to try it to see how it makes you feel. You can find it in most health food stores, the health food aisle of your grocery store, or online. Both the cacao nibs and the MCT oil are calorie-dense additions, but with the good kind of fat that helps you burn more fat. If this is going to be my entire lunch or I'm feeling like I just need some extra workout fuel, I'll usually add them.

As for the protein powder, I always include that, but I may vary how many scoops I use. There are a lot of good protein powders out there. I like the vegan ones, of course. Orgain is good, as is Garden of Life brand (Mike likes this one, too).

NUTRITION FACTS
(per snack-size serving)

173	calories
7 g	fat
11 g	carbs
14 g	protein
4 g	fiber
7.5 g	sugar

The point is that this smoothie is adaptable. If you have greens, throw in greens. You can use any berries, or even some other lower-sugar fruit instead. You could use a little unsweetened cocoa powder or cinnamon if you want to. Any healthy additions can help power up your afternoon.

Combine all the ingredients in a blender and blend until completely smooth. Sip and savor the nutrient density!

DINNER AT MY HOUSE

Carrie's Tortilla Pizza

Prep time: 20 minutes
(including chopping veggies)
or 5 minutes (if the veggies
are prechopped)
Total time: 20 to 35 minutes

Serves 1

Olive oil spray
1 sturdy whole-grain tortilla
(I like Ezekiel tortillas),
about 8 inches in diameter
¼ cup prepared spaghetti
sauce or marinara sauce
Handful of spinach

OPTIONAL TOPPINGS
(Choose based on your own
tastes, but be careful not
to overload your crust with
tomatoes, mushrooms, and
other "wet" toppings, or
your tortilla crust will get
soggy)
4 thin slices fresh tomato,
patted dry
2 tablespoons chopped
onion
2 tablespoons chopped bell
pepper
2 tablespoons chopped or
thinly sliced mushroom

Pizza is the best. I mean, who doesn't love it? If I could get away with eating it for every meal, I probably would. (Mike would say the same thing.) I'd eat it for breakfast, lunch, dinner, and . . . maybe throw one in for a snack somewhere, too! But of course, the "pizza diet" isn't a thing, and ordering it even semi-regularly isn't exactly part of a healthy lifestyle. So, I wanted to find a guilt-free way to enjoy one of the world's most beloved (and naughty) foods. I make my tortilla pizza a lot because everybody in my family likes it. This recipe makes one personal-size pizza, but you can make one for each person in your family so everyone can choose their own toppings. Personally, I pile on the veggies. Mike likes meat and some veggies on his. Isaiah likes meat and cheese (I slip in veggies whenever I can, though). This is a fun one for kids to get in on making as well. Let them choose their toppings and assemble their own pizza. I find that it's often easier to get a child to eat something they had a hand in making.

1. Preheat the oven to 425°F. Lightly spray a baking sheet or pizza pan with a little olive oil.

2. Put the tortilla on the prepared baking sheet. Spread the spaghetti sauce over the tortilla. Spread the spinach out evenly over the sauce. Sprinkle the veggie toppings of your choice evenly over the

1 tablespoon chopped or sliced pitted olives

2 teaspoons capers

2 slices vegan "meat" (such as Tofurky or Yves Veggie Cuisine) or other lean meat of your choice

¼ cup shredded vegan cheese (such as Daiya) or shredded cheese of your choice

Favorite Italian seasoning (garlic powder, Mrs. Dash Italian seasoning, basil, etc.)

NUTRITION FACTS

(per serving)

366 **calories**

14.5 g **fat**

33 g **carbs**

29 g **protein**

16 g **fiber**

5 g **sugar**

spinach. Tear up the "meat" and spread it over the veggies. Sprinkle the cheese over the top and shake some seasoning over the whole thing.

3. Pop the pizza in the oven and bake for about 15 minutes, rotating the pan once halfway through. The pizza is done when the edges start to crisp and the cheese is bubbling. Cut with a pizza cutter and enjoy!

what mike likes You could add organic lunch meat, ground turkey, or ground beef to this pizza.

Black Bean Quesadilla

Prep time: 6 minutes
Total time: 10 minutes

Serves 1

Olive oil spray
1 whole wheat tortilla,
    8 inches or larger
¼ cup Amy's Vegetarian
    Organic Refried Black
    Beans or low-sodium
    black beans
2 tablespoons chopped red
    or yellow onion, or more if
    you like
2 tablespoons chopped bell
    pepper (any color), or
    more if you like
¼ cup shredded vegan or
    dairy cheese
¼ cup cooked vegan "meat"
    (like Boca Crumbles
    or MorningStar Farms
    chicken strips) or your
    favorite lean meat
Handful of spinach
Mrs. Dash chipotle
    seasoning or your favorite
    taco seasoning
Salsa (optional)
2 tablespoons low-fat sour
    cream (optional)

I try to avoid eating at Mexican restaurants—everything I want to order is so fried and cheesy! Of course, it's all amazingly delicious, but I end up eating my weight in carbs and cheese. So I try to get my fix in other ways. Here is my healthy-swap recipe for quesadillas.

1. Lightly spray olive oil onto a griddle or large pan and turn the heat to medium. Add the tortilla. As the tortilla heats up, spread the black beans on one half, then add the onions, peppers, cheese, "meat," spinach, and Mrs. Dash. Keep everything on one side of the tortilla.

2. When the tortilla starts to brown, fold the empty half over the full half. Continue to brown it until the cheese melts, flipping it every so often so it browns evenly.

3. Transfer the quesadilla to a plate and cut it into 2 wedges. I like to spoon salsa and maybe even some sour cream on top of the quesadilla, but you can skip that if you prefer.

NUTRITION FACTS
(per serving)

291	calories
9.5 g	fat
34 g	carbs
11.5 g	protein
8.5 g	fiber
2 g	sugar

what mike likes Mike might substitute some cooked chicken breast or ground bison for the vegan meat in this quesadilla.

Healthy Taco Salad

Serves 1

2 big ol' handfuls of spring
    mix or any other mixed
    lettuce combo
¼ cup chopped red onion,
    or to taste
¼ cup chopped bell pepper,
    or to taste
½ cup halved or quartered
    cherry tomatoes, or to
    taste
¼ cup black beans or
    chickpeas
¼ cup cooked brown rice or
    quinoa (optional)
¼ avocado, sliced
½ cup vegan ground "beef"
    or "chicken" strips or a
    vegan black bean burger
    patty—or you could make
    Cara's Tex-Mex Quinoa
    Burgers on page 270

In my quest to make my favorite Mexican foods healthier, I decided to take on the traditional taco salad by making it . . . well . . . more saladlike. You won't find any empty calories here. This salad will fill any belly (even mine), and it has a lot more nutrition and a lot less fat and fewer calories than the version my mom used to make for us growing up. When I make this recipe for a group, I chop up veggies and let my diners assemble their salads themselves. This salad is super versatile and really works with whatever you've got in your fridge. You can increase the amounts in the recipe below depending on how many people you're serving.

Note: This salad is very filling as it is, but if you feel like you need a little something more in it, I recommend adding cooked brown rice or quinoa, especially if you already have some on hand.

2 tablespoons light sour
    cream (vegan or regular)
2 tablespoons shredded
    Mexican blend or cheddar
    cheese (vegan or regular)
Salsa

Put the lettuce in a bowl. Add the onion, bell pepper, tomatoes, beans, rice (if using), avocado, and protein. Top with the sour cream and cheese, and finish with salsa as your dressing.

what mike likes Mike might add some lean ground bison with taco seasoning to this salad.

NUTRITION FACTS

(per serving)

335	calories
18 g	fat
23 g	carbs
15 g	protein
11 g	fiber
6 g	sugar

Carrie's Ugly Slow Cooker Lasagna

Prep time: 30 minutes
Total time: 2 to 4 hours, plus 30 minutes

Serves 4 to 6 (or more), depending on how many veggies you use

1 tablespoon olive oil
1 medium yellow onion, diced
1 large bell pepper (any color), diced
Cooking spray
1 (24-ounce) jar spaghetti sauce or marinara sauce (you may not need it all)
1 (12-ounce) box no-boil whole wheat lasagna noodles (you may not use them all)
Big handful of spinach
Other veggies you might want to sprinkle in—you could sauté any of these along with the onions and peppers, or leave them raw: sliced mushrooms, chopped-up broccoli, more diced bell peppers,

Lasagna is most definitely a comfort food. There's just something about it: warm, thick noodles, sauce, and cheese—yum! Most of us have been eating it for our entire lives. Plus, it's easy to make in large quantities, so if you've got a big family, pasta dishes like this are probably no stranger to your table. Here is my healthier take on this comforting classic. I call it my "ugly" lasagna because when you scoop it out of the slow cooker into a bowl, it's not all nicely layered. It's just a big pile of comfort food!

Speaking of feeding big families, this recipe is pretty adaptable based on how many you want to feed and how big your slow cooker is. If you use all the noodles, all the sauce, and a ton of veggies, this could serve more than the 4 to 6 people mentioned above. If you use half the noodles, half the sauce, and not so many veggies, you could serve just a few. In general, estimate 2 to 3 ounces dry pasta and ¾ to 1 cup sauce per person.

1. In a large skillet, heat the olive oil over medium heat. Add the onion and bell pepper (and any other veggies you want to add) and cook, stirring, until the onion is just turning golden brown and the bell pepper is soft. Set aside.

quartered cherry tomatoes, half-moon slices of zucchini and/or yellow squash, sliced okra, shredded carrots, shredded cabbage, etc.

1 (8-ounce) package shredded vegan cheese (such as Daiya) or reduced-fat shredded cheese

Your favorite Italian seasoning

NUTRITION FACTS
(per serving)

309	calories
13.5 g	fat
35 g	carbs
7 g	protein
6.5 g	fiber
10.5 g	sugar

2. Spray a slow cooker with a light coating of cooking spray, then cover the bottom with a thin layer of the sauce (just enough to coat the bottom).

3. Break the noodles and fit them over the sauce to mostly cover the bottom in one layer. Spread a thin layer of spinach over the noodles and sprinkle with the onion–bell pepper mixture and whatever other veggies you have prepared. Top with a thin layer of sauce and then a thin layer of cheese and a few shakes of Italian seasoning.

4. Repeat layers of noodles, spinach, extra veggies, sauce, cheese, and seasoning, until you reach the top of the slow cooker or run out of ingredients. End with a final layer of sauce and seasoning.

5. Cover and cook the lasagna on high for 2 to 3 hours or on low for 3 to 4 hours. Check it periodically to make sure the edges aren't burning. It should be done within a couple of hours, but you can test to make sure the noodles are tender. When you're ready to serve it, scoop it out into bowls. It ain't pretty . . . but it sure is delicious!

DESSERTS BY CARRIE

Baked Apples

Prep time: 10 minutes
Total time: 40 minutes

Serves 4

3 Gala apples or your
preferred variety, peeled,
cored, and chopped or
sliced (see Note)
2 tablespoons real maple
syrup
1 tablespoon Earth Balance
buttery spread, melted
1 teaspoon apple pie spice
or ground cinnamon

Apple pie is as American as it gets, at least when it comes to dessert. This recipe is all about having that warm apple-cinnamon goodness without the guilt. It's easy to make and can be modified or topped in lots of ways. However you enjoy it, just keep it simple!

I put this in the oven when I start making dinner, and I turn off the oven after 30 minutes, but I let it stay in there so it's still warm when we're ready for dessert. Serve this with ½ cup Halo Top ice cream (or your favorite dairy-free ice cream or whipped cream), and it's a real treat! You can even top it with some chopped walnuts or pecans or ¼ cup of your favorite granola, or mix in some rolled oats. Use any leftovers for your oatmeal tomorrow morning.

Note: This would be a great time to use an apple peeler/corer/slicer like I mention on page 228!

1. Preheat the oven to 400°F.

2. Slice or chop the apples into large pieces and put them in a large bowl. Add the maple syrup, melted buttery spread, and apple pie spice and toss to combine. Transfer the apples to a small baking

NUTRITION FACTS

(per serving)

121	calories
3 g	fat
35 g	carbs
0 g	protein
3 g	fiber
20 g	sugar

dish with a lid (I use a 1-quart dish). Cover the dish and bake for 25 minutes, then give the apples a good stir and bake, uncovered, for 5 minutes more, until they start to turn golden. The apples should be just tender.

3. Serve with your favorite toppings, and make sure to scoop up and use the cooking liquid at the bottom of the dish as a sauce.

Healthy Pumpkin Chocolate Pudding

Prep time: 5 minutes
Total time: 5 minutes

Serves 5

1 (15-ounce) can pure
   pumpkin puree
½ cup chocolate protein
   powder
2 tablespoons unsweetened
   cocoa powder
½ cup unsweetened vanilla
   almond milk
3 tablespoons real maple
   syrup
Dash of pure vanilla extract
Dash of ground cinnamon

NUTRITION FACTS
(per serving)

172	calories
2.5 g	fat
16 g	carbs
16 g	protein
4 g	fiber
12 g	sugar

This is the recipe I invented when I was pregnant with Isaiah and craving pumpkin (see page 203). It's easy to put together and really satisfying, with lots of nutrition for a growing baby, or just for you! Mix this all together, and you can eat it immediately, or chill it for a while in the fridge for later. It tastes even better after spending the night in the refrigerator.

1. Scoop the pumpkin puree into a medium bowl.

2. In a separate medium bowl, whisk together the protein powder and the cocoa powder. Add the almond milk and whisk to combine.

3. Add the protein powder mixture to the pumpkin and mix well. Stir in the maple syrup, vanilla, and cinnamon. Enjoy immediately, or cover and refrigerate up to overnight before serving.

Recipes from Nutritionist Cara Clark

I've already introduced you to my nutritionist friend Cara, and she has graciously agreed to contribute some of her own recipes to this book. She is a bit fancier with her cooking than I am, so these recipes have a different flavor (so to speak), but they are all delicious and super healthy.

Best Smoothie Bowl

Prep time: 5 minutes
Total time: 5 minutes

Serves 1

½ cup unsweetened almond milk, plus more if needed
½ frozen banana
½ cup frozen berries
1 (3.5-ounce) packet frozen açai puree
Handful of any fresh greens (raw spinach is the least bitter)

TOPPINGS

2 tablespoons low-sugar granola (you could replace this with raw oats, muesli, or just some chopped nuts, if you prefer)
1 tablespoon natural almond butter, no sugar added
1 tablespoon hulled hemp seeds
1 teaspoon goji berries
Fresh berries and banana slices (optional)

Cara here—Carrie asked me to contribute some of my favorite recipes, and here is a go-to breakfast I often recommend. Smoothie bowls contain all the creamy nutritional goodness of a smoothie with more filling, chewy ingredients that make you feel like you actually ate something. It's almost like starting your day with a salad-dessert combo. The fiber from the greens and seeds will keep you full and satisfied for at least 4 hours, and all those color-rich veggies and fruits will energize you while they help build up your immune system.

Note that this recipe is much thicker than a smoothie you would drink because it goes in a bowl and you eat it with a spoon. Even with a high-speed blender, it can be hard to get this to blend easily, so you'll probably have to tamp it down a few times to get everything fully blended. You can always add more almond milk, but do so only a little bit at a time. The smoothie should have the consistency of soft-serve ice cream.

1. Put the almond milk in a high-speed blender, then add the banana, berries, açai, and greens. Blend the smoothie, tamping down as necessary, until smooth. Add more almond milk a tablespoon at a time if it's too thick.

2. Pour or scoop the smoothie into a bowl and add the toppings. Enjoy immediately.

cara says

AÇAI AND GOJI BERRIES . . . NOT IN THE PRODUCE SECTION

If you're into health food, you probably know all about açai and goji berries. But if you're not a health nut yet, you may not be familiar with these "superfood" berries.

› **AÇAI** (pronounced *ah-sigh-EE*) berries grow on açai palm trees. They are a vibrant purple color and they resemble blueberries or purple grapes. They have an extremely high antioxidant content. They are mostly seed and spoil quickly, so the best way to get them is to buy the frozen pulp or freeze-dried powder at a health food store or in the freezer section or health food aisle of a regular grocery store. Can't find them? You can always substitute blueberries.

› **GOJI** (pronounced GO-gee) berries are another superfood, and they come from China and surrounding areas. They are used in Chinese medicine and Asian cooking, but have recently caught on in the U.S. You can most easily find them in dried form—they are chewy, kind of like raisins. They taste a little like a sweeter version of cranberries, but with more nutrient density. However, if you can't find them or don't want to use them, you could always substitute unsweetened dried cranberries or dried cherries.

Chia Seed Pudding

Prep time: 5 minutes
Total time: 2 to 12 hours

Serves 2

---

1 cup unsweetened almond milk or other unsweetened nut, hemp, or oat milk

¼ cup chia seeds

2 tablespoons unsweetened raw cacao powder or cocoa powder

1 tablespoon real maple syrup (or a little bit more if you need it sweeter)

1 teaspoon pure vanilla extract

¼ cup chopped strawberries, for topping

¼ cup cacao nibs, for topping (optional)

NUTRITION FACTS
(per serving)

398	calories
19 g	fat
30 g	carbs
11 g	protein
19 g	fiber
18 g	sugar

This dish is delicious enough to serve for dessert, but since it is nutrient-dense, low in sugar, and will fill you up with the perfect ratio of protein to omega-3 fat (the good kind), along with fiber, it's perfect for breakfast! The maple syrup brings all the flavors together with its delicate sweetness, while providing you with minerals and antioxidants you can't get from refined sugar. And . . . chocolate for breakfast? I'm in! If you make five of these babies on the weekend and store them in the fridge, you can have an awesome grab-and-go breakfast every day all week long.

Note: Kids don't always like the texture of the whole chia seeds in this pudding, but if you blend it before putting it in the pint jars, it comes out smooth—a great breakfast or snack for kids.

In a medium bowl, stir together the almond milk, chia seeds, cacao powder, maple syrup, and vanilla. Divide the mixture between two 1-pint mason jars. Cover and refrigerate overnight or for at least 2 hours. When the pudding has thickened, top with the strawberries and cacao nibs (if using) and enjoy!

cara says

CACAO OR COCOA—
WHAT'S THE DIFFERENCE?

I recommend raw cacao powder and cacao nibs over cocoa powder and chocolate chips, and here's why: Cocoa powder is roasted, but raw cacao powder is the cold-pressed, ground version, so it has more of its enzymes and nutrients intact. Cocoa powder is good for you, too (as long as it's unsweetened!), but cacao has that little something extra. Cacao nibs are pieces of the cocoa bean, no sugar added, so they have that crunchy chocolate taste but no refined sweetener. It's easy to learn to love them. All that being said, if you would rather use unsweetened cocoa powder and dark chocolate chips (with at least 85% cacao), that works, too, although I would keep the chocolate chips to 1 or 2 tablespoons.

Healthy Quinoa Bowl

Prep time: 15 minutes
Total time: 15 minutes

Serves 4

¼ cup balsamic vinegar
Zest and juice of 1 juicy lime
   (3 to 4 tablespoons juice)
2 cups cooked quinoa
1 cup cooked black beans
1 yellow or orange bell
   pepper, diced
2 scallions, chopped
1 bunch fresh cilantro,
   chopped
Sea salt and black pepper

NUTRITION FACTS
(per serving)

204	calories
3 g	fat
30 g	carbs
8.5 g	protein
8 g	fiber
6 g	sugar

This happens to be one of my all-time favorite meals. It's filling because of the hearty quinoa and the delicious combination of flavors, so you don't need to eat a huge amount of it to feel satisfied. It's like going to your favorite Mexican restaurant, but better, because this doesn't contain any industrial seed oils (highly processed oils like vegetable, corn, and soybean oils) or unnecessary sodium. Quinoa is one of my favorite vegetarian proteins because it contains all nine essential amino acids.

1. In a small bowl, whisk together the vinegar, lime zest, and lime juice.

2. In a large bowl, combine the quinoa, beans, bell pepper, scallions, and cilantro. Pour the dressing over and gently toss to combine. Taste and season with sea salt and black pepper, then serve.

what mike likes Instead of or in addition to the black beans, Mike might add about a pound of chopped cooked chicken breast or ground turkey to this bowl.

cara says

QUIRKY QUINOA

Quinoa looks and tastes like a grain, and we cook it like a grain, but it's actually a seed. It comes from the flowers of the *Chenopodium quinoa* plant, which belongs to the same family as spinach, chard, and beets, and yes, it's gluten-free.

Some important things to know about quinoa: Always rinse it well in a fine-mesh strainer under cold water for at least a full minute before cooking it. Quinoa naturally has a bitter, soapy-tasting coating on it, so your quinoa will taste better if you rinse this off before cooking. Also, I suggest cooking up a big batch of this versatile food in your slow cooker,

Instant Pot, or rice cooker and storing it in the fridge to have on hand at all times. You never know when you might want to add some to a recipe.

Quinoa comes in many colors—white, red, black, purple, orange, and more. You can buy tricolor quinoa, which is a mixture of the black, red, and white varieties. They all taste a little different. It might just replace rice as your favorite side dish! That being said, you can always replace quinoa with a whole grain, such as brown rice, barley, or bulgur, if you don't like it or don't have it handy. But hey, take a chance on quinoa. You won't regret it!

Cara's Super Salad

Prep time: 25 minutes
Total time: 25 minutes

Serves 1 as a main course
or 2 as a side dish (or if you
don't like giant salads the
way I do!)

---

2 cups mixed greens
Chopped cucumber, bell
   pepper, and/or tomato
   (however much you like)
½ cup chopped or
   shredded cabbage
¼ cup shredded carrot
¼ avocado, diced
¼ cup fresh or thawed
   frozen corn kernels
¼ cup diced strawberries
2 tablespoons chopped
   walnuts (toast them if you
   want them to have more
   flavor, but don't worry
   about it if you don't have
   the time or inclination)
1 or 2 hard-boiled eggs,
   sliced (optional)
½ to 1 recipe Lemon-Tahini
   Dressing (recipe follows;
   optional)
1 or 2 scallions, sliced, for
   garnish

Forget ordinary green salads. I like to jazz up my salad with plenty of colorful, antioxidant-rich veggies full of essential micronutrients (vitamins and minerals). This adds not just color but texture and flavor to what might otherwise be a boring old bowl of lettuce. Added salad bonus: All that chewing is good exercise and can increase your metabolism! If salad is your main course, always add some carbs, fat, and protein from whole food sources. In this recipe, I've added corn and strawberries for carbs, avocados and dressing for fat, and walnuts for fat and some protein.

In a bowl, toss together the greens, vegetables, cabbage, and carrot. Top with the avocado, corn, strawberries, walnuts, and eggs (if using). This salad is fine plain, but if you like, drizzle it with the dressing; use half the dressing to serve one, or all of it for a richer salad or to serve two. Garnish with the scallions and serve.

what mike likes You could make this salad a side dish with grilled chicken breast or a grilled salmon fillet.

NUTRITION FACTS
(for the salad as a main course, to serve 1)

290	calories
14.5 g	fat
23 g	carbs
9 g	protein
15 g	fiber
12 g	sugar (from fruit)

Lemon-Tahini Dressing

Prep time: 3 minutes
Total time: 3 minutes, or a few hours with optional chilling time

---

Serves 2

---

3 tablespoons fresh lemon juice
2 tablespoons tahini
1 garlic clove, minced
Sea salt and black pepper
Dash of cayenne pepper

NUTRITION FACTS
(per serving)

75 calories
6 g fat
4 g carbs
9 g protein
1 g fiber
1 g sugar

I always like to have leftover dressing, which I keep in a jar in the fridge. This recipe makes two servings, so you can use half on your Super Salad (page 258) and save the rest for your next salad.

Combine all the ingredients in a small bowl with 2 tablespoons water and whisk together until well combined. For best flavor, cover and refrigerate for a few hours to allow the flavors to meld. This dressing can be stored in the refrigerator for a few days.

— *cara says* —

TA-WHO-NI?

Tahini is the sesame seed's answer to peanut butter. It's just sesame butter, and it's delicious. You can find it pretty much anywhere these days, even at Walmart. It comes from Middle Eastern cuisine, and it's one of the main ingredients in hummus. In fact, if you can't find tahini or don't want to use it, or if you want a lower-fat option, you can always substitute the same amount of hummus for tahini in recipes.

Cara's California Power Bowl

Prep time: 20 minutes
Total time: 20 minutes

Serves 1

1 tablespoon avocado oil
½ red bell pepper, sliced
½ red onion, sliced
½ teaspoon sea salt
Dash of black pepper
1 cup spinach or spring mix
Juice of ½ juicy lemon (1 to 2 tablespoons)
½ cup cooked brown rice
¼ cup cooked fresh or frozen corn
¼ avocado, diced
1 tablespoon raw sunflower seeds

NUTRITION FACTS
(per serving)

438	calories
24 g	fat
41 g	carbs
9 g	protein
9 g	fiber
7 g	sugar

To me, this bowl never gets old. It can satisfy any level of hunger. Sautéing the veggies makes them easily digestible—this can be helpful for people who have trouble digesting too many raw vegetables. Cooking also enhances the flavors and blends them together. This meal is sure to hold you over for at least 4 hours and may even feel like you're "cheating" the system, but trust me, you're providing your body with the fuel you need to check off every item on your daily to-do list. If you want something even more substantial with more protein, you could add some black beans, pinto beans, or baked tofu cubes.

1. In a small skillet, heat the avocado oil over medium heat. Add the bell pepper and onion and sauté for 3 to 4 minutes, until they are soft. Season with the salt and black pepper.

2. Put the spinach in a serving bowl and top with the lemon juice. Add the rice and corn and toss until everything is mixed. Top with the warm peppers and onions, then the avocado and sunflower seeds. Serve immediately.

what mike likes You could add some chopped cooked chicken breast or salmon to this bowl.

Cara's Cucumber Salad: Spiralized!

Prep time: 10 minutes
Total time: 10 minutes

Serves 1

2 medium cucumbers (10 to 12 ounces each) or an equivalent amount of smaller or larger cucumbers, spiralized or sliced into long noodles with a vegetable peeler
1 cup cherry or grape tomatoes, halved
1 medium shallot, thinly sliced
¼ cup crumbled feta cheese or goat cheese (for a vegan option, you can substitute vegan feta, or ¼ cup nutritional yeast—find this savory, cheesy flavoring in the health food aisle)
¼ cup sliced pitted kalamata olives
⅓ cup extra-virgin olive oil
Juice of ½ lemon
¼ cup red wine vinegar
2 teaspoons chopped fresh oregano leaves
1 garlic clove, minced
½ teaspoon sea salt
Black pepper

Have you ever noticed that eating the same foods over and over again gets old? Try them in a different shape, and you may get interested again. It's the same principle that applies when we give toddlers something new to keep their attention. Spiralizing any vegetable gives it a different texture and makes it even more versatile—try spiralizing zucchini, carrots, butternut squash, even broccoli stems. In this salad, it gives cucumbers a whole new lease on life and gives you the impression that you're eating noodles. However, unlike carb-heavy pasta that can make you crash, the energy you get from eating spiralized cucumbers will go on and on. Throw in some garlic for its powerful immune-boosting properties and the savory suggestion of an Italian dinner.

1. In a medium bowl, combine the cucumber "noodles," tomatoes, shallot, cheese, and olives.

2. In a small bowl, whisk together the olive oil, lemon juice, vinegar, oregano, garlic, salt, and pepper to taste until fully combined. (Or just combine it all in a jar, cover, and shake.)

3. Drizzle the dressing over the salad and toss to coat everything. Get out your fork and twirl those "noodles"!

NUTRITION FACTS
(per serving)

354	calories
30 g	fat
14 g	carbs
7 g	protein
4 g	fiber
7 g	sugar

Green Smoothie

Prep time: 10 minutes
Total time: 10 minutes

Serves 1

Big handful of any dark leafy greens
1 green apple, cored and coarsely chopped
½ frozen banana
1 celery stalk, coarsely chopped
Small handful of fresh parsley leaves
Juice of 1 lime
2 tablespoons hulled hemp seeds
1 teaspoon matcha green tea powder (optional)
6 to 8 ounces unsweetened coconut milk or nut milk
½ to 1 cup ice, if desired

NUTRITION FACTS
(per serving)

285	calories
11.5 g	fat
34 g	carbs
9 g	protein
9 g	fiber
24 g	sugar (from fruit)

Green smoothies look healthy, and they're packed with nutrients, but they taste like dessert. This is a power snack that only takes a few minutes to prepare but has huge nutritional benefits. Some hard-core health foodies like their smoothies made with vegetables only, but others (especially those new to the green smoothie concept) can't quite stomach that intense flavor. This smoothie has plenty of greens, but enough sweetness that they go down easy. If you can handle a little caffeine, add some matcha for nutritional bonus points.

Combine the greens, apple, banana, celery, parsley, lime juice, hemp seeds, and matcha (if using) in a blender. Pour the milk over the top and add ice if you want it frostier. Blend until everything is smooth and well combined. Pour into a glass. Sip slowly and savor the goodness.

GREEN TEA ON STEROIDS

Well, not really—matcha doesn't contain steroids, but it does have a stronger taste than regular green tea. Matcha is a high-quality green tea that is ground into a powder and whisked into hot water (as opposed to regular green tea, which is steeped in hot water). Originating in China, where it was called "beaten tea," matcha became popular centuries ago in Japan as a ceremonial drink, and its preparation is the basis for the Japanese tea ceremony, or "The Way of the Tea." Matcha is also a potent source of antioxidants. Because of its strong taste, I like to add it to smoothies rather than drinking it straight. The combination of other flavors from the veggies and fruits in a smoothie can make the matcha go down a bit easier. You might like the taste, but start small and work your way up. They say a cup of matcha has more than triple the antioxidants of a cup of regular green tea!

PB&B Rice Cakes

Prep time: 5 minutes
Total time: 5 minutes

Serves 1

2 tablespoons natural almond butter, no-sugar-added
2 brown rice cakes
Dash of ground cinnamon (optional)
2 teaspoons hulled hemp seeds
½ cup fresh blueberries

NUTRITION FACTS
(per serving)

340	calories
21 g	fat
26 g	carbs
11 g	protein
6 g	fiber
9 g	sugar (from fruit)

You can put a lot of different things on a rice cake, making this crunchy, low-cal snack the perfect palette for whatever you are craving. You can make a rice cake snack in 5 minutes and finish it in under a minute. This version combines protein, carbs, and fat for plenty of staying power—it's the perfect PB&B (that's peanut butter and blueberries). When you need something super quick and you want finger food, reach for the rice cakes, and feel free to change up the toppings depending on what you have stocked in the refrigerator.

Spread the almond butter over the rice cakes. Sprinkle with the cinnamon, if you like, and divide the hemp seeds and blueberries evenly between them. Crunch away!

cara says

HEMP SEEDS: 100% LEGAL!

Rest assured, not only are hemp seeds (sometimes called hemp hearts) perfectly legal and completely without any psychotropic effect, but they are mild-tasting and one of the rare plant foods that contains complete protein in one package. They also have the perfect ratio of omega-3, -6, and -9 fats: all of the nine essential amino acids. I often add them to snacks, smoothie bowls, smoothies, salads, and oatmeal for a protein boost.

Chocolate Chip Energy Bites

Prep time: 30 minutes
Total time: 1 hour

Makes 18 bites

3/4 cup natural creamy
    peanut butter
3 tablespoons raw honey
1½ cups rolled oats
½ cup mini dark chocolate
    chips
¼ teaspoon sea salt

NUTRITION FACTS
(per 3 pieces)

412	calories
27 g	fat
30 g	carbs
14 g	protein
7 g	fiber
15 g	sugar

Like a cookie with less sugar and more nutrients, energy bites won't send your blood sugar on a roller-coaster ride. And I'll give you a secret tip: These taste just as good coming from the freezer as they taste freshly made. This is a basic recipe, but it's very versatile and adaptable, so feel free to add superfood ingredients like chia seeds, hemp seeds, ground flax, or maca powder. Another bonus: These little guys will crush even the strongest hormone-based sugar cravings.

1. In a small saucepan, heat the peanut butter over low heat, stirring occasionally, until it gets runny. Remove from the heat and stir in the honey. Set aside.

2. Toss the oats and chocolate chips together in a large bowl. Drizzle the peanut butter–honey mixture over the top. Sprinkle with the salt, then mix everything together. Cover and refrigerate for about 30 minutes to allow the mixture to firm up. Remove from the fridge and form the mixture into eighteen 1-inch balls, or line a baking sheet with parchment paper, press the mixture into a rectangle, and cut it into 18 squares. Store the bites in a large resealable bag or bowl in the fridge for up to a week or freezer for up to a month.

Pumpkin Spice Granola

Prep time: 10 minutes
Total time: 30 to 35 minutes

Serves 12 (⅓ cup per serving)

1 cup rolled oats
1 cup raw pecan halves or pieces
1 cup unsalted raw sunflower seeds
½ cup raw almonds
¼ cup unsweetened dried berries
1 teaspoon pumpkin pie spice
½ (15-ounce) can pumpkin puree
1 tablespoon raw honey

NUTRITION FACTS
(per serving)

314 calories
22 g fat
17.5 g carbs
8 g protein
6.5 g fiber
8 g sugar

Welcome to heaven on Earth. This grab-and-go option does take a little more time to make than grabbing a rice cake, but it's so worth it. The taste is divine, and the satisfaction level is high. Even though it's pumpkin spice flavor, it never goes out of season! And you actually toast in the spiced pumpkin puree to make sure you're getting at least one fruit and one vegetable per serving. Store this in a jar in the refrigerator—although I bet it won't last long. This can be a snack (or even breakfast), or a topping on overnight oats, a smoothie bowl, or chia seed pudding. I predict the whole family will love this.

1. Preheat the oven to 350ºF. Line a large baking sheet with parchment paper or a silicone baking mat.

2. In a large bowl, combine the oats, pecans, sunflower seeds, almonds, dried berries, and pumpkin pie spice and toss thoroughly with your hands.

3. In a separate large bowl, whisk together the pumpkin puree and honey. Pour in the dry ingredients and mix with your hands or a spatula until the pumpkin puree is coating everything.

4. Spread the mixture out on the prepared baking sheet. Bake for 10 minutes. Stir the granola, rotate the pan 180 degrees, and bake for 10 to 15 minutes more, until the granola is mostly dry.

5. Let cool, then enjoy immediately or transfer to airtight containers and store in the fridge for up to a week or the freezer for up to a month.

Cara's Cowboy Caviar

Prep time: 20 minutes
Total time: 20 minutes

Serves 8

1 (15-ounce) can black beans, drained and rinsed
1 (15-ounce) can black-eyed peas, drained and rinsed
2 different colored bell peppers, chopped
3 Roma (plum) tomatoes, diced
1 cup thawed frozen sweet corn
½ small red onion, diced
¼ cup coarsely chopped fresh cilantro
¼ cup avocado oil
¼ cup apple cider vinegar
Juice of 1 juicy lime (about 3 tablespoons)
2 garlic cloves, minced
1 teaspoon ground cumin
½ teaspoon sea salt
¼ teaspoon cayenne pepper
¼ teaspoon cracked black pepper
Corn chips or plantain chips, for serving

If this doesn't have you salivating, I don't know what will! I'm no cowboy, but this is by far my favorite dip to eat on a chip or even straight from a spoon. Like the other snacks in this book, this one is rich in fiber and plant-based protein, and the pop of colors makes it even more appealing (and healthy). Eat this dip with your favorite organic corn or plantain chips. You can also throw it on top of a salad or mix it into your tofu scramble or scrambled eggs.

Combine all the ingredients except the chips in a large serving bowl and mix gently until well combined. Serve with corn or plantain chips for dipping.

NUTRITION FACTS
(per serving)

175 calories
6 g fat
18 g carbs
7 g protein
7.5 g fiber
7 g sugar

DINNER RECIPES

Cara's Tex-Mex Quinoa Burgers

Prep time: 35 minutes
Total time: 2 hours 10 minutes

Makes 8 burgers

Cooking spray
1/3 cup rolled oats
1 cup baked sweet potato chunks
1 (15-ounce) can black beans, drained, rinsed, and patted mostly dry
1/2 cup fresh or thawed frozen sweet corn (drained, if thawed)
1/2 cup finely chopped red onion
1/2 cup cooked quinoa
1 (4-ounce) can green chiles, drained
2 tablespoons natural almond butter, no-sugar-added
1 1/2 tablespoons taco seasoning (homemade or low-sodium store-bought with no additives, preservatives, or MSG)
Sea salt and black pepper

Quinoa (see page 257) is one of my go-to foods, and I especially like it for veggie burgers. Store-bought and restaurant veggie burgers can be questionable, because who knows what the heck is in them? Even with a label to read, you may not recognize some of those ingredients. That's why homemade veggie burgers are where it's at. With just the right ingredients, you can hide the "super-est" of superfoods. You won't even taste them because you'll be too distracted by the lusciousness of these Tex-Mex-style burgers. The whole family will enjoy them, and they have plenty of protein to keep your body functioning properly and burning fat. Make plenty of extra—the leftovers are awesome on your lunchtime salad.

Note: If making sweet potato chunks from scratch, you'll need 1 medium sweet potato to get a cup after baking, and you may have some left over.

Helpful hint: It's easy to make a batch of quinoa in your Instant Pot or slow cooker and store it in the fridge to have on hand for recipes like this. Don't forget to rinse it in a fine-mesh sieve before cooking!

1. Put the oats in a food processor and pulse them into oat flour. Add the sweet potatoes and half the black beans to the food processor and pulse just enough to form a coarse, chunky mixture.

2 eggs, whisked, or
   2 tablespoons ground flax
   mixed with 2 tablespoons
   water (for a vegan
   version)
Toasted whole-grain
   hamburger buns or pita
   pockets, for serving
Spinach, for serving
Toppings: bean sprouts,
   sliced tomato, sliced
   avocado, red onion slices,
   mustard, ketchup, cheese
   slices, or your favorite
   burger toppings

NUTRITION FACTS
(per serving)

124	calories
4 g	fat
16 g	carbs
5 g	protein
3 g	fiber
2 g	sugar

2. Transfer the mixture to a large bowl, add the remaining beans, the corn, onion, quinoa, chiles, almond butter, and taco seasoning, and stir it all up or mix it with your hands. Taste and season with salt and pepper. Add the eggs (or flax mixture) and work them in until everything is evenly mixed. Cover the dough and refrigerate for at least 1 hour or up to a few days.

3. Preheat the oven to 375°F. Line a large baking sheet with parchment paper and spray the parchment with cooking spray.

4. Spray a ⅓-cup measuring cup with cooking spray and scoop 8 roughly equal portions of the dough onto the prepared baking sheet. Coat your hands with oil and form the dough into patties. Bake for 20 minutes, then flip the burgers so they cook evenly and bake for 15 minutes more, or until they're just firm and easy to handle. If you're using cheese, add a slice to each burger during the last 5 minutes of cooking.

5. To serve, put a toasted bun or pita pocket on each plate. Put spinach on the bottom, top it with the burger, then add whatever toppings you want. Add the top bun and enjoy!

Cara's Slow Cooker Butternut Squash Chili

Prep time: 35 minutes
Total time: 35 minutes plus 4 to 8 hours

Serves 8

---

1 (28-ounce) can tomato sauce

1 (28-ounce) can diced tomatoes

1 small butternut squash, peeled, seeded, and chopped

1 Vidalia or other sweet onion, diced

1 green bell pepper, diced

1 cup low-sodium vegetable broth

1 jalapeño, seeded, membrane scraped out with a spoon, and finely diced

3 garlic cloves, sliced

2 tablespoons chili powder

1 tablespoon ground cumin

2 teaspoons ground cinnamon

Sea salt and black pepper

1 (15-ounce) can light red kidney beans, drained and rinsed

Butternut squash adds a sweet-savory, nutrient-rich special something to this chili. If you have extra time on your hands, peel and cube the butternut squash, roast it, then blend it to lend this chili a creamy texture— nice, although not required. Either way, this chili has added depth because of the squash. If you find yourself with leftovers, another fun idea is to stuff some roasted bell peppers with this chili for a whole different dinner. Don't be afraid to include the cinnamon, which is subtle but adds a Mediterranean flair, and also helps your metabolism burn faster (win-win).

In a slow cooker, combine the tomato sauce, diced tomatoes, squash, onion, bell pepper, broth, jalapeño, garlic, chili powder, cumin, and cinnamon. Season with a dash each of salt and black pepper. Cover and cook on Low for 7 to 8 hours or on High for 4 to 5 hours. Fifteen to 30 minutes before serving, stir in the beans. Taste and season with salt and black pepper. When the chili is done and you're ready for dinner, scoop it into bowls and garnish with your favorite chili toppings, like crushed baked tortilla chips, avocado cubes, plain yogurt, salsa, etc.

1 (15-ounce) can black beans,
   drained and rinsed
1 (15-ounce) can pinto beans,
   drained and rinsed
Your favorite chili toppings

what mike likes This recipe would work with the addition of 1 to 2 pounds lean ground bison or turkey. Cook the meat in a skillet before adding it to the slow cooker with the vegetables and seasonings.

NUTRITION FACTS
(per serving)

201	calories
1 g	fat
29 g	carbs
10 g	protein
12 g	fiber
9 g	sugar

Creamy Cashew Alfredo

Prep time: 30 minutes
Cook time: 30 minutes plus time to cook the pasta

Serves 4

2 cups raw cashews
1¼ cups water or low-sodium vegetable broth
¼ cup coconut milk, full- or low-fat
¼ cup nutritional yeast
2 teaspoons minced garlic
¼ cup fresh lemon juice
1 teaspoon dried thyme
1 teaspoon paprika
Sea salt and black pepper
12 ounces legume pasta or whole wheat pasta (or go light and use 4 cups of zoodles, which are zucchini cut into long noodle shapes with a spiralizer or vegetable peeler)

Pasta Alfredo doesn't have to be full of butter and cream. This version uses cashew cream and coconut milk to make a luscious, creamy, savory sauce. I would round this out with some steamed broccoli or cauliflower (or a mixture) on the side. This makes a lot of sauce, so you might have leftovers. If you do, store them in an airtight container in the refrigerator for up to 3 days.

Note: Toasting nuts and seeds is often optional, but it really enhances the flavor in this recipe.

1. Preheat the oven to 350°F.

2. Spread the cashews over a baking sheet and toast them in the oven for 10 minutes, or until they turn golden. Remove from the oven and let cool.

3. In a food processor or blender, combine the cashews, broth, coconut milk, nutritional yeast, garlic, lemon juice, thyme, and paprika. Blend until smooth and creamy, 3 to 4 minutes. If you'd like a creamier consistency, you can add more broth or water, a tablespoon or two at a time, and blend again. Pour the mixture into a

large saucepan and heat it over low heat, stirring occasionally, until warmed through, about 10 minutes. Do not let it boil. Taste and season with salt and pepper.

4. Meanwhile, cook the pasta according to the package directions (if you use zoodles, you don't need to cook them), then add the pasta to the sauce. Stir to coat the pasta, then serve immediately.

what mike likes *Make this a chicken Alfredo with the addition of 1 pound sliced cooked chicken breast.*

Lentil Sloppy Joe Sliders

Prep time: 35 minutes
Total time: 1 hour

Serves 6 (2 sliders per serving)

4 or 5 large sweet potatoes, peeled and sliced into 12 1-inch-thick rounds
1 tablespoon coconut oil, melted
Sea salt and black pepper for seasoning
2 tablespoons avocado oil
½ onion, diced
2 garlic cloves, minced
3 cups cooked lentils, drained
1 (6-ounce) can tomato paste
1 (4-ounce) can diced green chiles
2 tablespoons Worcestershire sauce
2 teaspoons paprika
1 teaspoon ground cumin

A recent food trend is to replace bread and buns with sliced sweet potatoes. Here is my version of lentil sloppy joe sliders, using toasty sweet potato rounds as the buns. Serve these open-faced. Of course, you could also serve these sloppy joes on regular whole-grain slider buns instead. I like serving these sliders with a salad on the side.

Note that you will have a lot of leftover sweet potato after making this recipe. You can typically get 12 decent-sized rounds out of the center of about 4 large sweet potatoes, which leaves you with a lot of scraps. Luckily, you can make these into mashed sweet potatoes or use them in any other recipe. Just sprinkle the leftovers with a little lemon juice and store them in an airtight container in the refrigerator for up to a day or two.

Note: If cooking lentils from scratch, use 1 cup dried lentils and cook according to package instructions.

1. Preheat the oven to 450°F. Line a baking sheet with parchment paper.

2. Space the sweet potato rounds evenly on the prepared baking sheet, then brush them with the melted coconut oil and season with salt. Bake for 12 minutes, then flip and bake until fork-tender, 10 to 15 minutes more. Set aside at room temperature. If you can, rewarm them in the oven for a few minutes just before serving.

NUTRITION FACTS

(per serving)

279	calories
7.5 g	fat
34 g	carbs
10 g	protein
10 g	fiber
9.5 g	sugar

3. While the sweet potatoes are roasting, in a large skillet, heat the avocado oil over medium heat until it starts to shimmer, then add the onion and garlic and cook for 4 to 5 minutes, stirring often, until onion is tender and lightly browned.

4. Stir in the lentils, tomato paste, chiles, Worcestershire, paprika, and cumin. Reduce the heat to medium-low and cook until completely warmed through, about 5 minutes more. Taste and season with salt and pepper.

5. Put two sweet potato rounds on each plate and spoon ½ cup of the lentil mixture (per serving) over them.

DESSERT RECIPES

Cara's Dark Chocolate Nicecream

Prep time: 10 minutes
Total time: 10 minutes,
and up to 8 to 12 hours

Serves: 2

---

2 frozen bananas
¼ cup coconut cream (or
  just scoop the solid part
  off the top of a can of
  coconut milk)
2 tablespoons cacao powder
1 tablespoon maple syrup
1 teaspoon vanilla

NUTRITION FACTS
(per serving)

275	calories
7.5 g	fat
42 g	carbs
5 g	protein
10 g	fiber
27 g	sugar

Hello, midsummer-night's dream! If you have a high-powered blender and some time to chill, then step away from the hot fudge sundae and enjoy this delicious and light treat instead. If you want some extra protein, feel free to add a scoop of pea-based protein powder, or sprinkle your Nicecream with hemp seeds.

Add all the ingredients to the bowl of a food processor or high-power blender. Blend on high until smooth and creamy, tamping down if it's too thick. Eat immediately for a softer texture, or put the mixture in an airtight container and freeze for 30 to 60 minutes, stirring every 10 to 15 minutes. The longer you freeze it, the firmer it will be.

Strawberry Shortcake

Prep time: *1 hour*
Total time: *1 hour 35 minutes*

Serves 10

Cooking spray
2¹⁄₂ cups whole wheat
   pastry flour
¹⁄₄ cup plus 1 tablespoon
   coconut sugar or palm
   sugar
1 tablespoon baking powder
¹⁄₂ teaspoon baking soda
¹⁄₄ teaspoon sea salt
6 tablespoons butter, Earth
   Balance buttery spread,
   or coconut oil, cut into
   small pieces and chilled,
   plus 1 tablespoon melted
1¹⁄₄ cups buttermilk
1 tablespoon lemon zest
4 cups sliced fresh
   strawberries
1 tablespoon fresh lemon
   juice
Whipped cream or whipped
   coconut cream, for
   serving (optional)

This recipe may be more involved than something that Carrie would typically want to make, but I promise you, it really isn't all that complicated! In early summer, when strawberries are at their peak, you can't beat this for a special seasonal dessert. It's not for every day, but it sure is pretty, it tastes great, and it's much healthier than standard strawberry shortcake. You may notice it doesn't contain much sweetener—the strawberries get to take most of the credit for this dessert's natural sweetness.

Note: You can substitute coconut or almond flour for the pastry flour, although 1 teaspoon xanthan gum can help hold this together if you do—look for it in the baking section of your health food store or your grocery store's gluten-free cooking aisle.

To make buttermilk, stir together 1¼ cups milk (or plant milk), and 1 tablespoon fresh lemon juice or distilled white vinegar, and let it sit for 10 minutes or so until thickened.

1. Preheat the oven to 425°F. Coat a 9-inch round cake pan or baking sheet with cooking spray.

2. In a large bowl, whisk together 2 cups of the flour, ¼ cup of the sugar, the baking powder, baking soda, and salt. Cut in the chilled butter with a pastry blender or two knives until the mixture resembles coarse crumbs.

continues

3. In a small bowl, combine the buttermilk and lemon zest. Add the buttermilk mixture to the flour mixture and toss gently with a fork to combine. (The dough should be wet and about the texture of cottage cheese.)

4. Sprinkle the remaining ½ cup flour in a shallow dish. Scoop 10 equal portions of the dough (about 3 tablespoons or a scant ¼ cup each) into the dish. Gently shape each portion into a round, tossing it in the flour to help shape it.

5. Arrange the rounds of dough in the prepared pan or on the prepared baking sheet (if using a baking sheet, place them about 2 inches apart). Brush the dough with the melted butter and sprinkle evenly with the remaining 1 tablespoon sugar. Bake for 22 minutes, or until the shortcakes are lightly browned. Let cool in the pan on a wire rack for 10 minutes. Use a paring knife to cut the shortcakes apart (if you baked them in a cake pan) and remove them from the pan one at a time, transferring them to the wire rack to cool. They can still be slightly warm when you serve them.

6. In a medium bowl, toss the strawberries with the lemon juice. Let stand for 15 minutes.

7. Split each shortcake in half and put it on a small plate; spoon about ⅓ cup of the strawberries over each cake. If desired, serve topped with whipped cream or whipped coconut cream (sweetened or not, according to your preference).

Almond Butter Brownies

Prep time: 25 minutes
Total time: 50 minutes

Serves 12

Cooking spray
2 large eggs
1/3 cup real maple syrup
2 tablespoons coconut
   sugar
2 teaspoons pure vanilla
   extract
1 cup creamy natural almond
   butter, no-sugar-added
6 tablespoons unsweetened
   raw cacao powder or
   cocoa powder
1/2 teaspoon baking soda
1/8 teaspoon sea salt
1/3 cup dark chocolate chips
   or chocolate chunks (or
   cacao nibs; see page 255)

NUTRITION FACTS
(per serving)

227	calories
15 g	fat
16 g	carbs
6 g	protein
3 g	fiber
15 g	sugar

I would take these brownies over birthday cake any day. There's no flour necessary, which means we're squeezing in more nutritional value. The nut butter in this recipe is not only loaded with all three macronutrients, but contains many minerals, vitamins, and antioxidants. Some nuts are high in omega-3 fat, which helps to reduce your risk of heart disease, among other health risks. Coconut sugar is an alternative to regular sugar and contains many more nutrients than white sugar. However, even though it's a better choice, it's still best used in moderation. Note that you should bake these until they're just set in the middle when you gently shake the pan. If you wait until a toothpick inserted into the middle comes out clean, they can be too dry.

1. Preheat the oven to 325°F. Line an 8-inch square baking dish with parchment paper and spray the parchment with cooking spray.

2. In a large bowl, using a handheld mixer, combine the eggs, maple syrup, sugar, and vanilla and beat on high speed for 3 minutes. Beat in the almond butter until well combined and smooth. Sift in the cacao powder. Add the baking soda and salt and stir to combine. Fold in the chocolate chips. The batter will be very thick.

3. Spread the brownie mixture evenly into the prepared pan. Bake for 25 minutes, or until the center is just set.

4. Let cool completely in the pan on a wire rack before cutting into 12 squares.

Dark Chocolate Sea Salt Freezer Fudge

Prep time: 5 minutes
Total time: 2 hours or overnight

Serves 10

---

1 cup natural almond butter, no-sugar-added
1/3 cup coconut oil
3 tablespoons raw honey
1 teaspoon pure vanilla extract
1/2 cup unsweetened raw cacao powder or cocoa powder
1/4 teaspoon coarsely ground pink Himalayan salt, for dusting

NUTRITION FACTS
(per serving)

209 calories
13 g fat
16 g carbs
6 g protein
4 g fiber
12.5 g sugar

Sometimes you need just a bite of something chocolatey, and sometimes you need a whole batch! You're better off going for something that uses cacao over cocoa powder (see the box on page 255) and that is a lot lower in sugar—you won't even miss sugar in this seemingly decadent fudge.

Note: Try different gourmet flavor varieties of sea salt for a fun twist.

1. Line a small loaf pan with parchment paper or waxed paper, leaving a few inches overhanging all four sides.

2. Combine the almond butter, coconut oil, honey, and vanilla in a microwave-safe bowl. Microwave for about 30 seconds to warm the mixture, then stir until smooth. Sift in the cacao powder and whisk to incorporate.

3. Pour the mixture into the prepared pan and spread it out evenly with a spatula. Dust it with the salt. Freeze it for at least 2 hours, or until it is firm and set.

4. Use the overhanging parchment to carefully lift the block of fudge out of the pan. Place it on a cutting board and cut it into 1-inch squares (there should be 10 to 12 squares). Serve immediately, or within 15 to 20 minutes. Store any remaining fudge in an airtight container in the freezer . . . for chocolate emergencies! It should keep for at least two months.

Harvest Apple Crisp

Prep time: 25 minutes
Total time: 1 hour 10 minutes

Serves 6

FOR THE FILLING:

1 teaspoon coconut oil, for greasing the pan
3 tart medium apples, cored and chopped
3 tablespoons real maple syrup
3 tablespoons unsweetened almond milk
2 tablespoons almond flour
1½ teaspoons pumpkin pie spice
½ teaspoon pure vanilla extract
1 scoop protein powder (optional, vanilla or plain, preferably unsweetened)

FOR THE TOPPING:

¾ cup chopped raw pecans or walnuts
½ cup unsweetened coconut flakes
¼ cup almond flour
¼ teaspoon pumpkin pie spice
2 tablespoons real maple syrup

Sugar? Who needs sugar? Reducing or removing sugar in a fruit dessert is fine because fruit is God's candy! Apples are a delicious, guilt-free way to enjoy the sweeter things in life, and they make this seasonal dessert perfect. I recommend Braeburn apples for this recipe, but if you can't find them, use any tart apple, like Granny Smith. Almond flour is a great alternative to regular white flour, as it will firm up and bind your baked goods without adding unnecessary empty carbohydrate calories. Add walnuts and coconut flakes for healthy fat, and I'd say this dessert is balanced enough to call a meal! (Why not have it for breakfast?) Serve this at a party with organic ice cream or vegan ice cream for a real treat!

1. Make the filling: Preheat the oven to 375°F. Grease an 8-inch square baking pan or glass pie dish with the coconut oil.

2. In a large bowl, combine the apples, maple syrup, almond milk, almond flour, pumpkin pie spice, vanilla, and protein powder (if using) and stir until the apples are fully coated. Pour the filling into the prepared pan. Smooth it into an even layer.

3. Make the topping: In a medium bowl, combine the pecans, coconut flakes, almond flour, and pumpkin pie spice and stir to combine. Gently fold in the maple syrup until crumbles form.

4. Spoon the topping evenly over the apples, making sure to keep the crumbles intact. Cover tightly with aluminum foil and bake for 30 minutes. Uncover and bake for 10 to 15 minutes more, until the top is golden brown. Let cool for at least 15 minutes before enjoying.

healthy swap practice

Now it's your turn! Think of a favorite recipe of yours that you *know* could be healthier than it is. Write it in your journal on the left side of the page, then on the right side of the page, rewrite it with all your ideas for what you could swap out or otherwise change to make the recipe healthier. Then . . . try it! Make your new healthy swap version and see how it tastes.

I suggest making just a few swaps at first, like whole-grain flour for white flour, cutting the cheese or oil or sugar in half, or adding a little less meat and replacing it with seafood or, better yet, a few more veggies. Then, as your palate adjusts, you can start making bigger swaps: replace traditional pasta or rice with zucchini noodles or cauliflower rice; cut out all the cheese or switch to fat-free cheese; replace all the meat with fiber-rich beans or even tofu; replace all the sugar with natural sweeteners like maple syrup or applesauce; replace all the oil or butter in your favorite baked goods with applesauce, mashed banana, or pumpkin puree. There are a million ways to make swaps. Your experiments might not *all* be successes, but the more you practice healthy swaps, the better you'll get, as you gain experience and a more refined sense of what works and what doesn't. Have fun with this—I know I do!

10

BEFORE YOU CHEAT

Vice Management and Derailers

heat? Who, me? When it comes to food, I'm as tempted as anyone. I have my weaknesses. I have my vices. And I certainly have a lot of elements in my life that threaten to derail me. I've learned that balance is more important than never letting so-called bad foods pass your lips. You can have vices and manage them, and you can handle derailers if you're ready for them.

You might like to kick back with a glass of wine at the end of the day. Maybe jumbo margaritas or Venti double mochas are more your thing. Or maybe your weakness is chocolate chip cookies, nachos, or a big bowl of pasta—I don't judge. Whatever your derailer food is, giving it up entirely may not be the answer. Having control over it rather than letting it control you *is* the answer.

But how do you control a vice? How do you resist that fancy coffee drink or that cookie when it's calling your name? What if your friends are always tempting you, or you can't resist the leftover macaroni and cheese on your child's plate, or *it's your birthday*?

Nobody can be perfect all the time. However, your greatest weapon against the temptations that threaten to derail you is, like the Boy Scouts say, being prepared. If you know there's a situation coming up that's going to test your willpower—like a holiday or a girls' night out—or if you know that temptation could strike for you at any time—like a sudden hunger craving or your husband deciding to surprise you by bringing home a *box of doughnuts*—be prepared. Have strategies in place that you can call on to resist temptation. It won't always work, but as long as it works most of the time—as long as your week balances out to be mostly good choices—you're going to be just fine. You'll stay on the Fit52 track.

Let's talk about some common derailers and how to combat them by being prepared. Most of these are food-related, but I'll throw in some exercise derailers here, too. Because sometimes, the couch is calling.

Derailer #1: Advertising

Oh, the lure of the billboard showing that plate of pancakes, the semi-truck with the giant photo of french fries on the side on its way to deliver food to a fast-food restaurant, those commercials that make food look so amazing . . . You can be doing just fine, feeling good about yourself, not even hungry, and then you see an advertisement for some naughty food and suddenly you *just have to have it.* Of course, companies want to make money, so they're very good at creating advertisements that make decadent food look irresistible. How do you resist the temptation?

Advertisements, especially for food, are geared to encourage impulse buys. You see a Frappuccino on a poster and you swerve right into the next Starbucks. You see a display of chocolate cupcakes with frosting at the store and you grab one and put it in your cart. You see a television commercial for a gooey, cheesy pizza, and you pick up the phone and order one. It's so easy to do, and that's what advertisers depend on. To save yourself from yourself (and from those ads), make a rule like, if advertising triggers you, you can't do anything about it for one hour (or even just half an hour). Use that hour to consider whether there's a healthy swap for the treat you're craving. Could you go home and make a lighter coffee drink or a healthier pizza, or just have a square of dark chocolate instead of a cupcake? Is there a healthier option right where you are, like an almond milk latte, veggie pizza (hold the cheese), or a mini cupcake you could savor? Or better yet, can you find a protein bar or an apple?

This isn't always foolproof because sometimes the idea of the cupcake will get stuck in your brain and you *will* still want it in an hour. But most of the time, after some time, the immediate effect of the advertising will have passed, and you will be more rational. You'll have time to think, *Wait a minute, I don't want to eat a delivery pizza. It will make me feel terrible later. Maybe I'll make a healthy version instead.* You've built in a window for making a better decision. If you make this a hard-and-fast rule for yourself, then you'll be less likely to end up a victim of your own whims or of advertising.

Derailer #2: Eyeballing It

If you've read this far, you know that I'm a planner, a tracker, a calculator, and an organizer. I want to know exactly what I'm eating and doing every day. But this isn't just because it's fun (although I do enjoy it). It's also because if I don't do this, I'll be totally derailed.

I've seen so many diet programs that tell you to "Stop counting calories! Don't track everything! You'll never keep it up!" I am living proof that this isn't true—at least not for me. I could eat just about anyone I know under the table and still not be full. I remember we had a pizza party in my choir class back in eighth grade, and I got into a pizza-eating contest with some boy. And I won. There has always been a disconnect between my stomach-fullness sensors and my brain. I've never had that switch that's supposed to tell you when you're full. Some people just know when to stop. They know because their bodies tell them they've had enough. Not mine. If I ever say I'm full, it's because I know, objectively, that I am full based on how much I've eaten. But I don't really feel it. I know I'm not the only one. Many of us just don't have that natural instinct.

To counteract this fact about myself, I make a plan for how much food I'm going to put on my plate and eat at every meal, and I stick to it. Whether it's a slice of pizza or a half cup of Brussels sprouts, I am accountable, and you better believe I'm going to quantify it. Eyeballing just doesn't work for me. If I try to eyeball portions, they creep up in size. If I put a cup of pasta on my plate but I don't measure it, you can bet that what I think is a cup is actually closer to two cups. You'd be surprised at how inaccurate eyeballing it can be.

You also might think that measuring is pretty black and white, and that 1 cup is always 8 ounces, but that is not necessarily true. First of all, liquid ounces (a measure of volume) are different than solid ounces (a measure of weight). And the weight of 1 cup (also a measure of volume) depends on what's *in* that measuring cup. A cup of green beans, a cup of yogurt, and a cup of popcorn all have different weights, and measuring

Body Image, Self-Esteem, and Motivation

I love that we are in a cultural moment of body acceptance. It's about time! We are all genetically different. We all have different shapes, and we all have our individual hurdles. I gain weight in my midsection first and lose it there last. That's my trouble area, so I have to watch out for that.

But I understand why some people have a problem with terms like "trouble area." They say you should love all of yourself, that there are no trouble areas, and I totally get that. If you feel good right where you are, that's awesome. But if you don't, I think it's reasonable to look at what you can't change and what you can. If you're not 100 percent happy with your current fitness or strength level or weight or general health, there are things you can do to optimize those aspects of

yourself, while still loving your body. There's nothing wrong with wanting to improve. It's still body acceptance. In fact, it's body love.

I feel best, strongest, fittest, and most confident when I *don't* let my midsection (or any other part of me) get out of hand. I feel better knowing I call the shots (for the most part) when it comes to managing my own fitness, health, strength, stamina, and shape. When I don't like what I see in the mirror, instead of beating myself up, I try to use it as motivation. When I know I've gone a little overboard and I don't like the way my body looks or feels as a result, I acknowledge that I made those decisions, and that I can make different ones. I have the power to change, and knowing that gives me confidence.

by cups or fractions of a cup isn't very accurate. Let's say, for example, that you're going to have a bowl of cereal. The label on the cereal box says that a serving size is ¾ cup (31 grams). How much is that, really? You can take out your measuring cup and fill it to the ¾ cup line. But how accurate is that measurement? Is it a heaping cup? Or should you be filling it to just below the line? There's a lot of uncertainty, which is why one of my favorite tools is a digital kitchen scale. A scale tells me exactly how much I'm eating in a way a measuring cup can't.

So about that cereal—if the box says that a serving is ¾ cup (31 grams), then you can put your bowl on your food scale and pour in cereal until you get to exactly 31 grams. It's way more precise. Then you know *exactly* how much you're eating, and therefore how many calories and how much fat, carbs, protein, sugar, and vitamins you are getting. If you don't do this, you could inadvertently end up eating double or triple the number of calories or sugar grams you thought you were eating, and over time, that will add up.

Of course, you can't always do this. If you're out to eat with friends or at someone's house, you can't exactly pull out your measuring cups and spoons and scale. But if you do this at home for a few weeks, you'll get better at estimating how much you're eating in situations where you can't measure. It's not something to get obsessed about. It's just something to keep you honest.

Derailer #3: Boredom

If you tend to snack out of boredom (or when you're doing something inactive, like watching TV), you should recognize that this kind of bored eating is a habit—and one that you can break. They say that the only way to truly break one habit is to replace it with another one. So my suggestion is to replace bored eating with a different, healthy habit.

Begin by making a list of things you can do instead of eating every time you're bored, or watching TV, or doing whatever it is that triggers you to snack when you're not hungry. Put the list on your phone, or somewhere you'll always have it handy, so that as soon as you get that feeling of wanting to eat, you can pull up that list and have an alternative right there in front of you. Some ideas might be:

> › **EXERCISE.** You can't stuff your face if you're on the floor doing sit-ups and push-ups. You can't wander into the kitchen if you're out

going out for a walk or riding your bike. You can't plow through a whole bag of potato chips if you're doing burpees. When you're bored, get up and move. When you're watching TV, get up and move (at least during the commercials).

› **DO SOMETHING WITH YOUR HANDS.** Do you know how to knit or crochet? Draw or color in one of those adult coloring books? Do something with your hands so that you can't eat. Go through a junk drawer and clean it out. Organize your closet. Go through your clothes to find things you don't wear anymore. Plan out your to-do list for the next day. Braid your hair. Polish your toenails or fingernails. Write in your journal. Go into the kitchen and do a little meal prep, like chopping veggies for the week. Keep those hands busy, and you might even get the bonus of accomplishing something you've been putting off.

Making TV Time Count

Every evening, I have my decompression time, when I finally get to sit down, relax, and watch some mindless TV. I love doing this. It is so relaxing to me. But if I sit there for too long, I start to feel guilty and unproductive. So what I do is I totally relax during the show—completely, no guilt—but as soon as there is a commercial break, I take things upstairs, or move that pile of books or clothes, or get laundry out of the dryer and fold a few items in the laundry room until I hear the show coming back on. Then I'm back on the couch, totally relaxed again. Until the next commercial, when I'm up and moving.

By the end of the show, the laundry is folded, all the things that need to be upstairs are upstairs, and I've gotten some things done. *And* I've totally relieved my stress. I feel relaxed and ready to sleep.

Derailer #4: Kids

Let's be honest: Kids are *not* great influences when it comes to your diet. Maybe you're one of those lucky moms whose kids eat vegetables all the time, but most of us really struggle with this. I've read all that advice about how to sneak vegetables into your kids' food, and I don't know about your kids, but mine *know*. I tried to give my son some of those tater tots with broccoli in them, and he was like, "What's wrong with these tater tots?"

And when he doesn't eat those yummy crispy broccoli tater tots, guess who does? Guess who finishes the chocolate chip waffle he didn't eat, or his spaghetti, or his fruit? Even if it's something healthy, I didn't plan for it, I don't really want it, and I certainly don't need it. I already had breakfast, so why did I eat his leftovers?

About Parental Guilt

Parents feel guilty about *so many things*, from feeling like we aren't feeding our kids food that is healthy enough to guilt over not spending enough time with them. Even when I work out, I feel guilty because I think, *That's an hour I could have spent with my kids.* Logically, I know that I'm a better mom because I work out. It makes me feel happier, calmer, and stronger, and it gives me the energy and endurance I need to be the mom my kids need. But parental guilt isn't always logical. It can really get you down if you let it. It can even trigger mindless eating, to try to relieve the guilty feelings. And then you feel even guiltier for not modeling good eating habits and not having more willpower.

Whatever you do, don't let guilt be an excuse to make bad decisions for yourself. You need that exercise. You need to eat well. Everything good you do for yourself is something good you do for your children, even if it's not directly spending time with them. That includes exercising, eating well, and even having a fulfilling career that makes you happy. There is nothing better for a child than happy, healthy, balanced, loving parents.

I'll tell you why: Because I hate wasting food. I really despise it. I will eat leftovers *for days*. So when I see that extra food on his plate, I can't bear to waste it. This is why I'm always finishing my son's food, but it's a complete derailer, and I really have to stop doing it. When you eat the leftover food on your kid's plate, you are playing the role of human garbage can. And a garbage can doesn't have fitness goals. When I find myself falling into this trap, I always log every bite that I ate. I have to face up to it and be accountable.

Conquering this one is really just a matter of either eating less at your own meal to compensate for the food you know you're going to eat off your child's plate, or getting used to throwing away a little bit of food. It's okay. Your child ate what he or she needed to eat. That old, cold food isn't benefiting anyone, so throwing it away is actually the best option. Just keep telling yourself that! (I keep telling myself that, but I haven't totally mastered this one yet.)

Derailer #5: Spouses, Partners, and Roommates

Don't think it's just the kids encouraging you to cheat. Spouses, or anyone you live with, can be big derailers, too. My husband is a (recently retired) professional athlete. He can eat a *lot* of food. He also snacks a lot. When we first got married, we would eat together all the time, until I realized I can't eat every time he eats because he eats ten times a day! He can eat pasta when I know I shouldn't eat pasta. He also loves to have dessert, but he can get away with having dessert every night, whereas I can't. (Now that he's retired and not burning a kajillion calories a day

playing hockey, however, he's starting to adjust the way he eats.) Also, he's not five foot three like I am.

Don't let yourself fall into the trap of thinking you can eat exactly the way your spouse (or anyone else, for that matter) can. Only you can know and decide what amount of food and what type of food is right for you. Decide, and stick to it . . . even when your husband is eating a huge tub of buttered popcorn or a bowl of ice cream the size of a small dog.

Derailer #6: Friends

Friends can be a major derailer. You can love your friends and still recognize when they are being a bad influence. For whatever reason, people feel more comfortable if other people are doing what they're doing, so if your friends are splurging and you aren't, they're probably going to try to convince you that you should, too. Even if you aren't in the mood. Even if you don't want it. There have been times when I ate something I didn't want to eat just because my friends were doing it, and I regretted that choice. Experts say that friends tend to end up similar in weight and health, so see if you can be the good influence instead of the victim. Maybe you can shift your whole group dynamic. It can't hurt to try!

But it can be tough. One of my best friends laughs whenever I comment on her bad food choices, but somehow, she never gains weight. I couldn't figure it out until I started watching more closely. When she has pizza, she piles two or three slices on her plate, but then she just kind of picks at it, so she really only eats the equivalent of one slice. When she talks me into ordering pizza and I put three slices on my plate, you know I'm going to eat them all. Or she'll talk me into opening a bag of M&M's, and then she'll only have a couple while I basically eat the rest of the bag. I finally had to tell her, "Please, you've got to stop! You're a derailer!"

I'm not saying you shouldn't hang out with certain friends based on their food choices. But I do think you need to recognize which friends are your health friends, and which are your health foes. And when your health foes want to order that pizza, pluck up the courage to say, "No, because I can't eat pizza the way you eat pizza, and I'm the one who's going to pay for it tomorrow." Then enlist your like-minded health friends into speaking up with you and convincing the others to order something healthier. You could also try to make your social times with your friends about something other than food. And if none of this works, talk to that friend who is derailing you. Let them know about your goals and ask for their support on your journey. If your friend loves you and wants you to be the best you can be, they'll understand. It's okay to put your own health first.

Derailer #7: Injuries

You're making great progress, getting stronger, in the habit of exercising every day, and then boom . . . you get injured. Derailed! You may have to completely stay off your feet for a while. You might have to get physical therapy that focuses more on rehab than real exercise, and before you know it, you've lost a lot of the progress you've made.

When you get injured or you're recovering from something like surgery, you may think you have a great excuse to skip your workouts. Think again! Injuries are one of the top reasons formerly fit people get out of shape, and it can take a long time to get back to where you were. Obviously, you should not do any exercise that could worsen your injury or compromise your recovery in any way. But find a way to work out your other parts while whatever part of you is healing heals. You just need to be a little creative.

I broke my wrist in 2017, and at first, I didn't know what to do, because a good portion of my regular exercises was off-limits. Sure, I could've lifted weights with my one good arm, but you don't want to build strength on only one side of your body because that can lead to other problems later. I couldn't do push-ups. I couldn't do pull-ups. I couldn't even hold a weight in my injured hand. This one injury made me rethink everything I was doing.

Getting injured showed me how much I used my arms while working out—I mean, of course you use your arms when you work out, but I hadn't really noticed that until I couldn't do it anymore. It only took a few days for my arm muscles to go lax. I could poke them, and they felt like Jell-O. I was losing all my muscle tone! It was surprising to me to see how little time it actually takes for muscles to start breaking down.

I wanted to keep working out, but with an injury, it's definitely important to be mindful and careful. You don't want to do anything that will aggravate the injury and make your healing time even longer. Then I got the idea of a weighted vest. If I wore it, I could at least do lower body exercises with some weight, to keep my legs strong while my wrist was

healing. That helped a lot. It gave me extra weight to do leg exercises like squats and lunges and step-ups without holding weights in my hands. I used the heck out of that weighted vest! I also tried to stay as active as possible and did my physical therapy religiously. As I got cleared to do more, I slowly built on my progress, increasing what I was doing and easing back in.

Even now, although I can finally hold a weight and do push-ups and pull-ups again, I still feel like I have to be careful when I'm doing anything fast that involves my wrist, like burpees. Sometimes I also think my right side and left side still look a bit different. It's a long road back after a serious injury. I don't know if my wrist will ever be all the way back to where it was, but at least I've been able to get back to my previous fitness level.

My husband, Mike, had this same problem in reverse. When he tore his Achilles tendon, he couldn't do any of his typical lower body workouts. He couldn't run or do the elliptical trainer or even ride a bicycle. How was he going to keep up with cardio? Enter the arm cycle! This machine lets you use your arms to "pedal" like you would on an exercise bike, so you can rest your lower body while still getting your heart rate up. He could also do weights while sitting, so he focused on his upper body while his injury healed.

If you aren't sure the best way to exercise with your injury, I recommend consulting with a physical therapist (your doctor may have already prescribed physical therapy) or a trainer who is experienced in exercising with specific injuries. There is always a way to keep going, even if you have to modify. When your injury is healed, you can ease back into what you were doing before, and it won't be as hard as it would be if you spent all your healing time sitting on the couch eating doughnuts.

Derailer #8: Stress

Stress is a huge reason why people eat when they don't really want or need to eat. The "high" from food can temporarily make you forget about the stress, but obviously, it's still there. Eating cookies won't get rid of the source of your stress. The obvious thing to do here is to figure out what's causing your stress and deal with it directly, instead of dealing with it indirectly and ineffectively with food.

You can also make a list of things you can do to manage your stress that might actually help it, rather than making it worse due to guilt from overeating. Exercise is one of the best ways to manage stress, so that would always be my number one recommendation. A good 30 minutes of cardio is my favorite way to blow off steam. Or just take a walk. Sometimes, being outside can make stress melt away.

Other ideas for stress management:

› Try yoga or meditation. These aren't really things I do, but they help a lot of people.

› Do some stretching and deep breathing on your own—no training necessary.

› Make a date with that friend you can pour your heart out to. Go have coffee or meet for a walk and talk it all out. Someone else's point of view might help you get perspective.

Keep in mind that a certain amount of stress is good (believe it or not). It trains you to manage the problems that inevitably crop up in life, and it can give you the energy and kick in the pants you need to recognize and solve problems. But it shouldn't go on and on. And we all need decompression time, a break from our stress for a while.

Remember that stress eating, no matter how good it feels in the moment, will do nothing to reduce your stress and will probably make it worse. Eating is the remedy for hunger, not stress. Instead, the next time you're stressed, sit back, put your feet up, breathe, and take a time-out. If

Sleep Deprivation

Studies have shown that people who are sleep-deprived are more likely to have carb cravings and binge on things like sugar and chips. Keep this in mind, and make sure that you're getting enough sleep. Now that I have little ones, I don't get as much sleep as I used to. I'm generally good with about six hours, but when I'm lucky enough to get seven hours, it's amazing. Eight hours may be that magic number for you. We all go through busy times in our lives when we're not getting as much sleep as we'd like. I take the opportunity to catch up whenever I can, and I'm not ashamed to go to bed early. If I'm traveling and not with my family, I'll go to bed at eight o'clock if I can, or I'll sleep in. I think this helps me a lot with discipline. I know that it's tough when you're busy, but instead of indulging that late night carb craving, why not just get in bed early and catch up on some z's?

you can't do this in the exact moment that the stress hits you, fit it into your day somewhere. We all need to do this. Make your decompression time sacred. You need it!

Derailer #9: Holidays and Special Occasions

This is a big one for me, because I am all about enjoying life. I gave you a lot of advice about how to indulge smartly in the last chapter, but here's another approach to holidays and special occasions: Instead of letting these big life events be traps for getting derailed, let them be motivators. Christmas is coming? Train for it. Thanksgiving? Train for it. Fourth of July barbecue? Train for it.

your derailers

What are your derailers? What triggers you to cheat? In your journal:

1. Make a list of all the situations and people that tend to derail you.
2. Next to each derailer, write at least one way you could manage it, to keep yourself from cheating or to balance it.
3. Write ten really pleasurable things you love to do that don't involve food.
4. At the end of your list, write one sentence (approximately) to remind you why your long-term goals are more important than the short-term thrill of a cheat. What do you want out of this life? What is your motivation? Whenever you're tempted, or life threatens to derail you, remember what you wrote here.

Maybe you have a vacation coming up. Instead of thinking, *Oh no, I'm going to eat everything!* you could think, *Hey, I want to rock a swimsuit. What a great goal for getting in better shape!* For me it might be an awards show. I know I want to feel and look my best on camera, so that motivates me to go hard. Maybe you're getting a family photo taken, or you have a class reunion or a wedding or a birthday coming up. Maybe it's just going to be summer soon and you want to wear shorts and a tank top. Let these occasions be your guiding star, your reason to be strong and make good decisions.

I train for the special occasions and holidays because I believe it's useful to have goals and finish lines. My mind-set is, "Okay, for the next two weeks, I'm going to be strict. Then, the night of this big event, I'm going to enjoy myself." The next morning, I know that I ate french fries or cake, but I trained for it, and it was only one night. It was worth it because I had fun. That's my attitude. Then I get right back in the gym. The trick is not to let it go on and on. I never think, *I splurged, so I might as well just keep going.* No way. I partied, I celebrated, and now it's time to get back to being responsible and accountable. It's one and done, then back on track.

You may have many occasions to add to this list. There is no reason why occasions meant for fun and celebration have to destroy you. There is always a way to participate without going overboard, and to enjoy your life while still being healthy. If you go off the rails, just get right back on. Don't waste time wallowing. You are strong, and you can keep getting stronger if you stay focused and plan. And always be accountable for everything you do, whether it's a victory or a cheat.

epilogue
SEE YOU AGAIN

The ideas, exercises, recipes, and advice I've put into these pages are strategies that have worked for me, and that I wanted to share with you. Everyone is different, and you may find that some ideas in this book speak to you and others don't. Above all, I hope that my Fit52 way of living has inspired you to get up, get out there, and get healthy, and that you are finding ways to apply some or all of its principles to your own life. I hope that in some small way, I have helped you to find your own path.

We are growing and changing all the time. At every stage of my life, there have been important people accompanying me on my journey, since long before anyone knew my name. Today, people still come up to me to say that they voted for me on *American Idol*. They were with me all along. Now that we're at the end of this book, I feel like you're with me, too—and I hope you know that I'm also with you.

Life isn't always easy. We will all have challenges, and we will always have things we need to figure out, but we're all capable of making positive changes in our lives. You just have to find your motivation, get yourself moving, and make healthy choices that will fuel and sustain your body while also making your life more enjoyable. There are hard times, but there are joyful times, too, and life can be rich and full of beautiful moments, gestures of love, periods of calm, and times for celebration.

You can participate in all of it. The goal of the Fit52 lifestyle is to live your best life—not a life of deprivation, but a life of nourishing plea-

sures, healthy adventures, active days, soul-satisfying food, and an ever-evolving sense of who you are and who you are meant to become.

Before you go, I would like to send you off with a few key things to remember about balance, pleasure, happiness, and health—some thoughts that I hope will stay with you on your journey:

> Remember where you came from.

> Dream big.

> Prioritize love.

> Know that you can always change, no matter where you're starting from.

> Try to be active on most days.

> Accentuate and celebrate the parts of you that you love.

> Anywhere you go, there is potential for movement.

> Food can be pleasurable and healthy at the same time.

> Anyone can cook.

> You can make your favorite indulgences work for you.

> Everybody needs a break. Take time to relax and decompress whenever you can.

> Live fully and embrace each God-given day on this beautiful planet.

> Loving yourself underlies all motivation to becoming a better person, so don't withhold your self-love. You matter.

Thank you for spending this time with me. I wish you all nothing but the most wonderful blessings for a healthy, happy life rich with love and goodness.

xoxo,

Carrie

appendix 1

MY JOURNAL ACCOUNTABILITY
TEMPLATE FOR TRACKING

This is the general setup I use for tracking my food and exercise in my journal every night. You can put this into your own journal or tweak it to work for your own needs.

As you can see, every day I record my steps and calories burned from both the apps I use. I write down everything I ate and the calories and macronutrients as calculated by the MyFitnessPal app. I write down which Fit52 exercises I did for each set and each suit, and any other exercise I did that day, such as walking, running, a different workout (like the leg workout or some other workout my trainer might give me while I'm on the road), or any "extracurricular fitness" I did that day, along with how much time I spent on Fit52 exercises and how much total exercise time I got that day.

Finally, that last section, Thoughts/Notes/Feelings, is for anything I want to remember about that day, like if I was on the road or at home, if I was feeling good or not so great, or anything unusual happening in my life that day that could account for any irregularities in my eating or exercise.

This may or may not work for you, so make yours any version you want in your journal. Or make copies of this template to use on your own every day. You can tuck them into your journal or three-hole-punch them and put them in a binder. Whatever works for you.

DATE:

Steps:	Fitbit calories burned:	MyFitnessPal calories burned:

FOOD I ATE TODAY:

Breakfast:	Snack:	Lunch:	Snack:	Dinner:	Evening:

NUTRITION:

Calories:	Fat:	Carbs:	Protein:	Fiber:	Sugar:

Water (ounces):

FIT52 WORKOUT

SET #1
Diamonds:

Hearts:

Clubs:

Spades:

SET #2
Diamonds:

Hearts:

Clubs:

Spades:

Fit52 time (minutes):

Other exercise:

Total time all exercise (minutes):

Thoughts/Notes/Feelings:

appendix 2

MODIFICATIONS
FOR THE FIT52 WORKOUT

MODIFY UP OR MODIFY DOWN

The exercises in the Fit52 Workout are designed for those who have a moderate fitness level, but that does not cover everybody. If you find any of the exercises to be too difficult, you can always decrease the weight or reps, or look here for a "Modify Down" version. If you find any of the exercises too easy, you can always increase the weight or reps, or look here for a "Modify Up" version. These are all simple modifications that can help you customize the Fit52 Workout to you and your current fitness level.

All comments below on these modifications come from my trainer Eve Overland, who has customized these levels just for you and what you need to do for yourself right now. Remember to meet yourself where you are—but also challenge yourself to keep progressing!

DAY #1

◆ PUSH-UPS

> › MODIFY DOWN: Do the push-ups from your knees, or on an incline (hands on bench).
> › MODIFY UP: Try more advanced push-up variations, such as decline, plyometric, alligator, etc.

♥ DOUBLE SUITCASE SQUATS

> › MODIFY DOWN: Do a bodyweight squat with no weight, or a Box Squat, sitting down on the bench and standing up.
> › MODIFY UP: Use the heaviest weight that will still allow you to maintain good form.

♣ REVERSE CRUNCHES WITH LEG DROP

> › MODIFY DOWN: Shorten the lever by making less distance between you and the "weight" (your legs), reducing the resistance. Do this by bending your knees at 90 degrees while lifting and lowering them. You can also drop one leg at a time.
> › MODIFY UP: Keep your legs straight. Work on control and try not to use momentum. Don't let your feet touch the ground on the leg drop. The lower you go, the more difficult this is.

♠ STAR JUMPS OR STAR JACKS

> › MODIFY DOWN: Do Squat Jumps (omit the "star" step) or do Jumping Jacks.
> › MODIFY UP: Use a mini band around your ankles.

TRICEPS BENCH DIPS

> › MODIFY DOWN: Keep your knees at 90 degrees.
> › MODIFY UP: Straighten your legs or perform an Elevated Triceps Dip between two benches of the same height, with your hands on one bench and your feet on the other. Be mindful of positioning. Make sure that the exercise focuses on your triceps and doesn't put an inappropriate load on your shoulders.

 STEP UPS

> › MODIFY DOWN: Do a Step Up to a box with a lower height.
> › MODIFY UP: Increase the load with dumbbells, kettlebells, or a barbell.

 PLANK AROUND-THE-WORLDS

> › MODIFY DOWN: Use a bent-knee plank position (instead of keeping your legs straight), or do Bird Dog: This is where you get on your hands and knees into a tabletop position (like you're getting ready to crawl). You lift up your right arm and left leg at the same time, return to tabletop, then lift your left arm and right leg at the same time, keeping your hips and shoulders square and your core engaged.
> › MODIFY UP: Use a mini band around your ankles or over your knees.

JUMP LUNGES

> › MODIFY DOWN: Fast Scissor Feet (front and back), or Alternating Step-Ups (as fast as possible).
> › MODIFY UP: Add weight with a medicine ball, sandbag, or even kettlebell or dumbbells. But when adding load to exercises where you are jumping (plyometric exercises) like this one, be mindful of choosing an appropriate weight.

DAY #2

 SET #1:

 LAT PULL-DOWNS

› MODIFY DOWN: Use a lighter resistance band.
› MODIFY UP: Use a heavier resistance band, or double up and use two bands. A pull-up would also be a great variation here.

 ALTERNATING CURTSY LUNGES

› MODIFY DOWN: Assist yourself with balance using a chair or other sturdy object, and only go down as far as your mobility and flexibility will allow. Continue working on strength, stability, and mobility so you can perfect your form and achieve a greater range of motion.
› MODIFY UP: Add resistance with dumbbells, a barbell, a kettlebell, or a medicine ball.

 SUPER PLANKS OR PLANK UP-DOWNS

› MODIFY DOWN: Perform the exercise on your knees (keeping a straight spine).
› MODIFY UP: Focus on bracing your entire core, avoid shifting your hips from side to side. You want zero rocking and rolling. Place your hand exactly where your elbow was. You will feel the difference. If you really want to get crazy, you could add resistance with a weighted vest, or you could "plyo pop-up" from your forearms to your hands in one explosive movement. This takes serious skill . . . but hey, it's a great party trick.

♠ SKATERS

> › MODIFY DOWN: Take out the jump. Take large lateral steps from side to side. Because this is the cardio section, the goal is to keep the pace moving.
> › MODIFY UP: Go for length and height. Keep the back foot elevated.

SET #2:

♦ BICEPS CURLS

> › MODIFY DOWN: Alternate arms, doing one curl at a time.
> › MODIFY UP: Go as heavy as possible with strict and deliberate form. No swinging and no momentum.

♥ BANDED SQUAT TAP-OUTS

> › MODIFY DOWN: Omit the band.
> › MODIFY UP: Use a heavier band or double up and use two bands.

♣ SIT-UPS WITH CROSS PUNCHES

> › MODIFY DOWN: Omit the dumbbells. Anchor your feet underneath the couch or another set of dumbbells.
> › MODIFY UP: Increase the weight, but not too much. I rarely give clients heavier than 10-pound dumbbells for this exercise, or for any punching or shadowboxing, for that matter. If you go too heavy, it decreases the range of motion in the arms, and form goes out the window. I find that the cross punches just become little jabs. This exercise's focus is on the core, so add some resistance with the dumbbells, but not so much that it just becomes a struggle for the arms. More is not more in this case, and not worth injury.

♠ LOG HOPS

› **MODIFY DOWN:** Start in plank position and tap one leg out to the side. Return to center, then tap the other leg out to the side.

› **MODIFY UP:** Place your hands forward on the bench, so you must hop over the bench and not behind it. Try not to double bounce.

DAY #3

♦ DIVEBOMBERS

› **MODIFY DOWN:** Up Dog to Down Dog (as in the warm-up).

› **MODIFY UP:** Go back the way you came, rather than swooping down and then immediately pushing your hips back up. When you look up with your chest up, bend your elbows and go backward through the same motions in reverse order.

♥ HAMSTRING ROLL-OUTS

› **MODIFY DOWN:** Lie on your back, bend your knees, and place your feet flat on the ground, hip-width apart (like you are setting up to do a basic crunch). Drive through your heels and lift your hips up off the ground. Squeeze your glutes and hamstrings at the top, then return to the starting position. To make it a little more challenging, try Glute Bridges with your feet on the ball: Set up the same as for Hamstring Roll-Outs, with your back on the floor, feet on the ball, and knees bent at 90 degrees. Instead of rolling out, just lift and lower your hips.

> › MODIFY UP: Do one leg at a time on the stability ball, right then left.

♣ BICYCLES

> › MODIFY DOWN: Turn this into Dead Bug exercise by taking out the twist. Lie flat on the floor with your arms by your sides, or lift them straight up to the ceiling. Lift your legs and bend your knees to 90 degrees. Your knees should be right over your hips and your lower back should stay connected to the floor. Lower one leg at a time, without touching the floor. Return to the starting position and repeat with the other leg.
> › MODIFY UP: Do this with straight legs.

♠ UP AND OVERS

> › MODIFY DOWN: Slow down the movement and perform lateral step-ups.
> › MODIFY UP: Jump high at the top and get some air. Or add a (lighter) set of dumbbells.

SET #2:

♦ CHEST FLYS

> › MODIFY DOWN: Use a lighter band.
> › MODIFY UP: Use a heavier band, or double up on the bands, but don't go so heavy that your form breaks down and the motion is recruited from the shoulders and not the chest. This could result in injury.

♥ ROMANIAN DEADLIFTS

› MODIFY DOWN: Body Weight Good Mornings. This is similar to a Romanian Deadlift, only you place your hands behind your head with your elbows wide and "take a bow," then return to standing.

› MODIFY UP: Use a heavier weight (for advanced), or do Single-Leg Deadlifts, right and left.

♣ MOUNTAIN CLIMBERS

› MODIFY DOWN: Do these slowly and with control, or on an incline with your hands on the bench.

› MODIFY UP: Do Decline Mountain Climbers, with your feet on a bench or up a wall.

♠ REVERSE LUNGES WITH HOP

› MODIFY DOWN: Omit the hop and just perform reverse lunges as quickly as you can while keeping good form.

› MODIFY UP: Add weight with dumbbells, a medicine ball, or a kettlebell. I would recommend not going too heavy if using dumbbells or a kettlebell.

DAY #4

SET #1:

SHOULDER PRESSES

› MODIFY DOWN: Press up one weight at a time, alternating arms, or use lighter dumbbells or bands.

> MODIFY UP: Go as heavy as possible with good form. If you perform this seated, you can't assist yourself with your legs or do a "push press," so I would argue that this variation is harder.

♥ SUMO SQUATS WITH UPRIGHT ROW

> MODIFY DOWN: Alternate single-arm upright row using a lighter weight.
> MODIFY UP: Work on making this exercise as explosive as possible in one fluid motion. Don't think of it as two separate exercises—the leg drive creates the power, and the arms and shoulders just go along for the ride.

♣ SIT-UP AND REACH

> MODIFY DOWN: Don't use any weights—just reach your arms overhead.
> MODIFY UP: Do this with straight arms and straight legs (this is called a Get Up Sit-Up).

♠ JUMP ROPE X10

> MODIFY DOWN: Jump in place and twirl a pretend rope. I know that it sounds silly, but it will get your heart rate up. If that is too much, do High Knees or run in place. The point is to bump up that cardio.
> MODIFY UP: Double-Unders (two rope spins per jump). If you do Double-Unders, only do singles, not x 10 . . . unless you are super advanced! For example, if your card is a 5, only do 5 Double-Unders.

♦ LATERAL RAISES

› MODIFY DOWN: Shorten the lever (the distance between you and the weight) by bending your elbows to 90 degrees. Or do one arm at a time.

› MODIFY UP: Instead of increasing the weight, work on tempo and time under tension. If you go too heavy, you may rely on momentum, and that's not doing you any service. Perform this exercise slowly, with control. An example of tempo is lifting the weight up for a count of 2, taking a 1-count pause at the top, then 2 counts down.

♥ THRUSTERS

› MODIFY DOWN: Use a PVC pipe or broomstick to work on form before adding weight.

› MODIFY UP: Increase the weight, and/or use a barbell.

♣ PLANK SHOULDER TAPS X2

› MODIFY DOWN: Perform this on your knees with a straight spine.

› MODIFY UP: Do this on a decline, with your feet on a bench, box, or BOSU.

♠ FROG JUMPS WITH OVERHEAD REACH

› MODIFY DOWN: Do Air Squats (fast bodyweight squats, no weight).

› MODIFY UP: Add a 180-degree turn—this is called a Snowboarder.

DAY #5

◆ LOW ROWS

> › MODIFY DOWN: Use a lighter band with less resistance.
> › MODIFY UP: Add an alternating reverse lunge and/or double up on the resistance bands.

♥ GOBLET SQUATS

> › MODIFY DOWN: Squat down to sit on a box or bench, then stand up again. This is called a Goblet Box Squat.
> › MODIFY UP: Use a heavier weight or do a Barbell Front Squat.

♣ CRAB TOE TOUCHES

> › MODIFY DOWN: Work on the reverse table top position and lift one leg at a time. (Omit the arm-to-foot reach.) You could also do this seated on the floor and perform Alternating Seated Tucks reaching for the opposite toe. Performing the tucks with one knee at a time mimics the alternating leg action of the crab toe touch, so you still get a similar benefit.
> › MODIFY UP: This exercise is challenging and does not require any up modification.

♠ BOX JUMPS

> › MODIFY DOWN: Use a lower box, alternate your Step-Ups, or do Tap Downs by starting on the bench and tapping one foot down at a time.
> › MODIFY UP: Use a higher box. Work on explosive power and string the jumps together without a double bounce. I am not so much in the CrossFit community anymore, but the language they use for this is "unbroken," in case that helps.

♦ SUPERMANS

> › MODIFY DOWN: Do one arm and one leg at a time, alternating opposite arm/legs (lift right leg/left arm, then left leg/right arm).
> › MODIFY UP: Do a Low Back Extension on a stability ball or a machine at the gym. You can also add weight by holding a plate, a medicine ball, or one dumbbell to your chest.

♥ BULGARIAN SPLIT SQUATS

> › MODIFY DOWN: Do a stationary (static) lunge (on both sides) without putting your foot on the bench. Keep both feet on the floor.
> › MODIFY UP: Use a heavier weight (that's challenging but that you can control) or do this with a barbell.

♣ RUSSIAN TWISTS

> › MODIFY DOWN: Keep your feet on the ground and don't use a weight.
> › MODIFY UP: Elevate your feet—challenge yourself without crossing your ankles, and hold a medicine ball, one dumbbell or two, or a kettlebell. You could also play around with keeping your arms as straight as possible to add more resistance.

♠ BURPEES

> › MODIFY DOWN: Step out to plank one foot at a time, don't do the push-up, and step back one foot at a time to starting position before standing. The jump is optional. You can also put your hands on an elevated surface, such as a box or bench (or dome-up side of a BOSU), when you come down to plank position. The push-up is optional here, too, but the incline will make it easier, so why not give it a try?

> › MODIFY UP: Try some of the many fun and challenging Burpee variations—there are a million of 'em! These are just a few:
>
>   › Burpees with 2 Push-Ups
>   › Burpees with Box Jump or Tuck Jump
>   › Burpee Pull-Ups
>   › Candlestick Burpees
>   › Broad Jump Burpees
>   › Lateral Jump (barbell or box) Burpees
>   › Burpees with weights, kettlebells, or dumbbells or a medicine ball
>   › Man Maker Burpees

DAY #6

SET #1:

◆ ALTERNATING FLOOR PRESSES, NEUTRAL GRIP

> › MODIFY DOWN: Use a lighter weight.
> › MODIFY UP: Use a heavier weight.

♥ WALKING LUNGES

> › MODIFY DOWN: Don't use a weight or do stationary (static) lunges (stay in place, don't move forward).
> › MODIFY UP: Use a heavier weight with dumbbells or a barbell, or hold the dumbbells overhead as you go—keep your arms straight for proper alignment (think of stacking bone on bone, and the dumbbells are just on top of a "shelf").

♣ BALL PASSES WITH STABILITY BALL

› MODIFY DOWN: Do Alternating Straight-Leg V-Ups by lifting your right leg and reaching for it with your left arm, then do the other side. Or just do this without the ball.

› MODIFY UP: Add weight by using a medicine ball instead of a stability ball.

♠ BROAD JUMP BACKPEDALS

› MODIFY DOWN: Take out the jump. Take a big step forward and low steps backward, but go as fast as you can, for cardio purposes.

› MODIFY UP: Hold a medicine ball at your chest during this exercise.

SET #2:

♦ RENEGADE ROWS

› MODIFY DOWN: Perform this on your knees, on an incline, or in an Alternating Bent-Over Row (on your feet, not in plank position).

› MODIFY UP: Use a heavier weight and work on core stability. Keep your hips square (same as in Plank Up-Downs and Shoulder Taps). To make it even more challenging, perform this with two kettlebells, holding the horns.

♥ TRIPLE CRUSHES

› MODIFY DOWN: Use a light medicine ball.

› MODIFY UP: Use one or two heavier dumbbells or one heavy kettlebell.

♣ SIDE PLANK HIP DROPS

> › MODIFY DOWN: Keep your knee (the one closer to the floor) on the floor for Side Plank, and/or do hip drops in a forearm plank, and just rock your hips side to side. (Right and left are 1 rep.)
> › MODIFY UP: Elevate your top leg a few inches.

♠ SQUAT TO TUCK JUMPS

> › MODIFY DOWN: Jump to a vertical target or do Air Squats.
> › MODIFY UP: Double the pulse on the squat at the bottom, and tuck jump as high as possible. Focus on landing soft in a low squat.

acknowledgments

I would like to give a special THANK-YOU to the following people who have supported me throughout the creation of this book, my health and fitness journey, and my life journey . . .

To my writing partner, Eve Adamson, thank you so much for your guidance and expertise!

Thank you so much to Eve Overland and Cara Clark for your incredible contributions to this book!

To everyone at Dey Street Books/HarperCollins, especially Jessica Sindler, Carrie Thornton, Ben Steinberg, Heidi Richter, Kendra Newton, Renata De Oliveira, and Suet Chong, thank you for putting your faith in me.

To Cameron Premo for your beautiful photography, and to everyone who worked together to help bring this book to life: Melissa Schleicher, Poni Silver, Louisa Shafia, Hannah Messinger, Mina Waller, Amy Garges, Terry Beasley, Rachel Ramsey, Angela Gleaves, Geoff Donkin, Amy Reynolds, Jeff Johnson, Ivey Childers, Mark Childers, and Don Schleicher.

Special thanks to Basheerah Ahmad and Erin Oprea for helping me learn how to become healthy and strong.

To Ricky Dallanegra for working out with me in many gyms around the world!

To my entire CALIA team at DICK'S Sporting Goods, you inspire me every day to Stay the Path!

To Ann Edelblute, you spent countless hours working on this project—keeping us all on track and encouraging me along the way. This book never would have gotten started or finished without you! Thank you, thank you, thank you! And to the rest of my management team at The HQ—Michelle de Leon, Jessica Dover, and Megan Watts—thank you for all your hard work and for always having my back.

To Cait Hoyt, Jeff Frasco, Steve Lashever, Mike Blank, and everyone at CAA—you are the best!

To Marc Chamlin, David Schmerler, and Ken Kraus at Loeb & Loeb, and to everyone at GRF, thank you.

To Brad Cafarelli and his incredible PR team, thank you for all you do.

I want to of course thank my parents, my sisters and their families, and everyone in Oklahoma who was a part of my journey while I was growing up. I'll always treasure where I came from.

And to my inspirations—Mike, Isaiah, and Jacob, you are my heart. And to our furry family members, too—Ace, Penny, Zero, and our growing farm of personalities!

And of a course a special thank-you to all my fans around the world, and anyone who is reading this book—I hope I've inspired you to find your path.

xoxo,

Carrie

ALL PHOTOGRAPHY BY CAMERON PREMO, UNLESS NOTED BELOW:
Ralph Larmann—p. xviii; provided by Carrie Underwood/Underwood Family—pp. 4, 5, 9, 13, 15, 25, 26; Ann Edelblute—pp. 6, 30; Steve Jennings—p. 16; Ray Mickshaw/FOX Image Collection via Getty Images—p. 24; Ray Mickshaw/WireImage via Getty Images—p. 27; Randy Walters Films—p. 39; Angelica Marie Photography—pp. 190, 251; Ethan Miller/Getty Images Entertainment via Getty Images—p. 140

FOR CAMERON PREMO PHOTOGRAPHY:
*Hair and makeup: Melissa Schleicher • Wardrobe stylist: Poni Silver
Fitness/lifestyle wardrobe: CALIA by Carrie Underwood*

DEY ST.

HarperCollins books may be purchased for educational, business, or sales promotional use. For information, please email the Special Markets Department at SPsales@harpercollins.com.

FIRST EDITION

DESIGNED BY SUET CHONG

Library of Congress Cataloging-in-Publication Data has been applied for.

ISBN 978-0-06-269091-3

20 21 22 23 24   LSC   10 9 8 7 6 5 4 3 2 1

Turn the page for a peek into my vegetable garden, and some extra recipes with veggies!

The more I learn about healthy eating and healthy living, the more my passion for it grows—and speaking of growing, my latest project at home has been vegetable gardening! Obviously, I love vegetables. They are what God made for dinner, so growing them in my own yard feels like the perfect thing to do at home with my family. It's fun, it's outdoorsy, and it's homegrown healthy food at its best.

But I must admit, I'm pretty new at the gardening game. Growing up, I had dreams of someday having my own farm where I would raise horses and chickens, and grow lush fruit trees and berry bushes and a huge vegetable garden. Well, we recently moved into a new home on a large piece of land, got some chickens and horses, planted a large orchard complete with blackberry briars and blueberries, and set up the vegetable garden behind our house. My dreams are becoming reality! Obviously, I have a lot to learn and not a lot of time to spend researching the magic of garden growing, so I have Joel (the dad of my friend and make-up artist, Melissa). He knows all about what to plant and when to pick it, and he takes care of things when I'm out on the road. I look forward to all that I'll learn from him and I hope someday to be able to fully plant and tend to my veggies all by myself. But until then, I ask questions, google, and do as much as my schedule will allow.

I love gardening for a lot of reasons. Weeding is one of my favorite parts. It might sound strange, but it kind of feels like meditation to me, sitting outside pulling out those weeds one by one. Gardening is also exercise, even if it's not a full-on workout. And, you know me, I get my

Compost Your Veggie Scraps

If you want free fertilizer for your garden, start a compost pile. Keep a little bucket or lidded container with a handle in your kitchen and throw all your veggie scraps in it when you're cooking. At the end of the day, you can dump it into a small pile in the corner of the yard, or you can get a fancy compost barrel that turns with a handle. Mix up your compost every so often and keep it damp, and those veggie scraps will transform into a rich dark "dirt" that will make your garden soil more fertile and healthy. Composting is also a great way to minimize what you throw away. Your veggie scraps will go back into the earth, where they came from. (Just don't put any scraps from meat or dairy products in there—they don't compost very well and they could attract pests.)

exercise everywhere I can! Walking, bending, lifting, stretching—it can even be strenuous, especially if you do the digging and tilling and planting yourself. Even just getting out in the fresh air and sunshine is good for you. I try to get out there every chance I get to check on the plants and yank out those weeds before they get too big. The best part, though, is the harvest! It's so satisfying to pick tomatoes, zucchini, cucumbers, or whatever is ripe, and have it for dinner within the hour. Food just doesn't get any fresher than that.

Gardening can also be a great family activity. It's a wonderful way to teach kids about eating healthy and about where their food really comes from. My kids are still very young, but our garden is next to the playset, so Isaiah can come out there with us and play while we're weeding. Sometimes he even wants to help and he's starting to get interested in what's growing. Mike and I love showing him how the veggies are getting bigger or changing colors and we've even noticed that he seems to be more excited to try new types of veggies (which can often times be like pulling teeth) when he helped grow them himself.

But I didn't grow up gardening. Even though my family owned a farm, we didn't grow fruits or vegetables. Our neighbors did, and I remember going over there sometimes to pick strawberries. I always thought it was so amazing that those beautiful red berries we would normally buy in cartons at the store were growing right there in my neighbor's yard. They tasted a million times better than those grocery-store strawberries. Now that I have my own garden, I'm learning as I go. I haven't tried to grow strawberries yet, but this year I did grow okra, bell peppers, zucchini (boy do those zucchini take over a garden!), yellow squash, cucumbers, cabbage, Brussels sprouts, beets, radishes, onions, celery, three different varieties of tomatoes (hey, I love tomatoes), and basil, which is awesome with those fresh sliced tomatoes. Some of my veggies did better than others, but overall, I think it all turned out pretty well. There's something about the whole process that feels magical. Every bright red (or yellow, or heirloom) tomato, every sunny yellow squash, every little green Brussels sprout or big green zucchini feels like a little miracle when you grow it yourself. When I plant vegetables in the earth and they grow into food I can feed to myself and the people I love, it feels like God and I are working together to do something good. I sure am grateful for the people who help me keep it going, and when those veggies are ready, it's fun looking up new recipes that will include all my garden goodness!

I know not everyone has the time or the space or a Joel to be able to make a garden possible, but there are a lot of different ways you can get the same benefits of a traditional home garden:

› CONTAINER GARDENING. In our last home, we didn't have a garden but I did grow some tomato vines and bell peppers and herbs like basil and rosemary in big pots out on our back porch. Our biggest nemesis was the chipmunks! Many days, they would snatch those tomatoes I was waiting on to turn red. To be honest, I just kind of let them do their thing. I didn't really fight it—I figured little Chip and Dale were just hungry. We also planted some melons, but we never got any melons. Sometimes gardening is about trial and error, and not everything you try is gonna work. It's still fun to try, and container gardens are a low-risk way to give gardening a shot. Just fill some big pots with dirt and get some starter plants (and maybe proactively think about some ways to keep the wildlife away). Tomatoes, peppers, and herbs generally work really well in containers.

› **INDOOR GARDENING.** Some plants work great indoors so you can garden even if you don't have any outdoor space you can use. Plant herbs in small pots and put them on a tray with a rim, then set it in front of a sunny window. You could also grow a little salad garden of different lettuces in a shallow, flat planter. If you don't have a sunny window, you can get a grow light at any garden store. One perk of inside gardens: no weeds!

› **SHARED GARDENS:** Gardening is a lot of work and honestly, most people don't really have the time to do it all. But what if you found other people who wanted the same thing and could share the work with you? Shared gardening is something a lot of people are trying. You lend out space in your yard to someone else, or someone else lends out space to you, and you do the gardening together, sharing the work and sharing the harvest. You can decide together what kind of garden you want and who will do what. It's not only easier than doing it yourself, but it's a great way to get to know your neighbors or spend time with your friends. Apparently, two million or more people are already doing this, and there is a website called Shared Earth (sharedearth.com) that can pair you up with others who want to share a garden.

› **COMMUNITY GARDENS:** A community garden is a big plot of land where people can rent small plots, or share the rent on a plot with others who want to garden together. This is a great way to have a garden of whatever size you want when you don't have yard space to do it or you live in an urban area where people don't generally have yards. Some of these are run by the city, so check locally to see if you have one near you.

› **VEGETABLE SHARES OR CO-OPS:** Maybe you're just not the gardening type but you like the idea of having the fresh vegetables. If that's you, look into vegetable shares or CSAs in your area. CSA stands for community-supported agriculture. You sign up with a local farm, pay a certain amount in advance or a monthly subscription fee, then every week or month throughout the growing season, you get to pick up a big box or bag of freshly harvested vegetables from the farm. Sometimes they include other goodies like fruit, fresh eggs from pastured chickens, fresh-baked bread, or bouquets of fresh flowers. Many of these farms also invite their subscribers to come out to visit the farm, so you can see where your food comes from.

› **FARMER'S MARKETS, FARM STANDS, AND U-PICK FARMS:** Even if you don't have vegetable shares, you probably have a farmer's market somewhere near you. You can visit the market on the weekends and pick up freshly harvested veggies to last you through the week— no gardening, but all the veggie goodness! Or stop at farm stands selling whatever they are harvesting right then, or U-pick farms where you get to go harvest veggies or fruits someone else grew— you never know what delicious locally grown veggies or fruits you can pick up right when they are at their absolute freshest. Plus, it's a great way to support smaller, local, family-owned farms.

The Harvest

Harvesting your garden is the fun part! You've watched those veggies getting bigger and brighter all summer long. There are few things more satisfying to me than picking veggies I grew and eating them for dinner.

But one problem with gardening is that everything gets ripe at the same time. You might end up with more than you can eat. If you get veggies from a CSA vegetable share or from the farmer's market, you might also get more than you and your family can consume. You can usually get really good deals if you buy larger amounts, but there's no point in that if your veggies spoil before you can eat them.

The solution is to preserve them for later. No waste! Some people love canning, and every once-in-a-while, my bestie, Ivey, and I will take a day to can (or "put up," as some people call it) our fresh veggies for later use. Canning can be a bit intimidating, though, so a simpler solution might be just to freeze the surplus veggies. Not every veggie freezes well. For example, cucumbers won't freeze, which is why people pickle them instead. Tomatoes don't freeze well, but a big batch of tomato sauce freezes just fine. Most other vegetables freeze well. All you have to do is get some sealable freezer bags and put enough for one family-size serving in each bag. Don't forget to label and date everything so you remember what's in those bags! Here are some easy ways to freeze your veggie bounty:

› **BRUSSELS SPROUTS:** Pluck them off the stalk, trim off the hard ends, soak them in water for 10 minutes, rinse them, pat them dry, and freeze.

› **CABBAGE:** Wash it really well, then cut it into big wedges. Freeze the wedges in bags.

› **CARROTS, ZUCCHINIS, SQUASH, OKRA, AND SWEET OR HOT PEPPERS:** Wash well, slice or cut into strips, and lay them out on a baking sheet covered in parchment paper. Put them in the freezer. When the individual slices are frozen (the next day), put them in bags and freeze.

› **HERBS (LIKE BASIL, OREGANO, CILANTRO, ETC.):** Chop them up and put them in ice cube trays. Cover them with water and freeze. Pop out the frozen cubes and store them in freezer bags. These are so easy to drop into any recipe while cooking.

> **TOMATOES:** Cut them in half, squeeze out the seeds, cook them until they fall apart (about 30 minutes at medium heat in a big saucepan), stirring often, then puree them in the blender to make tomato sauce. Freeze in one-cup portions.

MY FAVORITE VEGGIE RECIPES

Freezing eliminates waste and keeps my family in veggies during the winter, but my favorite way to use veggies is to make something out of them the day I pick them. Whether I'm in the mood to make something a little more involved or (more likely) want to keep it super simple, here are three of my favorite recipes that are perfect for using the veggies in your garden.

My Signature Roasted Veggies

Prep time: 20 minutes
Total time: 50 minutes

Serves 2 (or more)

1 bunch of asparagus, with
   the tough bottom parts
   chopped off
1 cup broccoli florets
1 cup Brussels sprouts,
   bottoms trimmed off and
   cut in half
About 6 ounces of small
   tender carrots, peeled
   or scrubbed. Keep them
   whole or cut them into big
   chunks
1 cup cauliflower florets
1 cup any potatoes, cut into
   big chunks (peeled or not)
2 tablespoons olive oil
Mrs. Dash, garlic salt, or any
   other seasoning you like
Salt and pepper to taste

This is my recipe that is hardly even a recipe, but that everybody seems to love and it is a huge part of my life—it really is my signature dish. I make this a lot and it is just about my favorite thing to eat. You can use whatever veggies you have on hand—the more the merrier. You can make a spring version with your spring veggies, like peas, asparagus, broccoli, baby carrots, and beets, or a mid-summer version with green beans, peppers, and potatoes, or a fall version with butternut squash, cabbage, Brussels sprouts, and kale. The more different colors you include, the better your variety of nutrients and vitamins. I always use Mrs. Dash to season my veggies (there are different flavors/ mixtures) or a bit of salt and pepper, but you can vary your spices each time. Find your favorites. Here is a basic recipe I often make—don't forget to use the veggies that are the ripest and most in-season when you make this irresistibly easy dinner.

1. Preheat the oven to 375°F, and lightly grease a cookie sheet or baking tray.

2. Arrange your veggies on the baking sheet, either in separate groups or all mixed together. Drizzle or spray with the olive oil and sprinkle with Mrs. Dash (or whatever seasoning you prefer).

NUTRITION FACTS

(per serving)

221	calories
14 g	fat
12.5 g	carbs
6.5 g	protein
8 g	fiber
8 g	sugar

3. Roast the veggies for 15 minutes, then give them a good toss using tongs or a spoon. Depending on the size of your veggies and how many you put in there, this could take anywhere from 20 to 30 minutes. The vegetables are done when the edges begin to crisp.

4. Serve warm with any protein and optionally (if you are extra hungry), some brown rice or quinoa. Helpful hint: If you're making your protein and it is finished cooking before your veggies are done, you can always set the oven to broil, to quickly get your veggies to catch up. But keep a close eye on them! That broil setting is no joke and you don't want to burn your vegetables to a crisp.

Ivey's Summer Squash Lasagna

Prep time: 20 minutes
Total time: 50 minutes

Serves 6

2 medium (or 3 small)
  summer squash and/or
  zucchini
15 ounces part-skim ricotta
  cheese
1 egg
2 to 3 tablespoons chopped
  fresh basil
1 bag Gardein meatless
  crumbles (optional,
  but adds a lot of filling
  protein)
1 teaspoon dried oregano
1 teaspoon Mrs. Dash Italian
  Medley
Salt and pepper to taste
2 cups shredded cheese
1 cup low-sodium marinara
  sauce (Ivey used Silver
  Palate brand)
1 tablespoon Parmesan
  cheese

This past summer we grew zucchini and summer squash, and we had so much that I gave some to my best friend, Ivey. That's also one of the wonderful things about gardening—you can share your harvest. It's so fun (and impressive) to visit someone's house and bring along a little basket of goodies from your own garden! Ivey is an incredible cook, so she made this amazing lasagna, but she still had so much squash that she made a second one and brought it over to my house. While she made enough for me and Mike to enjoy, unfortunately, Mike was out of town and I got it all to myself! Sorry Mike! It was delicious and healthy—the squash stands in for the noodles so you get extra veggie goodness without all the useless simple carbs. It looks especially nice if you use a combination of yellow summer squash and zucchini. She made it one more time just so she could write down what she did, for me to share with you. Here's her recipe. If you want to make this vegan, try making it with your favorite dairy-free cheese.

1. Preheat the oven to 350°F.

2. Using a vegetable peeler, knife, or a mandoline (a fancy slicing tool), slice the squash and zucchini the long way into shapes like lasagna noodles.

3. In a separate bowl, combine the ricotta, egg, and chopped basil. Mix well by hand. Set aside.

4. In a big pan, sauté 1 bag of Gardein crumbles as directed on the bag and season with oregano, Italian seasoning, salt, and pepper. Set aside.

5. Measure out 2 cups of shredded cheese, set aside.

6. Measure out 1 cup of sauce, set aside. (You can use more if you like it saucy-er)

7. Start layering:

   - In a 9 × 13 baking dish, spoon in a thin layer of sauce.
   - On top of the sauce, add one layer of squash "noodles," just enough to cover the sauce.
   - Over the squash, add ¼ of the ricotta mixture.
   - Over the ricotta, add ¼ of the Gardein crumbles.
   - Over the Gardein, add ¼ of the shredded cheese.
   - Repeat the layers in this order: zucchini, ricotta mixture, sauce, crumbles, and cheese. Keep layering until all the ingredients are gone—you should have at least 4 layers.

8. Sprinkle the Parmesan cheese over the top. Cover loosely with foil and bake for 45 minutes or until the lasagna is bubbling and the top is turning a nice golden brown. Of course, you could substitute some lean ground beef or bison for the Gardein crumbles . . . or just enjoy this yummy recipe as it is for a delicious "meatless Monday"!

Fresh Homemade Coleslaw

Prep time: 15 minutes
(less if your veggies are
pre-chopped)
Total time: 15 minutes

Serves 4

4 cups finely chopped or
  grated cabbage
2 large or 4 small carrots
  grated
1 medium cucumber, peeled
  and chopped
A few fresh basil leaves
  rolled and finely sliced
  (optional)
2 tablespoons rice vinegar
  (or apple cider vinegar)
2 tablespoons soy sauce (I
  use Bragg Liquid Aminos)
1 tablespoon toasted
  sesame oil
1 tablespoon sesame seeds

NUTRITION FACTS
(per serving)

97	calories
4.7 g	fat
12.3 g	carbs
2.2 g	protein
3.6 g	fiber
6 g	sugar

I'm not really a fan of fatty, creamy coleslaw, but I love a good fresh crispy coleslaw with a simple homemade vinaigrette or Asian sesame-flavored dressing, especially if it's made with cabbage and carrots from my own garden. This is a great way to use up cabbage and carrots. It's quick to make if you have a grater attachment on your food processor. Grating or chopping the vegetables is the part that takes the longest, but everybody loves this coleslaw so it's worth it!

Mix everything together. You can serve it right away or chill it for a few hours in the refrigerator.